S0-AQL-584

SUCCESSFUL TAILS

THE WONDERS OF THERAPY DOGS

PATRICIA H. WHEELER, PHD

AuthorHouse™
1663 Liberty Drive
Bloomington, IN 47403
www.authorhouse.com
Phone: 1-800-839-8640

Editor: Yong Suh

Published by AuthorHouse 09/27/2012

ISBN: 978-1-4772-6474-4 (sc)
ISBN: 978-1-4772-6471-3 (hc)
ISBN: 978-1-4772-6475-1 (e)

Library of Congress Control Number: 2012916320

This book is printed on acid-free paper.

TABLE OF CONTENTS

Dedicated to
all therapy dogs,
past, present, and future,
for their service
to our children and seniors,
to our troops and veterans,
to all of us
and for the wonderful work they do.

FOREWORD

When people see the therapy dogs with their vests on, they think they are working dogs like guide dogs and service dogs, and that they should stay back since they are busy taking care of their owner. But therapy dogs are there for anyone who wants to interact with them, and I have seen them at work firsthand.

I've visited the Livermore VA Medical Center when the handlers would come in with some of the therapy dogs, and the peoples' faces would light up immediately. The dogs bring solace and elevate the spirits of the service men and women who are oftentimes facing difficult recoveries.

When Pat told me she was writing this book, I was honored that she asked me to write this message. The stories and testimonials contained in these pages will open your eyes to the world of therapy dogs and how beneficial they can be for people.

The services that therapy dogs provide are far-reaching and can be life-changing. However, I have found that the obvious emotional boost that these dogs bring to people in recovery is the most remarkable part of their service. When handlers come into the Livermore VA with their therapy dogs, the veterans' moods instantly improve.

It was only in the last quarter of the 20th Century that we began to study in earnest the direct benefits of human–canine relationships. Through study and the development of the Lexington Attachment to Pets Scale, it has been shown that humans experience an increased quality of life and better psychological and social levels. These benefits manifest the most frequently and yield the best results in clinical settings, such as veterans recovering from physical and mental afflictions.

More than just veterans benefit from the love that therapy dogs provide. These dogs comfort children in reading programs, help young children cope with their challenges and fears, and teach children how to behave around dogs. For many seniors who cannot lead the active social lives that they did in their youth, therapy dogs provide much-needed friendship and companionship.

As I have heard when visiting with our service men and women, therapy dogs brighten their day and boost morale. The stories and testimonials contained in this book are uplifting and important for people to realize the true benefits and positive effects that therapy dogs can have. I can relate to that feeling, recalling how even our family dog was always a source of comfort when a family member was ill or injured.

Pat Wheeler has movingly and concisely brought together stories of how these dogs are an important part of our region. From being a part of Welcome Home Celebrations for our troops to providing solace to folks at local shelters, therapy dogs are a great benefit to our community. Contained in this important writing are the stories and testimonials not only of how therapy dogs bring smiles and raise the spirits of the people they come in contact with, but also how they help people recover from physical and emotional trauma.

Congressman Jerry McNerney,
California District 11,
United States House of Representatives,
Member of the Veterans' Affairs
Committee,
Ranking Member of the Subcommittee on
Disability Assistance and Memorial Affairs

PREFACE

After my husband passed away, I began watching *Animal Planet* on a regular basis. I really enjoyed the program "K-9 to 5," showing dogs at work. I was impressed with what the therapy dogs could do and thought I would like to be involved in something like that.

Looking into possible breeds, I decided on a Labrador Retriever (not realizing until later how much fur they can produce and shed every day!). A local veterinarian referred me to an AKC breeder. When he had a litter of eight Lab puppies available for adoption, I went to check them out. All were so adorable. Since I had always had male dogs, I said a male, but couldn't decide from among the four male puppies, as all were so adorable. So I asked him to select the one that would be the best therapy dog.

When the eight-week-old Black Lab arrived at my house, I asked my older son, Paul, for name suggestions. He immediately said, "Lawrence, the Livermore Lab." Great idea. So off Lawrence went for puppy socialization and basic obedience classes.

I realized early on that Lawrence would be a great therapy dog when I was taking him for a walk at a local shopping center. He saw a disheveled, drunk man sitting on the sidewalk by a trashcan outside a liquor store. Lawrence gently pulled me over to him and comforted him. The man was smiling and petting Lawrence.

The next step was to get Lawrence certified as a therapy dog. A neighbor told me about the program at Valley Humane Society. So I contacted Christine McDaniel, and she set up our evaluation at a site in San Ramon. We passed and immediately started going to an Alzheimer's/dementia facility in Livermore that had no therapy dog assigned to it. We went there every week starting in November 2002 until it closed in November 2011.

In 2004, we started going to the VA Palo Alto Health Care System (VAPAHCS) in Livermore. Lawrence started in July 2004. When other handlers learned about what he was doing, the program started to grow. Four other dogs, including my dog, Albert, joined that first year after Lawrence. And now my two dogs go to other sites, programs, and events on a regular basis.

Why do I keep doing this? I see what a wonderful difference my dogs and the other therapy dogs make for people facing challenges in their lives. I realized how important the therapy dogs are when I entered the room of a young veteran, withering away from cancer. As Albert and I entered his room, he said, "I wake up every morning wondering which dog is coming today and what time it will get here."

I started collecting numerous stories about how my dogs were making a difference for people. But then I became passionate about the need to make others aware of the wonders of therapy dogs, and started encouraging other handlers to collect stories and gathered testimonials from people who have seen the therapy dogs at work. My hope is that this book will promote such programs in various types of agencies—health, social service, educational, military, recreational, senior services—across the country and beyond; will encourage other dog owners to become therapy dog handlers; and will provide researchers with areas for further study on the value of therapy dogs.

The stories and testimonials have been provided to me by over 250 people including therapy dog handlers, residents and staff at various sites, students and clients, volunteers, and attendees at public events. Many are about my two dogs. But that is, in part, because I have been so passionate about collecting testimonials and stories, and because my two dogs have done many hours of therapy dog work (over 3,000 hours between them).

Patricia H. Wheeler, PhD

ACKNOWLEDGEMENTS

I am very thankful to the 250 plus people who provided testimonials, stories, quotes, poems, and photos to me over the past seven years during which I have been collecting materials. This book would not have been possible without them. Sadly, some of these people, and also some of the therapy dogs, have passed away. But, through this book, they will always be remembered. Others have moved or retired.

Some individuals went above and beyond simply sending me materials for themselves, their place of employment, or their dogs. They included, but are not limited to, John Flotten, Gail Turner, and Carol Weldin. Sue Jones and Gay Maestas provided me with information on the history of the Pet Therapy Program at Valley Humane Society and of the Paws to Read program.

Many individuals and agencies, in addition to the dogs' handlers, provided photos for the book and obtained needed release forms. They include Sue Day, Lynette Della Bona, Bud Donaldson, Duanne Ferrell, Reneé Freidus, Nathan Silva, Dawn and Shelby Thornton, Gail Turner, Carol Weldin, and Sherry Wiggins. I appreciate the following for allowing me to use their photos in this book: Dawn Schubert, Photographer (back cover); Diablo Valley Flag Brigade (the Welcome Home Celebration photos in Chapter 9); Doug Jorgensen, Photographer for The Independent (photos on pages 63, 212); and the Orinda Library (photo on page 63). Don Odle was wonderful, helping me deal with the scores of photos collected, converting them to grayscale, cropping them, blurring faces to protect identify, and advising me on which ones to use and not use.

The collection and editing of materials for this book has been a long process. I thank my editor, Yong Suh, for being patient with me, answering my numerous picky questions, and making sure that the text maintained the writing style and intent of those individuals submitting materials. My son, Paul Wheeler, was always helpful when Yong and I were unsure of editorial changes. I thank both Alicia Moore, Doctoral candidate in psychology, and Dr. Heather Moore, DVM, for reviewing content and directing me to appropriate resources. I appreciate the help from my son, Michael, in setting up the website (www.phwheeler.com).

Critical to this long-term project were people who kept me on course, checking in regularly to be sure I was making progress and providing advice when I hit brick walls. They included Sue Davis, Sandy du Pont, Hazel Jacoby, Dan Longnecker, Linda Rosen, Michael Sturdivan, Madeliene Ward, and Wy Weaver. Especially critical was my attorney, Sandra J. Shepard, Esq., who was always there to answer questions and provide valuable advice. Sadly, during the process of doing this book, she lost her dog, Jake. I wish I had been able to meet Jake.

I express much thanks to those who donated money to the Book Fund at Valley Humane Society to help pay for the production of this book. They included Sue Day, Jon and Rhonda Elliott, Emily Garcia of Easy Living Care Home, Clint and Jacqueline McFaddin, Joy Montgomery, Alicia Moore, L. Virginia Scholz, Luanda Sherman, Dawn Thornton, Ellen Waskey, Rose Wilkins, and David Wilson.

Last, but not least, thanks to my two dogs, Lawrence, the Livermore Lab, and Albert, who provided the inspiration for this book. They were often at my feet when I was at the computer or sorting through all the materials collected—not in my way, but comforting and encouraging me.

If I left anyone out, you know who you are. Thanks to you also.

I hope those of you reading this book appreciate what these people and dogs did to make this book happen.

~CHAPTER 1~

introduction

Therapy dogs are one of many types of working dogs. They are selected and trained, with their handler, to serve people of all ages and conditions, and, sometimes, to work with professional staff to help people achieve physical, emotional, social, and cognitive goals and objectives.

Therapy dogs are recognized as working dogs. The United States Postal Service (USPS) issued a series of stamps in 2012 honoring four types of "Dogs at Work"—guide dog, tracking dog, rescue dog, and therapy dog. The American Kennel Club (AKC) Humane Fund Awards for Canine Excellence recognizes five categories of working dogs—law enforcement, search and rescue, therapy, service, and exemplary companion dogs. The military is providing therapy dogs for our troops in Afghanistan and Iraq to help them cope with the on-going stressful conditions. Therapy Dogs International (TDI) has provided therapy dogs for several disastrous events. Called Disaster Stress Relief (DSR) teams, these therapy dog and handler teams were at the Oklahoma City bombing, the 9-11 World Trade Center attacks, Hurricane Katrina, and other disasters. For more information, see http://www.tdi-dog.org/OurPrograms.aspx?Page=DSR+%28Disaster+Stress+Relief%29.

Therapy dogs are often confused with service dogs and companion dogs. Service dogs are trained to work with one individual, usually one with a physical disability. Service dogs are permitted, under the Americans with Disabilities Act of 1990 (ADA) (www.ada.gov/), to go wherever the persons they are working for can go. This includes restaurants, theaters, stores, buses, and airplanes. They are considered a type of durable medical equipment, just like a wheelchair. Service dogs go through months of extensive training by professional instructors and are certified by various agencies throughout the country such as Canine Companions for Independence (CCI) in Santa Rosa (www.cci.org/). Most service dogs are Labrador Retrievers, Golden Retrievers, and German Shepherds because of their size, strength, temperament, and ability to learn quickly. Smaller dogs and mixed breeds are used for some types of service dogs (e.g., medical response dogs) and as other types of assistance dogs (e.g., hearing assistance dogs).

At times, companion dogs are recommended by professional health staff for persons suffering from emotional disorders such as depression and social isolation. The dog is usually the pet for that individual. However, companion dogs do not have the freedom to go wherever that individual goes, and they may or may not receive special training and certification.

Therapy dogs are someone's pet, but they serve other people. Any breed and any size dog can be a therapy dog, though not all individual dogs are appropriate to become therapy dogs. The therapy dog bios in Appendix B describe the 51 dogs featured in this book. They range in size from less than ten pounds to over 130 pounds. They include male and female dogs, purebreds and mixed breeds, from age two to mid-teens.

The dogs must be evaluated prior to being certified by an agency as a therapy dog. To be a good candidate, the dog must have an appropriate temperament, have no underlying health issues that could interfere with its work, exhibit basic obedience, and possess other characteristics and skills appropriate for the sites and programs where the dog will work.

The therapy dog is only part of the team, though. Each therapy dog has a handler, who might or might not be the owner. The handler is the person certified by an agency to take the therapy dog to various sites, programs, and events. Unless the owner is certified, that person should not take his/her dog to work as a therapy dog. Handlers include a diverse group of people from all types of career backgrounds and with a multitude of interests (see Appendix C for information on the 46 handlers featured in this book).

The therapy dog team should be certified and registered by a reputable agency. This agency trains and evaluates the handler, the dog, and the two of them as a team. It provides insurance coverage when the team is working. (Many homeowner policies also provide coverage for the owner and the dog.) The agency ensures that the sites and programs where the team works and the events to which they go are safe for all involved—the dog, the handler, the people being served, and the staff and others on site.

The certifying agency monitors the performance of the handler and the dog to make certain there are no handler or dog issues. For the handler, these can include failure to follow the rules and policies of both the certifying agency and the places s/he volunteers with the dog, rudeness, antisocial behavior, and inability to control the dog adequately. For the dog, the agency should watch for signs of fear, stress, aggression, and unfriendly behavior as well as new health problems that might limit its work as a therapy dog. Sometimes additional training and monitoring, or an assignment to another site, will address the problems. In other cases, they should no longer work as a therapy dog team.

Getting a Handler/Dog Team Ready for Certification—

How much work needs to be done to prepare a handler and dog for becoming a therapy dog team varies considerably. If the dog's or handler's temperament is inappropriate, then they should consider other volunteer opportunities. For example, I dismissed a Yorkie who practically tore my arm off when I first approached him. And I dismissed a potential handler who was very impolite to patients and staff. But most dogs and people are much better candidates for becoming therapy dog teams.

I encourage the handler and dog to take puppy socialization and basic obedience classes together. It is important that they take these classes together because they will be working as a team at all times. I have also found it very helpful to take my dogs for walks in busy locations such as shopping centers or down the main street of town. This will get the dog used to a variety of people and numerous distractions, and help the handler learn how to control the dog better.

The dog should be exposed to the things they might encounter in their work assignments. These can include sudden loud noises, automatic opening doors, elevators, medical equipment, wheelchairs, walkers (watch the tennis balls on them!), scooters, canes, crutches, beds that move up and down, food and linen carts, narrow spaces to pass through, playground equipment, motorcycles, etc.

All potential therapy dogs must have a complete health examination by a veterinarian to ensure that there are no underlying medical conditions which would prohibit such work. But even with some conditions, dogs can do a great job. I have seen dogs that are blind or have only three legs be a great inspiration to people with physical challenges. Assignments can be made to address such issues as allergies and difficulty walking on smooth surfaces. Some dogs don't get along well with other dogs. However, often assignments can be made to address this issue, and, if another dog comes on site, the handler can take his/her dog out or go to another area of that site.

The dog should have a health exam at least annually and always be current on the shots and tests required by the certifying agency as well as the sites and programs where the dog works.

I encourage potential handlers to shadow an experienced therapy dog team at a site that interests them. Some people think they will be fine volunteering at a certain type of site, only to find out they are uncomfortable once there. They could consider different types of sites or other volunteer opportunities.

Going to Work as a Team—

Dogs should wear their vest or bandanna showing that they are a certified therapy dog. The dogs should wear a standard nylon or leather collar, or a headcollar (e.g., Gentle Leader) or harness. They should not have decorations attached to the collars because people can get cut on them. A working therapy dog should never use a choke collar or electronic training collar because people could be pinched or injured by a choke collar, and the training collar could interfere with electronic signals in use at the site or the dog could be out of sight of the handler.

The handler should use a four-to-six foot nylon or leather leash, without decorative attachments. A retractable collar is inappropriate to use with a working therapy dog. No matter what size dog, they must always be close to the handler. There are situations where the dog might be off leash in an enclosed area, such as in group counseling sessions or in some physical therapy activities. But the handler must be nearby and have control of the dog.

The dogs need to be clean before going to work. I suggest regular professional grooming and nail trimming. In addition, they need to be cleaned every time before going to work and afterwards. This can be done with hand sanitizer, baby wipes, and certain shampoos. Special attention should be paid to their paws, especially if working in a health facility. They should also have their teeth brushed regularly and cleaned, as needed, by a veterinarian. I always carry a bottle of hand sanitizer with me, along with paper towels and plastic bags. Then I am prepared in case someone sneezes or coughs on the dog, or the dog steps into something that it shouldn't. I am also prepared to pick up after my dog, which all handlers should do.

The handler must be dressed appropriately for the assignment. Handlers should wear comfortable, sturdy walking shoes. I suggest wearing clothes similar to what the staff at the site or program are wearing. Handlers should not wear perfume or after-shave lotion. They should not smoke, use a cell phone, or text while working with their dog.

Some sites and programs have their own application process for volunteers, which should be completed before starting to work at a site. These might include background checks, references, and handler health exams as well as veterinary exams for the dog.

The handler should be adequately familiar with the site or program. This can include appropriate hours to come and which days of the week, where to park, where the dog can relieve itself, how to sign in and out, where the handler can safely leave their personal belongings (e.g., purse, backpack, coat), what areas of the facility are available for the team to go see people, where the handler and dog can get water and take a rest break, where the emergency exits are, which restrooms they can use, who the key staff members are and how to locate them when a problem arises, and the phone number to call when there is a problem. It is inappropriate to sit on a person's bed or wheelchair, so know where the chairs or benches are that are available to everyone.

People always enjoy seeing a dog do tricks. Each therapy dog must know basic obedience commands including sit, stay, heel, halt/stop, leave it, back, off, and down. Additional tricks are always welcomed, though jumping and barking are not appropriate. Twirl, dance, and tunnel are three popular ones that my dogs do. Sometime a toy can add to the fun that people are having.

It is reasonable to take breaks. Lawrence and I were at the VA for ten hours one day! He had no interest in leaving and wanted to see everyone. It was a very busy day there with a large public meeting going on about the future of the facility. He was certainly wound up that day, but I needed some breaks. I took them in areas where he could continue visiting the veterans while I relaxed (e.g., the lobby, the patio).

There are times that the dog needs a break. This can be a stressful job for them, especially when they have had to deal with a highly distraught person or a group of very active children. It is fine for the dog to "lie down on the job," as long as it is on a safe and clean surface.

The handler should keep the primary staff contact person(s) informed about their work at the site and report any unusual behaviors of clients, good and bad.

Sites, Programs, and Events—

Therapy dogs can work in many different types of settings. Often people think of them for hospitals and nursing homes. But there is a wide array of sites and programs featured in this book. They include the following:

- Camp Arroyo—operated by The Taylor Family Foundation and the YMCA, offers facilities for various groups serving people with special needs. Two programs involve the therapy dogs:
    - Exceptional Needs Network's Camp Arroyo—a camp for developmentally delayed youth
    - Kara's Camp Erin—a camp for children and youth grieving the loss of a loved one
- Community Assistance for Retarded and Handicapped—an agency that provides social and recreational programs and activities throughout the East Bay for special-needs clients, young children to seniors
- Easy Living Care Home—a set of five residential care facilities for seniors, including non-ambulatory and hospice
- The Friendship Center—now closed, was a daycare service program for seniors
- Library Programs—covers the Paws to Read programs at six libraries in the East Bay at which children and youngsters read to therapy dogs
- Livermore Manor—now closed, was an assisted living care facility for people with Alzheimer's and dementia
- Merrill Gardens—an assisted living and retirement community
- Military and Veteran Events—includes Welcome Home Celebrations for our troops, memorial services, Veterans Day parades and ceremonies, dedications, and other events honoring our military troops and veterans
- The Parkview—an assisted living and memory care facility for seniors

- School Programs—covers programs at four schools in three school districts which involve therapy dogs in reading programs, special education classrooms, tutoring programs, etc.
- Shepherd's Gate—a shelter for battered and homeless women and children
- VA Palo Alto Health Care System Livermore Division—a facility that has a community living center serving veterans who need long-term care plus short-term care and outpatient services in which the therapy dogs work

The chapter on other sites, programs, and events includes work at community events and in parades, with a police department, and at sites and with programs other than those listed above. Clearly, this listing shows that therapy dogs can work in many types of settings where they make a difference for the people they serve.

The Benefits of Therapy Dogs—

This book is full of testimonials and stories about the benefits of the therapy dogs. Each one tells of at least one benefit. The photos and poems express the benefits more. Even the short quotes often say a lot about what these dogs do for people and what they mean to them. The dogs help people in physical, emotional, social, and cognitive areas. They also help staff, family members, and others. Some of the benefits highlighted in this book are listed below. However, this is not a complete list of all the benefits of the 51 therapy dogs featured in this book and their work at the many sites, programs, and events covered.

Physical—lets the person touch and feel a responsive living being, encourages motion and stretching, motivates one to do physical therapy, provides warmth, lowers blood pressure, stops spasms, slows down rapid breathing, reduces pain because when touching a dog endorphins are released.

Emotional—generates unlimited amounts of unconditional love to everyone who wants it, helps people get over their fear of dogs, helps people control impulses, calms people, encourages people to be patient and obedient, brings back happy memories, elicits joy and laughter, helps people cope with anxiety and depression, encourages people to try to do things (e.g., walk farther, read hard words, do new crafts, play unfamiliar games), comforts and snuggles, brings humor and lightness to bleak situations, aids people who are dealing with traumatic experiences, gives people something to look forward to, lifts their morale, addresses feelings of loneliness and the need for friends, increases self-esteem, eases the transition for a person from life to death, helps people through times of grieving the loss of a loved one.

Social—focuses their attention on someone other than themselves (e.g., making eye contact, talking to a dog, being aware of something in their environment, smiling), brings a connection to the outside world, provides entertainment and does tricks which encourage people to group together to watch the dog, provides an opportunity to share stories about dogs with others, offers an opportunity to thank someone (namely the dog) through verbal praise or petting (or giving treats where permitted), serves as an ice-breaker in bringing people together, makes people more apt to open up and share their feelings and concerns with others, gives them an opportunity to interact with the dog and get it to do tricks at their command rather than the handler's, helps people practice social skills (e.g., making introductions, taking turns, thanking others, accepting responsibility), encourages people to appreciate our military troops and veterans for their service to our country, fosters a greater sense of national pride.

Cognitive—increases their desire to read and to participate in games and crafts, allows people to make decisions (e.g., to visit with the dog, to touch the dog, to talk to the dog, to ask the dog to do tricks), helps them focus on doing homework and preparing for tests, encourages them to ask questions, provides comfortable topics to share with others in oral and written format, exercises memory (e.g., recalling past experiences, remembering the dogs).

Staff reported that having therapy dogs present calms them down, which results in better service to clients. Some family members said they want to visit when the therapy dog is at the facility. The dogs encourage family members and friends to visit and make them aware that their loved one needs visitors.

The Rewards of Being a Therapy Dog Team—

The rewards are really hard to explain, but throughout this book, there are stories and testimonials by handlers about what this work means to them. The team brings so much joy and other benefits to those people it serves that the experience gives the handler a wonderful feeling of accomplishment.

There is no question that therapy dogs love their job. Handlers report to me how excited their dogs get when they get the vest out or when they are approaching the work site. When they were younger, each time I got a vest out for one of my dogs, both of my dogs ran toward it, trying to put their heads through it at the same time while their tails where shaking their whole bodies. As I approach a work site, they get very excited and start wiggling and yelping eagerly. If I drive past a work site, they stop wiggling and start whining. This even happened at a work site more than a year after we last went there—fantastic memories for something they really enjoyed.

I hope that readers who own appropriate dogs will consider having them work as therapy dogs. There are many resources available to prepare people and their dogs to be a therapy dog team. Ask a veterinarian or local animal shelter for referrals to programs and agencies that train and certify therapy dog teams.

I also hope that more sites and programs will consider adding therapy dogs to their offerings. As shown in this book, many types of sites and programs can offer therapy dogs for their clients. The descriptions, testimonials, and stories in this book contain information on how therapy dog programs operate at various facilities and give contact information to obtain additional suggestions for setting up such a program.

I hope all readers will learn about the value of dogs, and that they will respect dogs and do what they can to prevent dogs in their community from being abused or trained inappropriately.

In addition to the inspirational "successful tales" surrounding these therapy dogs, this book offers extremely valuable feedback to would-be therapy dog handlers in the form of actual responses from those people that the dogs are benefiting. Such feedback is an invaluable tool that can be used by facilities and programs to develop policies and to implement practices for therapy dog teams so they can best serve their clients.

One lesson the therapy dogs have taught me is that every person is important, no matter what their condition. All people have feelings, even if they can't express them. No matter how a person appears physically or how withdrawn and antisocial they are or how unpleasant they are acting or how disheveled they look or how poorly they are doing at a task such as walking or reading, we should give them that unconditional love. Be there. Listen to what they say. Show them you care about them. Learn from the dogs. They have so much to teach people. I hope all who read this book will learn lessons from what these therapy dogs do.

~CHAPTER 2~

camp arroyo programs

Camp Arroyo is a beautiful residential camp, serving children year-round as a place to explore, learn, and grow in an ideal outdoor setting. Nestled in the hills surrounding the 138-acre Del Valle Regional Wilderness in Livermore, the Camp was formally opened in 2000 and serves thousands of people each year.

Designed and operated on the principles of an ecologically sustainable community, Camp Arroyo's unique "green" camp design not only provides beautiful living, learning, and play facilities, but also serves as a tangible example of sustainable development. The Camp's design has been recognized nationally for its environmental architecture.

Owned by the East Bay Regional Park District, Camp Arroyo has two primary focus areas through the collaborations of The Taylor Family Foundation (TTFF) and the YMCA of the East Bay. Both groups have many years of knowledge and experience managing the Camp's life-changing experiences.

TTFF was founded in 1990. Its mission is to preserve the wellness and enhance the quality of life for children in Northern California with life-threatening and chronic illnesses and developmental disabilities as well as youth at-risk. This is done through unique therapeutic experiences and support. The camps are run during the summer months as well as several weekends during the rest of the year by TTFF with their skilled staff and volunteers. More information on TTFF can be found at www.ttff.org.

During the nine-month school year, from September though June, Camp Arroyo is an outdoor education center that introduces students, grades four and up, to important concepts about sustainable living. YMCA of the East Bay staff direct the programs provided to the young campers during this season.

TTFF has served children with HIV/AIDS, skin disease, heart disease, Crohn's disease, colitis, asthma, sickle cell, autism, hemophilia, cancer, brain tumors, and other chronic medical, developmental, and emotional challenges. One of TTFF's programs is offering a summer camp experience as well as weekend respites to these children and their families *at no charge*. TTFF serves children and families from all 49 counties in Northern California. At least half are from families at or below the poverty level.

TTFF's summer camp program was created in 2000 at Camp Arroyo. The Exceptional Needs Network (ENN) and Kara are just two of many groups that TTFF partners with to create lasting memories and a respite for children and families in need. These two agencies and their programs at Camp Arroyo are described in this chapter.

Exceptional Needs Network Program at Camp Arroyo—

The Exceptional Needs Network (ENN) was founded in 2001 as a volunteer organization by a group of parents of special needs children. ENN started its program at Camp Arroyo in 2002. ENN's Camp can accommodate up to 45 developmentally delayed youth, ages 6-22 years, per session. ENN has one counselor for each youth at the Camp. In addition to the camp program, ENN also offers a therapeutic horseback-riding program. In the past, ENN awarded grants to special education teachers. More information on ENN can be found at www.ennetwork.org.

Up to eight specially selected therapy dog teams visit the ENN program at Camp Arroyo for two sessions each summer and sometimes one session in the fall. The teams have been participating in this program since 2004, with Carol Weldin having coordinated the visits since 2006, working closely with Laura McSheffrey and one of her assistants in hand-selecting the therapy dog teams that participate. Each of these teams has undergone an additional evaluation, inclusive of temperament evaluation of the therapy dog and the handler's interactions with the target population, to determine the team's effectiveness in interacting with children with disabilities.

Visitations are planned for one-hour increments, with children coming and going in the prescribed visitation area, depending on other activities they have scheduled. Visits are held in an open area that allows for free circulation among the therapy dog teams and the children. Children mingle among the individual therapy dog teams, often spending more time with one team, depending on their interest and interaction with a specific therapy dog. Some prefer the smaller dogs; some prefer those with long hair; and some have no particular preference. The overriding facts are that the therapy dogs are very calm and do not initiate the approach and that the handlers are conversant with these special-needs children.

—Testimonials—

Therapy dogs are very popular with the groups hosted by The Taylor Family Foundation at Camp Arroyo. When requested by a group, the dogs and their handlers come in for a few hours at a time to hang out with the kids on the grass under a shade tree. Their presence with many of our campers, especially the campers with autism, brings a calm and a joy, and enhances the kids' stay at camp. The dogs are very popular, and the handlers are wonderful to work with, and, to our delight, many come back all summer long. The therapy dog program is a wonderful addition to the activities that we can offer.

Angie Carmignani, Executive Director, The Taylor Family Foundation

Since 2004, the therapy dog teams have been coming to ENN's Camp Arroyo. The handlers bring their therapy dogs to visit with the campers. It is always rewarding to see the campers' interaction with the dogs. When the campers are visiting with the dogs, they seem to be less anxious and more calm and relaxed.

I have also seen campers that I have been told are afraid of dogs able to overcome their fear with the help of the handlers and their dogs. The smiles are never-ending when the dogs are at camp!!

Laura McSheffrey, Director, Exceptional Needs Network

It is very heartwarming to see the response of a child who was previously reluctant to approach a dog, due to a bad experience, or who was uncomfortable because of having had no prior interaction with a dog, being very comfortable with the calm and soothing nature of these exceptional dogs. Children who are non-verbal can often be observed with big smiles on their faces. This exemplifies the power of and the importance of these visitations with the therapy dogs.

Carol Weldin, Therapy Dog Team Coordinator for Exceptional Needs Network at Camp Arroyo

—Stories—

Below are stories about four therapy dogs and their work at Camp Arroyo—Ella, a Cavalier King Charles Spaniel; Kane and Lucky, both Golden Retrievers; and Mojo, a Welsh Corgi.

Not Afraid of These Dogs—

The counselor for a 13-year-old girl named Judy was telling me that Judy had always been afraid of dogs. Judy had another friend sitting near her. This friend told me that she has always had to lock her dog up when Judy was at her house, even though her dog is soooo friendly.

The counselor directed Judy to Lucky, who was very gentle and friendly with Judy. After several minutes, Judy was eventually able to touch Lucky, and, therein, began a mutual admiration between them. Judy was thrilled to finally pet him, and she could hardly wait to tell her mother that she had indeed petted a dog. She was so proud, as evidenced by her ear-to-ear smile, when she looked down at Lucky. It was the beginning of a great new accomplishment with Lucky, a new kind of friendship.

Judy came home from camp telling her mother about the therapy dogs. Her mother asked her, “Weren’t you afraid of the dogs?” Judy replied, “No, they were therapy dogs!!!!” She then told her mother how much she enjoyed visiting with them. I got tears in my eyes when I learned about this.

Can’t Forget This Dog—

Two boys with autism had participated in the Paws to Read program when they were younger with my dogs, Bizi (now deceased) and Lucky. Years later, when the boys were at Camp Arroyo, I heard one of them calling “Lucky.” Both boys were at the camp and both remembered Lucky, their listener in the early years of the Paws to Read program. He apparently was very special to them.

Responding to the Dog—

At each summer camp, Diane, a teenage girl in a reclined wheelchair, came to visit with the dogs. She was memorable because she didn’t speak and could barely move her arms and legs. Diane expressed herself by tongue movements and throat sounds. Her counselor asked me to lift Ella close to Diane so she could feel Ella’s fur on her arms and hands.

I'll never forget the joy on Diane's face the first time Ella's fur contacted her skin. She vocalized and moved her tongue in all directions. Her body spoke volumes about her excitement of Ella's softness. She especially liked Ella's tiny feet on her arm and didn't want them to be taken off her arm. Her counselor said the dog visits were the highlight of Diane's camp experience each summer.

Time for Laughs—

Kane really likes going to Camp Arroyo. Sometimes, Kane and I would sit on the ground together, and Kane would go from one person to the next. If they weren't paying attention to him, Kane would just do something silly, like turn over on his back and wiggle around until they laughed. It's nice to hear children laugh.

Almost Too Late for the Dog—

One afternoon, the therapy dog teams were leaving, and we were the last team to leave the lawn area. For some reason, I turned and looked back. I saw a child who had arrived late, standing on the lawn. Bryce was upset and telling the staff member that he had missed the dogs. I turned and asked if Mojo could sit with him for a while.

I told Bryce that Mojo didn't get enough petting today and would love to get some loving. The smile on Bryce was amazing. He dropped to the ground, and, of course, Mojo climbed onto his lap. Bryce talked to and petted Mojo telling him that he was the best dog ever. I was walking on a cloud after that experience. You see, we, as volunteers, get as much joy from these programs as the children do.

From Fear to Friendship—

A tall teenage boy named Brandon was very afraid of dogs. He circled the outside of the group of campers who were petting dogs, too afraid to approach any dog. I thought of a way to approach the fearful teen. Since Ella is small, I held her in my arm at my side with her head behind my elbow and her tail facing forward. I asked Brandon if he would like to pet Ella, and his counselor encouraged him by showing him how to pet Ella's back.

After awhile, he reluctantly put out one finger to try, approaching cautiously, with a wincing look on his face like it would hurt. His finger brushed Ella's back softly and quickly. Brandon smiled. He considered it awhile and came back to try with his whole hand extended.

He was so surprised at Ella's softness and that she didn't even move. When her tail started wagging, Brandon laughed. After a few more pats, he let me turn her around, and he watched while others petted her. He waved to Ella from a few feet away and came closer to watch her face. He touched Ella's ear and told her she was his friend. Brandon made my day.

—Quotes—

- Seeing the doggies is the best part of camp. *(six-year-old child)*
- My favorite memory of camp was seeing the animals because I love animals. *(14-year-old youngster)*
- The things I liked best at camp were the Rock Wall and the animals. *(nine-year-old child)*
- My favorite thing to do at camp was petting the animals. *(ten-year-old child)*

Kara's Camp Erin Program at Camp Arroyo—

The Moyer Foundation, headquartered in Seattle, Washington, is a public, 501(c) (3) nonprofit organization founded in 2000 by Major League Baseball (MLB) World Series-winning All-Star Pitcher Jamie Moyer and his wife, Karen. Camp Erin is the largest network of bereavement camps for children and teens in the country with over 40 camps nationwide, including Canada. Four are specifically for youth who have lost a family member in the military.

The Moyer Foundation partners with healthcare and bereavement organizations in local communities, such as Kara, to help fund, develop, and grow the Camp Erin program nationwide. The Foundation is leading the effort to help establish as many as 60 Camp Erin bereavement camps nationwide because no child should grieve alone. For more information on The Moyer Foundation, go to www.moyerfoundation.org.

Kara is a nonprofit organization, located in Palo Alto, and has been serving the San Francisco Bay Area since 1976. Its services are provided primarily by volunteers who have experience in healing from personal loss. With the aid of professional staff and ongoing training, Kara's volunteers facilitate others' journeys during life-threatening illness and bereavement. Kara is supported primarily by tax-deductible donations from individuals, corporations, and foundations. For information on Kara, go to www.kara-grief.org.

Kara's Camp Erin is partnered with the San Francisco Giants. The Taylor Family Foundation (TTFF) donates the use of Camp Arroyo to Kara's Camp Erin. TTFF's mission is to preserve the wellness and enhance the quality of life for children in Northern California with life-threatening and chronic illnesses and disabilities, as well as youth at-risk, through unique therapeutic experiences and support.

Kara's founding is rooted in the early 1970s, when a growing awareness swept through the United States, England, and other countries that the way contemporary society handled death, based on the medical establishment's practices, was inadequate. The seminal work of Dr. Elizabeth Kubler-Ross and the emerging hospice movement stimulated discussions about death and dying in Palo Alto and other communities.

Today, over 150 volunteers provide services that support those who are grieving, dying, or anticipating the death of a loved one. Kara has come a long way since the fledgling group of 17 volunteers began the service. Yet it remains true to its roots, dedicated to the healing process of supporting people during times of grief and loss. One of Kara's programs is Camp Erin, which it started in 2008.

Camp Erin is the largest bereavement camp program in the country, designed for youth, ages 6-17 years, who are grieving the loss of a family member or someone close to them. The weekend-long experience, held annually by Kara at Camp Arroyo, usually in the summer, is filled with traditional and fun camp activities, combined with grief education and emotional support, facilitated by grief professionals and trained volunteers. The campers learn that they are not alone and that their feelings are normal and similar to those of others. They also have an opportunity to address their feelings and learn how to honor the person who died.

While at Camp Arroyo, the children and teens in the Camp Erin program run, laugh, and make friends with others who share the same grief experience. Therapy dog teams were involved for the first time in 2011.

—Testimonials—

We were so excited that the therapy dogs would be coming to Camp Erin in 2011. Often a child can find it difficult to express feelings about their loss and they might be unsure about ways to find comfort. The therapy dogs are perfect for these children in particular.

Yet, all of our campers seemed to find comfort with the dogs. Nothing needs to be said. Rather, there is a feeling of mutual love, understanding, and trust between the camper and the dog. It was the ideal match. We are ever so grateful to the dogs and their handlers for coming to Camp Erin.

Deb Gitlin, Kara Assistant Director of Youth and Family Services

After the death of their dad, my children have had the opportunity to attend Camp Erin. This weekend-long love fest has been very helpful for my kids in processing their grief, and, most importantly, for them to see that they are not the only kids to experience a big loss. The power of standing in a room with 100 other kids, all of whom have had a sibling or parent die, and knowing that each of those kids has an understanding of how you feel is beyond measure.

While I hate the fact that my children meet the criteria for attending, I'm overwhelmingly grateful for the chance for them to attend Camp Erin. They come away from camp knowing that they are loved and that they are not alone. The therapy dogs were a great distraction from some of the more feeling-based activities—just a demonstration of play and love! Both of my kids loved playing with and petting the dogs.

Carol Pugh, Parent of two campers

—Stories—

Those dogs participating have included—Buddy W, a Golden Retriever/Yellow Lab mix; Lady, a Border Collie/Aussie mix; P.I.P., a Border Collie/Cattle Dog mix; and Tioga, a Labrador Retriever/Golden Retriever mix.

Lifting the Burden of a Lost Loved One—

During our visit with the children at Camp Erin, the children mingled with the therapy dogs, individually and in groups. They smiled, laughed, and enjoyed the company of the therapy dogs. For an afternoon, it became apparent that the burden of their recent loss was lifted and that the presence of the dogs enhanced their experience at Camp Erin. At the end of the day, literally all of the kids expressed their thanks to us, and many asked if they could hug Buddy W as a thank you for his visit. Buddy W graciously accepted. It was a very special day "at work" for Buddy W.

Fun Times—

Lady absolutely loved Camp Erin, mostly because she loves kids. She took to all of them really well, and they quickly took to her also. She seemed to have a group of kids around her most of the time.

The fun really started when the Frisbies ® came out. The children took turns throwing them for her, and she made a few dazzling catches that drew some oohs and aahs. Different groups of children were brought out throughout the day, and Lady loved all of them. I could tell from the look on her face when we left Camp Erin after three hours that she was already looking forward to going back to Camp Erin next year.

Play Ball—

P.I.P. (Pretty Impressive Pooch) and I were invited to Camp Erin. It was a hot day, in the 90s. We were there from 3:00 to 6:00 PM. When we arrived, they told us that children would be rotating through in groups. Some of the dogs were lying in the shade, and the children were petting them. Other children were walking dogs around the camp area.

P.I.P. is a hands-on dog, and his game is "Play Ball." He leaps into the air or chases the ball. P.I.P. can also do many tricks. P.I.P. was having the time of his life chasing the ball and bringing it back. Each child wanted to be the one to throw the ball. P.I.P. would choose a different child each time he brought the ball back and drop the ball at their feet. Everyone got some turns.

Bringing Out the Quiet Children—

I took Tioga to Camp Erin along with his best friends, Carolyn Vane and her dog, P.I.P. He is always a showstopper with lots of tricks that everyone enjoys. While P.I.P. is wowing his audience with leaps to catch his toy, Tioga quietly works the crowd to ensure that someone's hand is always scratching his lower back or his head. He seems to instinctively be drawn to the introverts in a crowd and then works gently and relentlessly to draw them out. He is also completely comfortable with four to five children all massaging some part of his body simultaneously, though some dogs would feel uncomfortable in this situation.

Special Dog—

I heard Lucy telling the next group to get the black and white dog named P.I.P. She said, "P.I.P. is the best!" I later heard Lucy say to her friend, "I wish P.I.P. was my dog." Lucy's friend agreed. I hope the time they spent with P.I.P. brought them as much happiness as they brought to him and that they both feel that P.I.P. is now their friend.

—Quotes—

- The dogs were great! *(young camper)*
- I really liked the dogs. *(young camper)*
- I love petting the dogs! *(six-year-old girl camper)*
- It was really fun to play Frisbee with Lady! She can jump about three feet off the ground. *(eight-year-old boy camper)*

~CHAPTER 3~

community assistance for retarded and handicapped

Community Assistance for Retarded and Handicapped (CARH) is a private, not-for-profit organization founded in 1972. Its mission is "to enrich the lives of local citizens with intellectual disabilities by providing social and recreational services that may not be offered by other private or governmental agencies." CARH provides social and recreational activities for its over 2,000 special-needs clients, young children to seniors, almost every day except Sunday. These opportunities allow clients to make friends and socialize with them, and to be part of their own community.

Programs and activities include bingo, crafts, movies, parties, picnics, and special events. They are held at various locations throughout the East Bay. Most are conducted by CARH's team of trained volunteers. CARH also has special services such as the Mobile Dental Hygiene Program, the Campership Tuition Program, and A Wonderful You Day when clients can get their hair and nails done by volunteer hair stylists/ barbers and manicurists. It also provides financial assistance for basic needs such as wheelchairs, eyeglasses, and special beds.

CARH receives no government funding and relies primarily on tax-deductible donations of gently-used household items and clothing from residences in five counties and recycling to fund its program. CARH's administrative office is located at 20513-17 Almeda Street, Castro Valley, California 94546. For information, call 1-877-537-6611 or fax 510-537-8668 or go to the website at www.carh-inc.org.

Two Newfoundlands go to CARH activities. Starting in 2007, Tedi Bear and Chex Mix attended the summer picnics, one for seniors and one for the developmentally disabled. Since then, they have attended numerous CARH events. For example, Tedi Bear went to the Halloween Party in 2007 and Chex Mix has been at St. Patrick's Day parties. In August 2011, Chex Mix was named "Volunteer of the Month."

—Testimonials—

When Chex Mix, a beautiful black and white Newfoundland pup, attends CARH's special events and activities, it is delightful to watch the pleased and excited faces of those we serve who are living with intellectual disabilities. A large majority of the individuals we serve live in residential care homes. Some care homes do not permit pets. Many of our clients have never had the privilege of experiencing the benefits of pet ownership and are thrilled for the chance to experience the unconditional love and joy a visiting gentle dog can offer. Chex Mix brings additional happiness to our functions. He is without a doubt a "huge" and popular attraction.

Our clients cannot get enough of the gentle giant, aka "big teddy bear." We have had clients eagerly wait in line for their turn to spend time with Chex Mix to give and receive hugs and kisses too. Chex Mix is a bit of a ham and seems to bask in all the doting. It is a joy to watch our clients interact with him. We had one client who does not speak, and who rarely smiles, but she smiled when it was her turn to visit with Chex Mix.

Jennifer Feeney, CARH Program Coordinator

Having Chex Mix come to these different events put on by CARH makes my son, Kevin, relaxed and very calm. He enjoys having the dog there. It is a good thing what Hazel is doing with her dog here and also the kids in the reading program at the Castro Valley Library. It makes it like home. That's great for the kids at the library and for the people at the CARH events.

There are people who are afraid of dogs, but Chex Mix comes in and plops down with a gentle greeting sound as if to say, "Here I am. Pet me on my head." He licks their hand or puts his paws up. Then they realize he is not going to hurt them and that he actually likes them. So the people aren't afraid of him anymore.

Bev Mello, Mother of a client, and Kevin Mello, Client

—Stories—

Below are stories for the two Newfoundlands who have gone to CARH activities—Tedi Bear and Chex Mix.

A Bear in the Park?—

Tedi Bear's first therapy dog assignment was to attend a picnic held by CARH. It was in a park area. As we walked in, many of the attendees came to see what this "bear" really was. They enjoyed the petting and many talked to her.

Tedi Bear seemed to know what they wanted. Gwendolyn, one of the senior clients, called us over, saying, "I always had dogs and miss them so. Can I please pet her?" "Of course," I said, and Tedi Bear just laid her head in Gwendolyn's lap and rested it there. Her lap was just the right height for Tedi Bear's head, and Tedi Bear filled up her lap!

Knowing When to Seek Attention—

Chex Mix is very forward in begging for attention. However, he also seems to know when pushing is not appropriate. Thus, his work with the clients at CARH is great to watch. He accepts attention from those who wish to give it, but never pushes those who are concerned about him. He is willing to cuddle by putting his head on a lap, and will shake hands when invited to do so.

Making St. Patrick's Day Special—

Our 2011 St. Patrick's Day dances were a great success and Chex Mix certainly added to the excitement. Chex Mix gave big wet kisses and was a "huge" attraction. When the DJ played "Who Let the Dogs Out," Chex Mix made his debut by pulling a cart full of gifts for our guests. He was so popular, I almost had to do crowd control. One client said, "I love him!" It was precious watching the clients interact with Chex Mix. Everyone gathered around to pet, hug, and kiss him. One of our clients actually lay on the floor to snuggle with him.

A Winner on Bingo Day—

Chex Mix attended Bingo Day at CARH. One lady came over as soon as Chex Mix walked in. She petted him and chatted with him. Soon several others came over to see him. Even Edwin, who said to me, "I am afraid of big dogs, but he seems so gentle," came over to pet him. Edwin came over several more times while we were there. It is wonderful to see how Chex Mix can warm up a room!

Interested in the Dog—

One Saturday afternoon, Chex Mix and I went to a CARH event with several activities and services available to its clients. Three men had come to play bingo and to have dental cleanings. All three men came over several times during the afternoon to pet Chex Mix gently and to ask me questions about him. They were fascinated by Chex Mix's size and gentleness. One of the men even enjoyed the kisses from Chex Mix! And Chex Mix didn't mind doing it before and after the teeth cleaning.

Words Come Out—

Lois, a lady in a wheelchair, was at CARH one afternoon for bingo. She is facing both physical and mental challenges, and her caregiver was with her. Chex Mix is at bingo for the break between the first and second sessions so people can come see him and pet him. Lois's caregiver was standing next to her, and I asked her if she thought Lois would like to pet the dog. The caregiver said, "No." Lois came up to Chex Mix and said, "Doggie! Good Doggie!" When the caregiver heard Lois talk, she commented, "I didn't even know she knew those words. That is great!"

—Quotes—

- Chex loves people and getting attention. Even though he is a large dog (135 pounds), he is so sweet, gentle, and loving. *(staff)*
- Chex is an adorable and spectacular dog who creates a lot of smiles wherever he goes. *(staff)*
- Hi Chex. Do you remember me? *(client)*
- Oh good. Chex is here today. *(client)*

~CHAPTER 4~

easy living care home

Easy Living Care Home (ELCH), located at five sites in Livermore, is a residential care facility licensed by the California Department of Social Services. Founded in 2006, its mission is to fill the gap between independent retirement living and skilled nursing care.

ELCH provides long-term care for up to six seniors, including non-ambulatory and hospice, at each site. They live in single and double bedrooms in a house that has been modified to meet the needs of the residents in terms of accessibility, care, and comfort. They share the rest of the house with the other residents.

By developing a personalized care plan for each resident, ELCH staff offers nurturing and dignified care to seniors who can no longer live on their own. Staff is available 24 hours a day, seven days a week. They are trained in creative approaches to and skilled in helping those with physical and mental disabilities. They promote and improve the wellbeing of the residents while implementing their individual care plans.

The sites in Livermore are located at 2863 Carmen Avenue, 417 Jillana Avenue, 281 Lloyd Street, 3536 Murphy Street, and 1285 Norwood Place. For more information, go to http://easylivingcarehome.com/.

The therapy dog visits started in September 2006 when the mother of one of the handlers' friends was at the ELCH on Murphy Street. Her mother missed seeing the dogs and asked to have them brought by. Everyone enjoyed them so much that they started going once a week to the ELCH Murphy Street site. Now three therapy dogs—Albert, Lawrence, and Thunder—visit that site and each of the other four ELCH sites at least once or twice a month.

—Testimonials—

The residents are much more responsive and pleasant during the days that the dogs visit the facility. Often times, I wish we could keep one of them because I know they would make our jobs as caregivers a lot easier.

Judy Baxter, Caregiver

I provide activities for seniors at the five Easy Living Care Home sites and about 20 other sites from Walnut Creek to Livermore. I am always amazed at the therapeutic value that the therapy dogs have on the elders. I worked at a local hospital for ten years. I have observed many visits by trained dogs and saw that this was the time that the seniors reacted the most. They reacted in an obviously happy way, always a reaction of joy! These dogs bring back many good memories for the people. They are not threatening, so the elders feel good about loving them, and the benefit of the dogs' showing affection to the seniors is huge.

The touch therapy helps with depression found in so many seniors. Depression is very common in the aging process. It is usually healed with activity. Any activity presented that makes the elderly happy releases chemicals in the brain that helps them heal and feel wellness. When a person is mingling with an animal, they are moving, stretching, petting, feeling, touching, and, most of all, observing a wagging tail and loving eyes. It is all good and therapeutic for seniors!

I love the therapy dogs meeting the needs of our seniors. The last stages of life, unfortunately, have little newness or activity, so this is a blessing to all. Thank you for your work.

Theresa Cleaver, Owner, Plan B Senior Resources

I wanted to take this opportunity to write to you regarding the use of therapy dogs in visiting the elderly and infirm in board and care facilities such as Easy Living Care Home.

I have been present when the therapy dogs have been interacting with elderly and dementia patients. For the residents, this is often a highlight in their day. People who have difficulty responding verbally to their family and/or caregivers seem to be able to react positively to these dogs.

As the daughter of a dementia patient, I have experienced this firsthand. At times, when my mother has had great difficulty communicating verbally, a visit from the therapy dog has been something she has remembered and is able to share verbally with me. At Easy Living Care Home, the therapy dogs encourage fellow residents to come out of their rooms just to interact. The residents are more talkative with one another and with the caregivers and family members after a therapy dog visit. The dog allows them to touch an animal and to feel physical closeness and personal interaction in an acceptable, monitored environment.

Many of these residents had a close relationship with a family pet in their earlier years. Some have had to leave their pets behind when they moved to a more secure environment. The visits from the therapy dogs remind them of those close relationships in a positive way. They look forward to these visits. Being with the dogs also calms them and allows them to focus better on their daily activities.

I hope that you will be able to continue this important and meaningful service for our families and residents.

Barbara Correa, Daughter of a dementia patient

We love animals, and so I like having the dogs come here. They're so friendly. And nobody else comes to see us.

I used to be deathly afraid of dogs, but I don't seem to be in my old age. I turned 100 last August. When I first saw Thunder, I instinctively touched him because of his demeanor. He was very calm.

Katherine (Kate) Dalessi, Resident

When the dogs come to see me, I feel good. I love dogs. Thunder, Albert, and Lawrence are well behaved. I like seeing Albert watching for squirrels, Lawrence sleeping, and Thunder looking out the window. I feel sad when they leave here.

Barbara Farren, Resident

My mission is to provide proper care for seniors. I opened Easy Living Care Home to allow seniors who can no longer live in their own homes to have a place to live where they could feel comfort and elegance, and be in a homelike setting.

Knowing that there have been many losses in their lives, I try to put things in place for their enjoyment that will compliment who they are today, honor their integrity, and help them feel worthy and hopeful. Depression and decline of health stem from feelings of hopelessness and helplessness—nothing for them to look forward to (future) and unworthiness (loss of capabilities to accomplish tasks).

The dogs visiting the Easy Living Care Home sites have not only brought joy to our residents, but the visits are something for seniors to look forward to. Having animals to pet, kiss, hug, and squeeze is therapeutic for seniors. They respond to the touch and the playfulness which is projected by the dogs unconditionally. The seniors feel alive when they are watching a dog play. The dogs make them feel loved which ultimately helps them forget about their pain. The feeling of hope is healing to them, and the dogs are not bothered by their frailness, so the seniors feel adequate and whole again for the moment.

It is a wonderful thing that takes place between a senior and a loving dog. It is finer than riches, stays in their system longer than the strongest drug, and brightens them up like the presence of a loved one entering a room. Nothing else has this power. I believe the dogs make them feel alive and youthful again. It probably even smoothes their wrinkles as they smile from ear to ear.

Thank you for all that these therapy dogs have accomplished with our seniors. Without these dogs, their lives would be emptier.

Emily Garcia, Administrator/Owner

The therapy dogs are good help to some of our clients. The dogs give joy to them as well as to the staff whenever they come around. They're so cute and awesome. It gives us something relaxing whenever you touch the dog. When you call his name, he comes to you as if he knows you.

Ricardo Gerena, Direct Staff Professional

One of the many joys of living at Emily Garcia's Easy Living Care Home on Murphy Street was Pat bringing Albert and Lawrence over for a visit. I'm so glad they come to Norwood now too. The "boys" go around to each of us with their tails wagging the message of "HAPPY TO SEE YOU AGAIN!!" The individual greeting continues with a warm head in the lap and "kisses" on our hands, or a leaning into our legs to encourage long strokes and scratches from ears to tail.

Likewise, the visits with Laurie's dog, Thunder, are treasured by me. I especially like those rolling deep tones announcing his arrival and his joy of being with all of us again.

I enjoy each visit and would stop the activity I was doing in my room to come out for a visit with whichever therapy dog was brought that day. It is great therapy for all of us, especially me.

Thomas Marshall, Resident

It's nice to have the dogs here. They make me feel good. I like to see them when they come in. I like all the dogs; I don't have a favorite. They do a good job of making us feel good.

Marge Ramano, Resident

I really appreciate your bringing your dogs to see my friend. She has been here for a long, long time. She has no relatives nearby and hardly gets any visitors. She looks forward to seeing the dogs. I love seeing the smile on her face when the dogs come in. The dogs are a highlight in her day. It's wonderful seeing her reach out to pet the dogs on their heads.

Jane Rasmussan, Friend of a resident

It is favorable having the dogs here. It's a pleasure to pet the dogs. It reminds me of when I was growing up on the farm. I had two dogs and a pony. I recommend that people be friendly with dogs and horses. And I like seeing Albert swishing his tail and doing the twist.

Henry (Hank) Reeves, Resident

For years, one of our residents who had Alzheimer's would not take her pain medication. Then one day, we noticed her demeanor was happier every time Pat brought one of her dogs here. From then on, she would take her medication so she wouldn't be sick whenever the dogs were around. I truly believe that she lived longer because of the dogs. They are miracle workers.

Liberto Vergilio (Vher) Ventenilla, Caregiver

There is something peaceful and calming when a dog comes to you. The dog is your friend at the start. I like seeing them here. Thunder and Lawrence get along together.

Charles Walker, Resident

—Stories—

Below are stories for the three dogs that go to the Easy Living Care Home sites—Albert, a Border Collie/Lab mix; Lawrence, a Black Labrador Retriever; and Thunder, a Boxer/Great Dane mix.

Time with the Mirror—

On sunny days, Mabel likes to sit in another resident's room where she can be in the sunshine and stay warm. When Albert comes in, he stands next to the chair that Mabel is in and looks at himself in the full-length mirrors on the closet doors. He wiggles around, walks closer, and then backs up. Albert repeats this routine several times. Mabel is convinced that Albert sees himself in the mirrors, and she really enjoys watching Albert watch himself.

Arrival Time—

Lawrence walks in and up to Allison, the only resident awake upon his arrival. Allison says, "Hello. How are you today?" Lawrence immediately goes plop on the floor. "Oh, so you're tired already," concludes Allison.

Giving Commands—

Leroy loves giving commands to the dogs and seeing if they do what he asks. One day, he told Lawrence to lie down. He had to repeat it a couple times before Lawrence did lie down. Later that morning, as soon as he told Lawrence to lie down, Lawrence hit the floor with a thud. "Good dog, good dog," said Leroy as he bent over to scratch Lawrence's head. I said, "Doesn't it feel good for someone to do something as soon as you ask them?" "YES!" replied Leroy, with a hearty laugh. He added, "But don't tell my wife."

Need to Stay Warm—

When the dogs are at ELCH, they are wagging their tails much of the time. Clara asks them not to do it because they are making her cold. What she really likes is for then to lie down on her feet and keep them warm.

A Special Scratch—

Karen loves scratching the dogs on the top of the head and down the top of their muzzle with one finger. And the dogs really enjoy it. She always has a wide smile on her face when she does this. The tails tell us that Albert, Lawrence, and Thunder all like it, but it apparently feels good to Karen too.

Listen to Me, Albert—

Joseph looked down at Albert, lying peacefully on the floor by his feet. Joseph leaned over and said, "Albert, you are so pretty." No response from Albert. So Joseph leaned over and lifted up Albert's floppy ear, commenting on how clean his ear was. Joseph again said, "Albert, you're so pretty." No response. "Listen to me, Albert! I want you to know how pretty you are!" said Joseph in a louder voice. Albert looked up at Joseph and happily wagged his tail.

Where Did the Thud Come From?—

We were in the living room watching TV when we heard a thud from the kitchen. Janet said, "Sounds like Lawrence just lied down." But Lawrence was already lying down, keeping Janet's toes warm.

Showing Off—

Albert enjoys doing tricks. He likes to show off for the residents and to entertain them by dancing, twirling, tunneling (between my legs), and, when younger, rolling over. They enjoy his show, and he gives them a good laugh.

Special Reunion—

At his first visit to an ELCH site, Lawrence saw one of his long-time friends who moved there from another ELCH site. Both were quite excited to see each other, with Lawrence's head between Oscar's knees and his tail wagging rapidly while Oscar gave Lawrence a nice backrub.

Oscar then introduced Lawrence to the other residents and told the other residents about the tricks Lawrence likes to do. He asked me to have Lawrence do a "tunnel," which Lawrence promptly did. Then Oscar had Lawrence sit, lie down, and shake. Even though Oscar hadn't seen Lawrence in months, he knew what tricks Lawrence would do.

Thunder's Head—

Every time Thunder and I go to the Murphy house, I take Thunder down the line of the residents sitting in their chairs watching TV. Whenever we stop to see Charlotte, Thunder *always* puts his head in her lap, whether she is awake or not. If she is awake, she always has the same comment, "He sure has a heavy head." Thunder's head is quite large, and I know that it is heavy. But the smile on Charlotte's face tells us she likes having Thunder do this.

Going for a Walk—

Sally was determined to go for a walk one morning and kept going to the front door and opened it a couple times. I finally decided maybe Albert could go on a walk with her around the house, circling through the family room, dining room, living room, and front hall, back to the family room.

We went over to where Sally was sitting. She got up and took Albert's leash. I tried to hold onto Albert's leash too, but she was determined to get it away from me. So we walked around, my giving Albert commands like "Left" and "Forward," so he could lead the way. Then Sally said, "I want to take him home," as she proceeded down the hallway with Albert and into one of the bedrooms. I don't know if it was her room or not. But Sally sat on the edge of the bed and played with Albert a few minutes. Then a caretaker came in to help me get the leash back from her. At least she settled down for awhile, back on a couch in the family room, after that.

A New Friend—

Lawrence had just met Dale at the Norwood site. After visiting the other residents there, Lawrence went over to Dale and lay down on the floor in front of him. I said to Dale, "I think you have a new friend." Dale replied, "Couldn't have a better friend than Lawrence," as he leaned over and scratched Lawrence's back.

Watching Sports on TV—

Cameron wanted to watch the baseball game on TV. I told Cameron that Lawrence likes to watch football, but that I had never seen him watch baseball. Lawrence was lying on the floor in front of the TV. Cameron pointed out several times that Lawrence's eyes were looking at the TV and that he occasionally rolled his eyes while watching the game. Apparently Lawrence enjoys baseball too.

Missing the Dogs—

We hadn't been to one of the sites for a few weeks while work was being done there. Then I learned that it was clear for us to take our dogs there again. Before having a chance to go back to that site, I saw two of the residents from that site at a holiday party at another site. One exclaimed, "Just seeing you guys will be enough for Christmas!" Another said, "I am really glad I had the bookmark so I could look at their pictures when they weren't there." When I told her we would be giving her a new bookmark with their pictures on it for this Christmas, she was all excited. It seems like they really missed our dogs.

A Big Smile—

On our first visit to the Jillana site, Otis was sitting in a chair in the family room watching TV when Thunder and I arrived. I walked over to him, said "Hi," and introduced Thunder to him. He immediately had a great big smile on his face, which stayed there the entire time we visited with him. I asked him a few questions about the animals he has seen in the backyard, and I received some very short answers from Otis since he was watching TV.

A short while later, after Thunder and I had visited another resident in his room, we came back out to the family room where Otis was still watching TV. In the meantime, a woman had arrived to visit Otis. She was his daughter. She was pleased to see that Thunder was there. I told her that we had already visited with her father earlier this morning. Her first response to me was, "He doesn't talk much." I quickly responded to her that I had asked him several questions, and that he had answered them. She looked a little surprised and pleased at the same time. I felt elated that, with Thunder at my side, I was able to get responses from her dad that she thought might not be possible. Thunder has a way of bringing people out of their shells, because all he does is give someone unconditional love and listen attentively.

Time to Dance—

Albert loves to be scratched on his back near his tail. When he is scratched there, he wiggles back and forth. One day when Harry was scratching Albert there, he said, "Albert is dancing. Albert, you are doing the twist." Harry continued doing it several more times that morning, hoping Albert would learn to twist on command. We'll keep trying. Maybe one of these days he will.

Article on Missing Dog—

Rosa was reading the morning newspaper while Lawrence rested on the floor next to her. An article about a lost, small dog that disappeared five years ago caught her eye. The dog was found earlier in the month and taken to a shelter. Since it had a microchip, the shelter was able to locate its owners. The dog was returned to the owners two days before Christmas. Rosa loved this story and kept telling us about it as she looked down at Lawrence on the floor next to her. She was very happy to learn that Lawrence also has a microchip.

Breaking Out Into Song—

Albert was happily wagging his tail and going around to see everyone. Suddenly Edith broke into song, singing "Everybody Loves Somebody Sometime." She added, "Albert loves everybody all the time!"

Have to See You Before You Leave—

Albert arrived at Norwood just when Gilbert was being picked up by his daughter for an outing. It was a sunny day, though the wind made it feel chilly. The caregiver wheeled Gilbert down the ramp and then helped Gilbert's daughter move him into the front seat. Albert was watching attentively the entire time.

As soon as Gilbert was comfortably in the front seat, Albert wanted to get into the car with him. He put his paws up on the base of the doorframe and nudged Gilbert with his muzzle. Gilbert was so glad to see how much Albert wanted to be with him, and his daughter was pleased to see her dad receiving love from Albert.

No People Food!—

Lawrence is always searching for crumbs on the floor. That's why my kitchen has no food on the floor, only dog hair and mud that Lawrence sheds or brings in. Emma wanted to give Lawrence some crumbs left from her breakfast. As she held a small piece of food in her hand, I said, "No people food for Lawrence," although he had already cleaned some off the floor under the table. Emma put it back on her plate. She remarked, "Now look at Lawrence. He's not going to forgive me." I suggested she gently drop it on the floor. She did, and Lawrence was quite happy about that, as was Emma.

Great Massages—

Albert loves to get massages, especially since he has arthritis in his back legs. And Randy is good at giving massages. Randy was in his room when we arrived, but when the caregiver told him Albert was there, he came out of his room and started rubbing Albert. Albert wiggled around in delight, as if doing the twist that Harry was trying to teach him.

Randy gave him a massage from head to tail. When Randy stopped, Albert turned around and looked at him. "Oh, you want me to go through the same routine again," said Randy, and Albert wagged his tail as if saying, "YES!" Kent, another resident, said, "I'll give you 30 minutes before he lets you stop that." Randy continued the massaging, and Albert kept doing the twist when Randy was rubbing him on his back near his tail. Kent said, "Oh boy, you're a dancer." After Randy stopped, Albert stretched and then plopped onto the floor. "I like the way Albert is so fully relaxed now that he has had two massages," said Randy. Harry added, "He's perfectly happy."

Melodic Music—

Juan is a fairly new resident, and Thunder and I had not met him before. Juan talked about how he used to be a ballroom dancer, competing all over the state. Then spontaneously, the caretaker brought Juan his harmonica. As soon as he started to play, Thunder put his nose right up to the harmonica, being very inquisitive.

Juan played it very well, and the music was very soothing. After a couple of minutes, Thunder laid on the floor next to him. Thunder's ears stayed perked up because he really enjoyed the music. This was the first time that Thunder had ever heard a harmonica, and apparently he really enjoyed the music, as we all did.

Great Day for Squirrel Patrol—

Albert was visiting Joan and Mary at Lloyd one sunny March morning. Both ladies were reading their newspapers when we arrived. Albert made himself comfortable on the floor near each of them. Suddenly, Albert was up and looking out the patio door near Joan's chair. Joan pulled the curtain back so she could look out and so Albert could see even more.

He looked very intently out at the backyard. Joan and I couldn't see what he was looking at, but he obviously saw something. We assumed it was squirrels. Whenever I say the word "squirrel," his ears perk up. Joan said, "He is really intent on looking at something. Albert's eyes are really focused on something, and his tail isn't moving. I don't see what he is seeing."

Suddenly, Joan and I saw two squirrels playfully jumping from tree to tree in the backyard. Obviously, Albert was aware that there were squirrels in the backyard that morning. Both Joan and Mary complimented Albert on the wonderful job he had done keeping an eye on the squirrels for them. We all had a fun time watching the squirrels playing as well as watching Albert watching the squirrels.

—Quotes—

- I'm so glad you came today. Where have you been? *(resident)*
- Even though you're ten years old, you're a puppy at heart. *(resident)*
- Do you know how much joy you bring to people, Albert? *(visitor)*
- No people can love the way these dogs do. *(resident)*

- Your fur looks so soft. Oh, it is soft. It feels so good. *(resident)*
- The dogs are so cute. They are wonderful. *(visitor)*
- You're ten years old? You have a history, don't you! *(resident)*
- If I had a dog like you, I'd put him in a place with a silver lining. *(resident)*
- It's so nice of you to bring the therapy dogs here. They make everyone happy. *(family member)*
- If a dog licks you, you know you have a friend. If a cat licks you, you have chicken on your face. *(resident)*
- The therapy dogs are wonderful. We talk to them like they are people. *(visitor)*
- I love dogs. I want to have one to stay in my room. Let me know if you want me to be his dog sitter. *(resident)*
- The temperament of these dogs is the best! *(resident)*
- You get all attached to these dogs, and they get attached to you. They become your best friends. *(resident)*
- I have to tell my family that I met a really special dog today! *(resident)*

Albert

~CHAPTER 5~

the friendship center

The Friendship Center Adult Day Care Program was opened in 1992 by the Livermore Area Recreation and Park District (LARPD). The adult day care services included organized daily activities as well as personal care services. The Friendship Center provided social stimulation and health services to seniors who required supervised care. This program offered caregivers a break from their normal care giving responsibilities. Services included coordination of transportation to and from The Center, social activities, meals and snacks, and assistance with activities of daily living.

The Friendship Center was open during normal business hours, five days a week. It was located in a former school building at 543 Sonoma Avenue in Livermore. On May 14, 2008, the LARPD Board of Directors made the tough decision to close The Friendship Center when its lease with the school district was terminated because the school district needed the facilities for its growing charter school program, and no other suitable location could be found for The Center.

Therapy dogs visited The Friendship Center for several years. Augie went once a month from 2001 until The Center's closing in 2008. Buddy H went there from 1998 to 2000 on special occasions. Schnoz visited the clients at The Friendship Center twice a month in 2006 and 2007.

—Testimonials—

I have witnessed the very positive effects that these animals have on elderly people in day programs such as The Friendship Center in Livermore as well as in board and care facilities. A visit with the therapy dog was the highlight of the day for clients at The Friendship Center. Not only did the people benefit from touching, petting, and being close to these dogs. It encouraged them to share their visits and experiences with their families and friends.

As a past client of The Friendship Center, my mom bonded closely with Augie, one of the therapy dogs that visited The Center regularly. Mom would always tell me when Augie had been to visit. She looked forward to seeing Augie, and I enjoyed hearing her tell me about Augie's visit.

Barbara Correa, Daughter of a client

The dogs were very nice. There were five of us there one day, and, of course, we all loved seeing the dogs. I remember Schnoz and Augie.

Barbara Farren, Former client

I love dogs, and I also love talking and working with older adults. I was pleasantly surprised to be able to enjoy both at various times when visiting The Friendship Center. The therapy dogs who visited The Center had a profound effect on the clients. I observed that even the most withdrawn clients would smile and want to pet the dogs when they saw them.

The other noticeable effect that I observed was the calming influence they had. Several of the clients could often exhibit anxious, nervous, and agitated behavior. Whenever the dogs came, all of those who were at The Center were noticeably calm. I believe the dogs knew that some of the clients were anxious, and, in their own special way, they reached out to them as if to say, "It's all right."

It was truly a blessing to have the dogs come to The Center, and many clients, as well as staff, benefited greatly from their participation.

Steve Goodman, Member and 2011 President, LARPD Board of Directors

Almost all clients at The Friendship Center had some form of dementia. The visits from the dogs were a special time for the clients as they evoked memories, conversations, and stories from the clients. For those clients that could only live in the present, they brought smiles and laughs. The dogs would visit with the clients and "lead" an activity such as musical chairs whereby a staff member and Augie would circle a chair while music played. When the music stopped, we would see who was faster—Augie sitting on the ground or the staff person trying to sit in the chair. Augie always won.

Sandra Kaya, Former Activity Director, The Friendship Center; Administrative Aide to the Assistant General Manager, LARPD

Although we were not using the term "therapy dog" when we had our first canine visitor in 1992, everyone recognized the benefit of having Sunshine, a beautiful Spaniel, visiting with us. This loving dog was part of the family who had a loved one in our program. Sunshine was so popular with the clients and staff that we used photos of him on the cover of our first brochure. Our canine visitors were popular through the years and seemed to be like music to the adult day care participants—they were universally loved. Even participants who said they were not interested in petting the therapy dogs usually changed their minds after watching others with the dogs.

The dedicated volunteers who were willing to bring their dogs to our program added a special element to our program that brightened everyone's day at The Friendship Center.

Maureen Gandara Swinbank, MSW, Supervisor, Senior and Volunteer Services, LARPD

—Stories—

Below are stories for three dogs that went to The Friendship Center—Augie, a Golden Retriever; Buddy H, a Queensland Heeler/ Golden Retriever mix; and Schnoz, a Standard Schnauzer.

Preparing for Augie—

There was a routine when Augie arrived. There would be an announcement that "Augie's here!" This was followed by the staff immediately removing all trashcans from the floor since Augie had an uncontrollable urge to scout for snacks in the trashcans. Next, he would go around the room and greet each client. At that point, the trashcans were the farthest thing from Augie's mind because now he was focused on his friends.

Knowing When to Behave—

Buddy H was a feisty puppy at home, but as soon as he went to The Friendship Center, he seemed to understand that he needed to be calm. The clients would always ask, "Is he always this good?" I would respond, "Apparently when he wants or needs to be!" That always seemed to make them laugh.

Getting People to Move—

Augie instinctively knew that some people had limited mobility and would patiently sit still for literally minutes so that they could move their hands in slow motion from their laps to the top of his head. These clients would grin from ear to ear at their accomplishment and the reward of being able to pet him. I guess he was a "physical therapist" too!

Puppy News Updates—

I have female Schnauzers at home, and one of them had a litter of puppies. Schnoz brought in stories and pictures of the puppies. These were a big hit with the clients, and would bring back memories and prompt them to tell stories. It was difficult to tell the puppies apart, so I identified them with colored rickrack trim. But the clients gave the puppies names as they didn't like calling them green boy, red girl, etc. On days when the clients drew pictures as part of their artwork activities, some drew pictures of Schnoz and the puppies.

Showtime—

During each visit, Augie performed for about an hour. He displayed many of his talents which included jumping through a hula hoop, dancing with a tutu, and playing hide-and-go-seek, to name a few. Clients got good laughs out of watching Augie.

Doing His Job—

Rodney refused to believe he was a client, but instead said he was an employee of The Friendship Center. Even though he was afraid of dogs, he insisted on meeting Schnoz and me at the door and escorting us to the recreation room because he said that was his job. Although he was very shy around Schnoz at first, he gradually warmed up, and, before we knew it, Rodney and Schnoz were best friends.

Birthday Party for Augie—

Augie especially liked celebrating his birthday at The Friendship Center because not only did everyone sing "Happy Birthday" to him, but he also got to eat a sugar cookie in the shape of a dog bone. We would share these birthday treats with the clients. One year, this posed a problem when a client became distressed because she thought I was feeding dog food to her rather than Augie eating people food. But we assured her it was people food.

Special Communication—

When Buddy H came in for a visit, the expressions on the clients' faces changed. Most of them were delighted to have a young dog around the facility to interact with. His presence seemed to bring back memories of their own pets that they had in the past.

In particular, I remember a beautiful female resident by the name of Dorothy. She did not appear to be elderly, like most of the other clients, and, if I am not mistaken, she might have been recovering from a stroke. Dorothy rarely showed any expression on her face, but one day Buddy H snuggled up next to her. I gently led her hand to Buddy H's head so that she could pet him, and, as soon as she felt his soft fur on her hand, she smiled! It was as though there was some underlying communication between her and Buddy H that allowed the two of them to connect. One time, Dorothy, who could only speak with great effort, said in a soft voice, "Good boy!" It was truly amazing and so incredibly rewarding to hear her speak!

Performance Routine—

Since Schnoz had graduated from obedience school, he has some talents. On nice days, after lunch, the clients would go outside to the courtyard at The Center. Schnoz would go through his routine, and the clients would smile and clap. Schnoz made them come alive. He would go around, shaking hands with them, and then take a bow. All clients were delighted with his performance. Schnoz would repeat his routine over and over again, but to the clients, it was always seen as a first time performance since they usually had forgotten his last one.

How Old Is the Dog?—

One of the most frequent questions from the clients was "Is Buddy old?" I would respond, "No, why do you ask?" And they would reply, "Because he has a grey muzzle," and then they would always laugh about it.

How Schnoz Got His Name—

One activity for the clients at The Center was showing them movies. I brought in a DVD of Jimmy Durante one day. He was a great comedian of the 1950s and known as "The Great Schnozzola" because of his large nose. I told them that Schnoz was named after him. Although it was a short program, it struck a cord with the clients, and they really enjoyed it.

~CHAPTER 6~

library programs

In October 1999, Sue Jones was the Library Assistant II with Children's Services at the Pleasanton Public Library and the Humane Education Director (a volunteer position) for Valley Humane Society (VHS). She was invited by Nathania Gartman, Humane Educator for Best Friends Animal Society, to make a presentation on one of her humane education programs to other educators at a conference in Utah.

After a morning of visiting classrooms with a therapy dog team from Inter-Mountain Therapy Animals, the handler mentioned to Sue that they were going to try something new that evening. Since Sue worked in a library, the handler encouraged Sue to come and see what happened when therapy dogs were welcomed into a local bookstore and children were invited to read to them. Sue did attend, and what she witnessed that evening was the light-bulb moment of her life.

With one foot in the Pleasanton Public Library, which was hungry for community collaborations and unique programming, and the other in the Valley Humane Society's Pet Therapy Program, Sue put the two together to create something wonderful.

In November 2002, Paws to Read was launched, the first program of its kind in California. On October 15, 2004, the *San Francisco Chronicle* ran a story about the Paws to Read program. The article hit the Internet (http://www.sfgate.com/bayarea/article/Pleasanton-Dog-eared-companions-2687460.php). It took only one day for the Pleasanton Public Library and VHS to be inundated with inquiries from throughout the United States and around the world, from Canada to England and Germany to Australia and New Zealand.

Although the Pleasanton Public Library's program had been painstakingly built from the ground up through trial and error, under Sue's leadership, Paws to Read was shared with many other libraries throughout the San Francisco Bay Area and beyond. Now similar programs can be found worldwide.

Research has shown that when children read to dogs, their reading skills improve, they become more interested in reading, and it helps improve their self-esteem. Links to studies include:

http://blog.sfgate.com/jscarlett/2011/07/07/dogs-and-young-readers-on-the-same-page/

http://www.vet.tufts.edu/pr/20110810.html

Therapy dog teams visit several libraries in the Bay Area as part of the Paws to Read programs. Libraries welcome the opportunity to have therapy dogs and their handlers come for reading sessions. Children can bring their own book or select a book from the library. They sit on a mat or pillow, next to the dog and near the dog's handler.

The Paws to Read program is offered in five communities. Both the Danville and Orinda libraries are part of the Contra Costa County Library system. The Castro Valley Library is part of the Alameda County Library system. The Livermore and Pleasanton libraries are city libraries. Below are descriptions of the programs at these libraries, in the order that their Paws to Read programs started.

The **Pleasanton Public Library** is proud to be the first library in California to provide such an innovative and valuable program, offering Paws to Read to the public since November 2002. It has inspired many local and national libraries to implement similar programs.

The library is an especially popular destination for first through fifth graders attending the Paws to Read program on Tuesday evenings. This much-in-demand program is offered for six consecutive weeks during the fall, winter, and spring as well as for four weeks in the summer. Between 18 and 22 handlers, together with their dogs, participate each week in two 25-minute reading sessions. In partnership with local schools, reading specialists are given priority registration for their students. Once open to the public, this program usually fills within a few hours. Those children who are not formally registered are encouraged to come to the library on the night of the program and add their names to a drop-in waiting list.

Since 2009, Paws to Read volunteers have also visited a special day class at one of the local elementary schools. A new special day class teacher approached the Pleasanton Public Library with the hope that the Paws to Read program could be brought into her classroom. Beginning that fall, two volunteer teams visit each week to facilitate students' ability to communicate. The program has had such a profound impact on the children, resulting in numerous breakthroughs, that it has become part of the school's educational program for these students. (see Chapter 11 on School Programs).

The Pleasanton Public Library is located at 400 Old Bernal Avenue, Pleasanton, California 94566. For information, call 925-931-3400 or go to www.ci.pleasanton.ca.us/library.html.

At the **Orinda Library**, Paws to Read has three runs a year, in the spring, summer, and fall. The program started in September 2006. Each run is usually six weeks long. Most sessions are on Wednesday afternoons, and some are on Saturdays. The Wednesday sessions are 25 minutes long, with two sessions each day. The Saturday ones are 15 minutes long, with three sessions each day.

The number of therapy dog teams varies, with anywhere from one to five dogs in the library's small meeting room. Of the 19 available teams, eight come from TherapyPets (out of Oakland), five from the East Bay SPCA, and three from Valley Humane Society (VHS). The rest are from Therapy Dogs International (TDI), Animal Rescue Foundation (ARF), and Guide Dogs for the Blind breeder program.

The Orinda Library is located at 26 Orinda Way, Orinda, California 94563. For information, call 925-254-2184 or go to http://ccclib.org/locations/orinda.html.

Since January 2009, the **Danville Library** has offered the Paws to Read Literacy Program. The sessions are held in the Mt. Diablo Room, a small room that can accommodate eight therapy dog teams and eight children. Paws to Read meets on Monday afternoons from 4:00 to 5:00 PM, providing two 25-minute reading sessions. Participating children must be in grades one to five and be registered by their parents.

The library staff provides an assortment of books for various reading levels. Children pick out the books that they can read. No instruction is provided in this program. The program meets for five or six weeks, three times a year, in early spring, during the summer, and in the fall. The program is supported by the Friends of the Danville Library, and, in 2011, it received a generous grant from the San Ramon Valley Kiwanis Club.

The Danville Library is located near downtown and next to the Community Center at 400 Front Street, Danville, California 94526. For information, call 925-837-4889 or go to ccclib.org/locations/danville.html.

The **Livermore Public Library** has Paws to Read programs at both the Civic Center library and the Rincon branch. During the summer of 2009, library staff decided to expand program offerings by involving more volunteers. One of the programs they focused on was Paws to Read. Kathleen Waelde, a Leadership Livermore graduate, was recruited to facilitate and oversee a Paws to Read program at the Livermore Public Library. Library staff and Kathleen decided to model their program on those at the Danville and Pleasanton public libraries.

The program was launched in the fall of 2009 at the Civic Center Library, starting with sessions on two Saturday mornings. In 2010, sessions at the Civic Center library were moved to Wednesday evenings from 7:00 to 8:00 PM (two 25-minute sessions, with a ten-minute break for the dogs), which was found to be a better time slot both for families attending as well as for the dog handlers. The Rincon branch was added to the program in the spring of 2010, but their hours were set for 3:00 to 4:00 PM on Fridays, which worked best for serving the neighboring Marylin Avenue School after Friday dismissal.

The Civic Center program is offered in eight-week segments, one in the fall and two in the spring, and the Rincon program is offered in shorter segments, one in the fall and one in the spring. The average number of dog handlers at the Civic Center programs is twelve, and the average number at Rincon is six.

Library staff set out an assortment of books of various reading levels for children to choose from, but children are also welcome to bring a book from home. Signups usually start about ten days before a session begins. When children arrive and check in, they are assigned to specific therapy dogs.

In January 2011, it was decided to invite autistic children in the Livermore area to attend specially-scheduled, closed sessions of Paws to Read, since working with therapy dogs has been shown to be beneficial to children with autism. The volunteer handlers who agreed to work in this special program attended a presentation at Las Positas College by Temple Grandin, noted autistic author and speaker. Many of these volunteers also give of their time at The Taylor Family Foundation (see Chapter 2 on Camp Arroyo Programs). This special program has grown since its inception. It now involves two or three separately represented groups of autistic/special needs children in the Livermore area.

The Livermore Paws to Read program has proven to be very popular with youngsters perfecting their reading skills. Drop-ins may be accepted on a first-come, first-served basis. Participating children must be able to read, and children up through grade five are welcomed. Children should also not be fearful of dogs or have allergies to pets.

The Livermore Civic Center Library is at 1188 South Livermore Avenue, Livermore, California 94550, near the City Hall. The Rincon branch is at 725 Rincon Avenue, Livermore, California 94551 near Marylin Avenue School and May Nissen Park. For more information, call 925-373-5504, or visit the website at www.livermorelibrary.net.

The **Castro Valley Library** started its Paws to Read program in May 2010. It is designed to help young readers gain self-confidence and improve their reading skills. Usually on the first Monday of each month, children in grades K-6 congregate in the Chabot Canyon room at 6:30 PM to wait for their "date" with a canine friend. There are two 25-minute reading sessions for every Paws to Read evening, and they both operate in the same manner.

Each participating child is assigned to one of the 20 dogs that volunteer for the program. Once the child enters the room, they choose from a multitude of books of various reading levels, selected by library staff, and then partner up with their assigned dogs. Once the 25-minute reading session has ended, the meeting room doors are opened, allowing the children's parents, grandparents, and guardians to enter the room and to have a five-minute meet-and-greet photo op with the dog and its owner. The Paws to Read program has been supported by the Friends of the Castro Valley Library since its inception in May 2010.

The Castro Valley Library is located at 3600 Norbridge Avenue, Castro Valley, California 94546. For information, call 510-667-7900 or go to www.aclibrary.org/branches/csv/castrovalleyhome.asp.

—Testimonials—

We began the program at the Danville Library in January 2009 at the request of a patron who was familiar with the program. After discussing the possibilities of having the program here, I contacted Reneé Freidus, who is in charge of the program at the Pleasanton Public Library. Reneé was invaluable, helpful, and generous with her ideas and information. After some investigation into the Paws to Read program, I felt it would be useful and fun for children who could benefit from extra reading practice.

With that in mind, I notified the reading specialists in the San Ramon Valley Unified School District about the program. I described the program in a letter to each specialist as well as a letter to the principal of the school. I also let the specialists know that any students they recommended to the program would be given the opportunity to register early for the reading sessions. I have had support from some reading specialists, which has given me a chance to work more closely with the local school district, thereby facilitating communication regarding our mutual programs. Partnerships with groups like Valley Humane Society and local schools provide unique opportunities to develop stronger community ties, which benefits the children.

Several children have come in to read and simply to be by a dog if the family cannot have a dog for whatever reason. Others come in to practice reading and have found that this is a fun way to do it. Volunteers are not enlisted to teach. So we encourage the children to read very easy books because this is reading practice and not for reading instruction.

About a year ago, a mother told me that her daughter had signed up to read to a dog on her birthday. She dressed up and came to read. She told her mother that it was the best birthday she had ever had. Another girl has signed up for every reading session since we began. She has been dubbed by one of our volunteers as our "best customer."

The program has been successful with many children returning for each session, and many of them for the maximum number of allowable reading sessions. The value of this program lies in the fact that children are reading both for extra practice and for the joy of it while being near a dog. Reading successfully is such an important part of a child's ability to do well in school that programs which encourage reading will enhance the child's future accomplishments. Studies have shown that reading to dogs and extra reading practice enhance and improve reading competency and those skills associated with reading like spelling and writing.

Kathleen Baritell, Youth Services Librarian, Danville Library

I have referred first graders to the Paws to Read program at the Pleasanton Public Library to read aloud to therapy dogs for several years. My students love reading aloud to the trained dogs for several reasons: the element of silliness in reading to a dog takes the stress off for a beginning reader, the dogs are not judgmental so they increase the comfort level of the reader, and it makes a positive memory that reading and libraries can be fun.

Laura Bennett, First Grade Teacher, Donlon School, Pleasanton

My son and I are very happy to have the experience of learning to read. It is a great idea to have the dogs as therapy. My son loves animals, especially dogs.

I want to thank all the volunteers for the great job. They are changing the life of the kids. My son is special and is a little bit behind in reading. He really loves this program. Thank you very much.

Isabel Casillas, Parent of a reader, Livermore Public Library

My involvement with Paws to Read at the Pleasanton Public Library is a joy and a blessing. I began my happy association as a volunteer at the very first pilot session in November 2002. For the first few years, I volunteered with Mopsey, an adorable little Shih Tzu. Mitzi, a cute Lhasa Apso/Terrier mix, became my Paws to Read partner after she joined our family in 2005. When Sue Jones retired in May 2007, I was given the honor of facilitating this transformative program. Mitzi was forced into early "retirement," but still enjoys being a back-up on the odd occasion!

My most memorable experience is the time a deaf, speech-impaired little girl read her book by signing to Mopsey and me. Her mother sat nearby with her newborn baby, interpreting the signing for us. The mom was very appreciative that her child could participate in the program, explaining how much courage it took for her daughter to join us that evening. To this day, I still think of that loving and dedicated mother and how she drove all the way from Berkeley to enable her child to participate in the program. Listening to that little girl read her stories was a life changing evening for me!

Reneé Freidus, Library Assistant, Pleasanton Public Library

The dogs are so cute. I love to see them and read to them!

Dylan Irby, Six-year-old child, Castro Valley Library

It was fun being able to read with the therapy dogs. They are so cute and friendly. And every session is always exciting because I get to meet a new dog.

Haley Irby, Nine-year-old child, Castro Valley Library

I am very impressed with the Paws to Read program at the Castro Valley Library. Not only are the pets adorable, but the kids just love being so close to the animals. My son is a struggling reader, and, after experiencing just one session in the Paws to Read program, he is much more excited to return. His teacher has mentioned that he has grown from a level 12 reader to a level 14 reader in only two months. Too bad the program isn't weekly instead of monthly. It is a great program, and we are fortunate to have it available at our local library.

Tresa Irby, Parent of readers, Castro Valley Library

In 1999, when Paws to Read was just a germ of an idea for the Pleasanton Public Library, I must admit that I had more business in mind than "warm and fuzzy." At the time, we were a new city library seeking unique and relevant children's programming as well as ties to the local school district.

In November 2002, Paws to Read began, and, on every count, exceeded our wildest dreams. In no time at all, we knew something much more was happening in our meeting room than simply the introduction of friendly dogs to eager children.

Parents and teachers reported definitive reading score improvements. Children displayed patience, gentleness, and good manners around the dogs. The library's collection of books on the care and training of dogs was always empty. Parents and their children returned to the library on non-Paws to Read days for more of what the library had to offer.

We were also happy to hear that our loving dog handlers were getting as much out of the program as the children. Friendships formed among the handlers. Some handlers became mentors to children with special needs. Some handlers, who were without children or grandchildren nearby, found a type of family in us. In the event of the loss of a beloved dog and family member, there was a whole community there to support them with understanding and empathy.

I won't presume to know *how* it works. And I don't know *why* it works. Certainly something special happens between a dog and a child that's real, not pretend. All I know is that there is some type of pinch-yourself, goose-pimpled, hair-on-the-back-of-your-neck magic going on—something mysterious and enchanting.

There is a multitude of people deserving of thanks for this program. But in the end, it's those wonderful therapy dogs—mixed breeds to purebreds and champions, rescues and family pets—who effortlessly forge those invisible connections to children and make it all work. They share all their love and joy for nothing more than a kind word or a pat on the head. Every one of them is in my heart. To have been a part of creating something magical like Paws to Read has been the blessing of my life.

Sue Jones, Former Library Assistant II, Pleasanton Public Library; Founder of VHS's Paws to Read program

We are very proud of the Paws program at the Orinda Library. We have a very supportive Friends group and some generous donors who have funded blankets, pillows, and floor chairs. They also provide water for the handlers and books in honor of the Paws teams. After every five visits, a child gets to choose a paperback of their own from a selection of books provided by our supporters.

We have a mix of readers. Some are fluent readers; others are beginners. Some have allergies, but the limited exposure and the careful cleanliness of the dogs allow these children to experience the pleasure of petting and talking to a dog. Some children find this form of reading more fun than doing it alone or for a parent; others treasure making a canine connection. One parent said her child is reluctant to read at home for many reasons, but, when at the Paws program, she is really motivated to read. It doesn't feel like homework to her, and she likes snuggling with the dog. Reading goes from work to pleasure when the dog is there.

Lin Look, Youth Services Librarian, Orinda Library

We can always tell when children walk into the Children's Room to read to the dogs—the children's excitement can hardly be contained. Many children have participated in the program for several years, yet their enthusiasm never seems to diminish. For library staff, it is very rewarding to see the beaming face of a child who is new to the program and has read to one of the dogs for the first time.

After their session, these children often run to their parents and ask to be signed up for more Paws to Read time. Parents also have talked about their joy in seeing growth in their child's confidence in reading and reading aloud, a skill that they say positively impacts their success in the classroom. Paws to Read is a positive family experience.

Vicki Miller and Anne Gove, Library Assistants, Children's Desk, Pleasanton Public Library

Paws to Read started at the Livermore Public Library under my predecessor, Rosemary Dukelow. We were looking for ways to meet the needs of the community that we had not previously met, but experiencing budget cuts, we hoped to do this by means of volunteers. Library staff researched and discovered a number of opportunities, and one of these was Paws to Read.

As soon as the library announced the planning of this program and the need for volunteers, the library was blessed with several highly-motivated individuals who stepped forward to coordinate and assist with this program—Kathleen, Gail, Linda, Marni, Jenifer, Sue—you know who you are. They have scheduled and coordinated dog handlers and their certified therapy dogs. They have researched special dog quilts (which the Friends of the Livermore Library financed) for the dogs to lie on. Kathleen found a community contact who has large washing machines and who launders the quilts regularly.

Our volunteers came up with the idea of bookmarks featuring a photo and name of each dog. These bookmarks soon became a "hot item" among the children, who vie among each other to collect complete sets! Our volunteers brainstormed ways to get the word out into the community so we could reach those children who needed the reading practice the most. We have made great progress in reaching those children through working with every parent and school organization in the area.

The dog handlers take great interest in the children who come to read. While adhering to the program goal of a "non-judgmental atmosphere," they find ways to support the children in their reading efforts and in building relationships with their dogs. They are a dedicated group, and we feel very blessed that they take part in this program.

I have heard from a number of parents that their children's reading skills have improved enormously since they started coming to our Paws to Read program. We have collected a number of written testimonies from parents and children describing the positive impact that reading to dogs has had on them.

I love seeing the faces of the children, full of anticipation and excitement as they rush in for their time slot to read to the dogs. And they come away equally excited, lining up to sign up for the next session, and treasuring the Paws to Read bookmarks they have just received.

This has probably been the most fulfilling service I have rendered to children in my career as a librarian.

Gary E. Myer, Supervising Librarian, Youth Services, Livermore Public Library, Civic Center

My daughter is a curious, affectionate, fun, and intelligent eight-year-old girl. She is a voracious reader. She started reading chapter books before age four. She knew all her alphabet letters before eighteen months even though she barely talked. One of our favorite pastime activities was to visit animal shelters in Dublin after school and pet stores like PETCO and Pet Food Express.

Since she loves animals, I thought it would be such a wonderful experience for her to share her love for books with one of her several favorite animals. Paws to Read has benefited my daughter in four ways: improving her social skills with people, increasing animal awareness for her, calming and relaxing her, and making her happy. I look forward to seeing her enjoy her journey and share her love of books.

Thuy-Hong Nguyen, Parent of a reader, Castro Valley Library

Our family is multi-cultural, multi-lingual. Our children are growing up tri-lingual. As great as that is in the long term, it is harder on the children in the early school years. Our daughter could not read at the same pace as her classmates when we started first grade at Lydiksen Elementary School in Pleasanton. It was very difficult for our family to see our daughter struggling at such an early age. The teacher was not very sympathetic about our situation, but the reading specialist was great and suggested that she go to Paws to Read at the Pleasanton Public Library. It seemed like a great idea that she would read to non-judgmental dogs, but we could not even imagine how great this program really was.

We walked into a large room, where there were many dogs sitting on comfortable pillows and blankets with their owners. The registered children lined up, and each child was assigned a dog. They read to the dogs while the parents waited outside in the library. Then, 25 minutes later, the doors opened and the parents went inside to see their children, many of us taking a picture of our child with their reading partners. All of the children were giggling and happy. The dog owners, the dogs, and the library staff are very supportive and patient with us as we sometimes forget that there is another session five minutes later.

I asked my daughter what she does in there. She tells me that the dogs she reads to love her! And the dogs love to be stroked while she reads to them. Sometimes they even lick her and wag their tails. She reads and reads. Oftentimes, she, who is struggling to read, will read eight books to her reading partner for the evening. When I asked her if she feels worried about making mistakes, she answers that it doesn't make a difference, because, even when she makes mistakes, her reading partner continues to let her stroke its fur and lick her. The program's intention is to boost confidence in the hearts of our little readers, and it sure made my little reader much more confident. She says that, even if she picks a book that is too difficult, she can show the pictures to her reading partner, and the dog would still be as interested in her book as if she was reading it. She says that she needs to explain the pictures to the dog though, because it might get bored. :)

My daughter is one of the first to go register in the guest book at the front table. She always writes the name of her reading partner of the evening and draws a heart, then writes her name. :) She is now in second grade and I can see her self-confidence return to us. She is still slightly behind, but she is catching up at a fast pace. We will continue going to Paws to Read for as long as they let us. She is always excited to bring home a flyer for Paws to Read, which her reading specialist at school sends home with her.

We are very grateful that we were given this opportunity to boost our daughter's confidence with the help of reading to dogs. They and their owners are such a wonderful addition to our family. Thank you.

Mona Osman, Mother of a reader, Pleasanton Public Library

I am a speech-language pathologist and the founder of a therapy and educational program for children, both typically developing and those with special needs. The children at the School of Imagination had the opportunity to attend the Paws to Read program at the Livermore Public Library. We brought the children, who are all on the Autism Spectrum, to the program once a week for three weeks. Many of the children have difficulty with communication, behavior, and transitions to new places, so getting them there was a challenge. After the first session, they were in love with the dogs! They were each given bookmarks with pictures of the dogs that they read to.

On the drive back to school, we talked about their favorite dogs and who they wanted to read to next week. The bookmarks were treasures, and they shared them excitedly with their parents upon pickup. Some of the children who had a fear of dogs the first week were, by the third week, sitting close to the dogs, and, even if they couldn't read, they were petting them.

The volunteers were patient and understanding. They encouraged the children and welcomed them no matter what their ability level. It is such an amazing program run by fantastic volunteers! The children that we work with are often isolated due to their inability to communicate and respond appropriately in social situations. The Paws to Read program allowed them to make a connection with a wonderful animal and its owner, who accepted them and appreciated them for the unique individuals that they are.

Charlene Sigman, Co-Founder and Program Director,
School of Imagination & Happy Talkers, Dublin

When we moved into the new Castro Valley Library in October of 2009, one of the first tasks assigned to me was to start up the Paws to Read program. Having little to no idea of what this program actually entailed and how it was going to function, this was a pretty daunting task. However, one could see that there were many key elements that led one to believe that this was going to be a winner of a program. Over two years later, that belief has become a reality.

Paws to Read is one of the most rewarding programs I have been involved with. Every first Monday of the month, there is a palpable energy in the building as 6:30 PM draws close. It's a blast to see the kids, some of which are repeat visitors, visibly excited in line, anxiously awaiting their dog assignment, and then, once they get it, talking to their peers about which dog is really nice, or really cute, or which dog is a good listener, etc. Parents seem to really enjoy this program also. Beyond just the joy that it brings to their kids, I do get a sense that they are fully aware of the immense benefit that this program provides.

One particular exchange with a parent that has stuck with me was when a mother enthusiastically approached me and told me how great this program was for her son because he was really shy. She said that reading to the dog helped her son get more confident in reading aloud and led to overall improvement in his reading skills. Unbeknownst to her, she had basically repeated verbatim the Paws to Read mission statement. That was incredibly satisfying because it seemed to validate why we were offering this program.

Nathan Silva, Library Assistant II, Castro Valley Library

I have observed the children that come to the library to give their love and time to the dogs. It is a piece of time for them when everything is right with the world. The owners of the dogs bring them because they love children and want to help enrich their lives. In this triangle, each is giving and receiving something valuable—love and the joy of reading. The rewards are exponential.

Gail Turner, Volunteer Coordinator, Livermore Public Library, Rincon branch

The first night that we participated in the Paws to Read program, I was anxious to meet the other dog handlers and their canine counterparts, and to learn from those with more experience. As we entered the Pleasanton Public Library, I saw the 20 plus blankets nicely arranged in the main meeting room of the library with two pillows neatly placed at each reading location. After getting my nametag and card to be placed in front of the blanket (so that the children could identify the dog and dog handler), we were off to our blanket.

As the handlers settled in with their dogs, it was quite a sight. Here we were in the Pleasanton Public Library with 20 plus dogs of all breeds, sitting on blankets in the library with children lined up, anxiously awaiting their turn to read to dogs! I later learned that there was a considerable waiting list for the sessions, and, that often times, each Paws to Read night was filled the day that registration opened to the public.

As I look back at our first night, Buddy W seemed a little confused. After all, at 7:00 PM, he would normally be on his blanket in front of the fireplace or on one of his beds, sound asleep for the night. He was more anxious than normal as if to say, "What is this all about?" After a few minutes, he curled up on both pillows (one of which is intended for the child and one for the adult) with his eyes wide open and never taking an eye off of me.

A few minutes before 7:00 PM, Reneé Freidus made a few program announcements regarding first-time participants, and, at exactly 7:00 PM, we were ready for the first Paws to Read session. Reneé opened the doors, and the kids lined up, several clutching as many as four books. Others would choose books from a table in the room before they went to their assigned locations.

Reneé read each child's nametag and proudly announced which dog that child would be reading to that evening. Some walked and some ran to their assigned dog and handler, and those children that obviously were repeat readers sat down immediately, familiar with the program and ready to read to their canine friend. Each week, I waited and watched the children go through the line to see who would be assigned to Buddy W and me.

In future weeks, I learned that Buddy W would become increasingly comfortable with the routine. In fact, from time to time, I would look at him only to see his eyes slowly closing as the child concentrated on their reading. More than one child said, "I think Buddy is sleeping," to which I learned several responses including, "Buddy is listening, but when you read well it relaxes him," or "I think his eyes are open" (at which point I would talk loudly in an attempt to wake him up). In one case, a little boy exclaimed, "It sure looks like he's sleeping to me!"

I must admit that until I became involved in this program, few things brought tears to my eyes. I can't remember shedding tears at the movies and rarely at weddings. I am not embarrassed to say that, for some reason, this has changed as a result of my involvement with these programs. The feeling of joy that I experience as a result of the joy that Buddy W brings to others is almost indescribable. Not only has Buddy W become an unbelievably important part of our household, but he has brought considerable joy and comfort to those that he has had the pleasure of meeting in his capacity as a therapy dog.

Paul Wankle, Therapy dog owner/handler; Member, VHS Board of Directors

As a reading specialist, I have referred my students to this wonderful program, and I also had the opportunity to participate in the program with my dog, Kody, for seven years. The one thing that struck me immediately about the Paws to Read program was the fact that dogs of all shapes and sizes were sitting on mats, fairly close to each other, and there were no sounds from the dogs at all—no barking, no growling, no whining. They each sat on their mats, eagerly awaiting a child to bring over a cherished book that they wanted to share with their assigned dog. It was a magical hour. The only voices you could hear were those of the children reading quietly to their special dog.

Children love this program because they have an opportunity to practice their reading in a non-judgmental environment. Children are free to take risks because a dog never criticizes their reading. It never matters if a child misses a word or has to sound it out. The dogs make the children feel special. This program improves the children's confidence and self-esteem. When the pressure is taken off of reading, then it becomes fun. And the more the children read, the better readers they become. My own students can't wait to share their experiences and show me the picture of the dog they read to the night before.

Ellen Waskey, Reading Specialist, Lydiksen Elementary School, Pleasanton

I think that Paws to Read is an outstanding program for our students! The children I've worked with have greatly enjoyed going to read to the dogs. They feel comfortable in the setting and feel safe to make mistakes. The dog owners are incredibly patient and kind, and often offer encouragement to the students (not to mention, helping them with an occasional unknown word!).

Some of my students have gone on their own on a regular basis. I've also gone with my students as a whole group. Their excitement is contagious! I plan on bringing my students back this spring.

Mary Wyosnick, Reading Specialist, Livermore Valley Charter School

I had a fun time reading with you. Thank you for letting me read with you. Did you like *Smasher* and *R.I.P Ripsqueak*?

Child, Pleasanton Public Library

Buddy, you were a nice dog. Your ears and head were very soft. Thank you for being my buddy.

Child, Pleasanton Public Library

Paws to Read is so fun! I've been here before, but just discovered this book. My dog was Mitzi. She's so cute!

Child, Pleasanton Public Library

The girls love the Paws to Read program! It has been especially beneficial for one of my daughters as she hates reading. It's usually a battle to get her to do her reading homework, but it's a different story when she is reading to the dogs. It's nice to see her show enthusiasm for reading for a change!

My other daughter enjoys reading, but she gets very excited about meeting the dogs and their owners. Participating in the program makes her feel special.

Please thank all your wonderful volunteers for us.

Parent of a reader, Livermore Public Library

Thank you for offering the program. Maria loves it! Even though she's only participated in your program twice, I've noticed a big improvement in her reading. I hope you can keep this program going so that many other kids can benefit.

Parent of a reader, Livermore Public Library

My daughter is a huge fan of your program, and I've been so pleased. She's currently in first grade, and, although she likes reading and stories, she's not as confident with her aloud reading skills as I'd like her to be. One night, after reading to one of your wonderful pups, my daughter told me that she especially likes reading at Paws to Read "because no one ever stops me and fixes my words." Please, please, please continue this program. We will continue to sign up for as long as you'll have us.

Parent of a reader, Livermore Public Library

My children are reluctant to read for 20 minutes at home for all kinds of reasons. But at the Orinda Library, with the dogs here, they are really motivated. It doesn't feel like doing homework when they are snuggling with a dog. This program makes reading a pleasure instead of work and gives a new meaning to the term "dog-eared books."

Parent of a reader, Orinda Library

Used with permission of Doug Jorgensen,
Photographer for The Independent

Used with permission of the Orinda Library

Mojo

10

19
10

—Stories—

A large number of therapy dogs go to the Paws to Read programs at the participating libraries. Those dogs for whom there are stories about their work in Paws to Read programs include the following—Bella, a Shetland Sheepdog; Bosco, a Black Labrador Retreiver; Buddy H, a Queensland Heeler/Golden Retriever mix; Buddy W, a Golden Retriever/ Yellow Labrador Retriever mix; Cabo, a Yellow Labrador Retriever; Chex Mix, a Newfoundland; Christy, a Norwegian Elkhound; Dixie, a Labradoodle; Ella, a Cavalier King Charles Spaniel; Elsa, a Black Labrador Retriever; Gandalf II, a Chihuahua/Schipperke mix; Gunther, a Norwegian Elkhound; Kane, a Golden Retriever; Kody, a Samoyed; Lucky, a Golden Retriever; Maggie, a Golden Retriever mix; Mitsy, a Havanese/Poodle mix; Mojo, a Welsh Corgi; Mopsey, a Shih Tzu; P.I.P., a Border Collie/Cattle Dog mix; Schnoz, a Standard Schnauzer; Tedi Bear, a Newfoundland; and Tioga, a Labrador Retriever/Golden Retriever mix.

Comfortable with the Dog Now—

A little girl named Tina couldn't read and was afraid of dogs. So her mom came and sat with Kane and me. Kane rested there quietly, waiting for Tina to touch him. This happened each time we went to the Paws to Read program and saw her. But then one time, Tina said to her mother, "You can go out now because I am with my friend Kane and so I am okay." That sure made us feel good.

A Bilingual Dog?—

One young girl could only read in Spanish. Elsa, of course, didn't care that she wasn't reading in English and listened so attentively that it seemed that the girl thought Elsa knew Spanish. The problem was when she was stuck on a word, neither Elsa nor I could help her.

Sleeping on the Job—

With his many years working for the Police Department, Gandalf II is glad to settle down with children at the Paws to Read program and get some snoozing in. He has learned that he can do this job while sleeping. He snuggles up next to the children reading to him and comforts them. I'm sure he is listening to the story, though, because he is a dog that is always on alert. And his sleeping doesn't seem to bother the children either.

What a Great Story—

Art Linkletter said it best—"Kids say the darndest things." Paws to Read is such a joy. Some of the children are tentative, some shy, some good readers, some actors. One little boy came into the room, plopped onto the pillow with a large book, gave Schnoz a hug, and proceeded to read a wonderful story, page turning and all. It was one of the best stories I've ever heard. Not a word of it was printed on the pages, though. When he was done with the story, he gave Schnoz a huge goodbye hug, grabbed his bookmark, and left.

Protecting the Dog from a Sad Story—

We keep a large collection of dog-related books inside the library meeting room where we hold the Paws to Read sessions. The children may choose from this collection or bring other stories to read or even bring in their homework. One night, a little girl named Susie brought a story of her own choice and began reading it to a particularly joyful and affectionate Golden Retriever named Apple. But in this book, a dog gets hit by a car. At the point in the story where this was about to happen, Susie paused, put her hands over the dog's ears, and said, "Apple, you can't hear this." She continued to read the story, and, when the bad part was over (and the dog survived), Susie lay back down next to an oblivious, cuddly Apple and finished the story.

Paws to Read as a Prize—

I received a call one day from a remarkable teacher at a school in Vallejo. She had a unique request. She wanted to offer attendance at a Paws to Read session as a prize to each of 15 students whose reading had most improved. For one night, parents and students would carpool 43 miles to Pleasanton for their reading session, followed by ice cream at a local shop.

Since the children would have only one opportunity to visit us, both the library staff and the therapy dog teams wanted to make this a night to remember. A welcome banner graced the meeting room entrance. We arranged for each of the 15 winners to read to two different dogs instead of one so they could have different experiences. We encouraged the dog handlers to bring their dogs in colorful, fun costumes for photos.

All the dogs seemed to sense a special mission that night. They charmed our dazzled guests with gentle affection and focused attention.

Afterwards, the children left with goody bags of book-related prizes, and we honored their teacher with flowers and a gift for her efforts. The joy on the faces of those children, as they proudly read to their special dogs, was simply indescribable. The entire room glowed with their pride that spring night! I think the dogs even walked a little taller!

Paying Attention—

Bosco was known for rolling around on his blanket while at Paws to Read at the Pleasanton Public Library. The kids reading to him would get a kick out of his demeanor, as he would start out upright, and, by the end of the 25-minute session, his four paws would be straight up in the air, with his tongue hanging out the side.

I would tell the kids, "Don't worry. Bosco is listening. He just has an odd way of showing it." This was a great way to make the kids laugh and to break the ice a little for some of them.

Knowing How to Comfort a Child—

Even though she was a very large dog, Tedi Bear was occasionally assigned to a child who was uncomfortable with dogs. She instinctively knew that she should be quiet and not move too much so she would not bother the child. One parent said, "We were betting on whether our daughter would make the full 30 minutes or not, but Tedi Bear was so quiet that she apparently felt okay." Tedi Bear enjoyed giving kisses to those who read to her, but she never tried kissing the children who were scared of dogs.

Big Dog or Little Dog

One evening, Andrew, a ten-year-old boy, was walking towards our mat, and I thought, "Bet he wishes he was reading to one of the big dogs." But to my surprise, he was smiling. Looking down at Mitsy, Andrew said, "I am so happy that I get to read to a little dog." He looked at Mitsy, showed her the book, and said, "Mitsy, tonight we are going to read *Sean and Keeper Show-and-Tell!*" It was so cute seeing Andrew and Mitsy together.

Respecting Others' Beliefs—

During registration for Paws to Read, a father came in to schedule his two sons at the recommendation of a reading specialist. But there was a big problem. Their faith prevented the boys from coming into any physical contact with the dogs! No petting, no wet kisses, no using dogs as pillows. Although he would do anything to help his sons, including allowing them to be in close proximity to dogs, this father, and me too, wondered if our program could be as effective for the boys without contact with the dogs.

With a heads-up to the handlers who owned exceptionally calm dogs, those sweet boys read their little hearts out, fearlessly sitting close to their assigned dogs without touching or even asking questions about dogs. It took only respect for their faith and the nearness of the dogs to work their magic once again. Their father trusted the program after that and brought his sons back to read many more times.

Trying to Make a Deal—

A very sweet and gregarious eight-year-old girl named Cindy settled down next to Schnoz. She wanted to know his history. Cindy had three books to read and did her reading well. When it was time to finish, she pointed to my wedding ring and said, "That's a pretty ring." I replied, "Thank you." Then Cindy asked, "Can I have it instead of the bookmark?"

Deaf Child Reads to the Dog—

In the early days of the program, we were still discovering how to be helpful to every child who wanted to participate. One day, a mother called me from Berkeley, 33 miles away. She had heard about our program from a friend who lived in Pleasanton. Her young daughter, Angela, was profoundly deaf with severe speech impairments. This sullen little girl was having a great deal of trouble in school and had no enthusiasm for reading. Her mother hoped that Paws to Read might just be the program to spark Angela's interest.

A quick survey revealed that none of our handlers knew sign language, so we weren't exactly sure how this was going to work. So, with an infant in her arms, this dedicated mother and her reticent daughter sat down with Mopsey, a little Shih Tzu. Angela began to sign the story to Mopsey as her mother translated the book aloud to the handler. It was a scene both surreal and wonderful to witness.

At the end of the story, when her signing had stopped, right on cue Mopsey offered her enthusiastic affection, wordlessly telling this child, with instant praise, that she had done well. Angela left our library for the long drive home, smiling from ear to ear! Even ten years later, I still tear up at that memory.

Being Examined by a Child—

Chex Mix listens intently when he is at the Paws to Read sessions. Sometimes, the children even think he is asleep because his eyes are closed! One time, Kirk, a young boy about five years old, read to him and then became very curious. He poked his fingers into Chex Mix's ears. Kirk felt his nose several times and informed me it wasn't cold like it should be. He also checked out his tail and sides, and felt the pads on each paw. Chex Mix stayed quiet the entire time. After that session, several other handlers came up and said to me, "We are so glad you had that child. Our dog would not have been so tolerant." Maybe Kirk will become a veterinarian some day.

Dogs Like Reading Time—

If you look for Cabo on a Friday afternoon, more than likely you will find him at the Rincon branch library for the Paws to Read program. Cabo has been "reading" at Rincon since 2011, and looks forward to spending an hour with the other six therapy dogs and the children that line up at the door waiting to read to him.

Cabo's demeanor with these children is one of love, care, and attentiveness. Cabo often sprawls out on the blanket with his head on the lap of the child reading to him. Although Cabo takes up almost the entire blanket space, the children don't seem to mind. They are just happy to have a dog pay attention to them!

Which Book Will the Dog Like—

Maggie loves to lie on her back (maybe a habit from when she nursed all her puppies). One day, we were at the Danville Library where a little girl named Julie was quietly reading to her as Maggie lay on her back. All of a sudden, Maggie turned over and her paw came up, and she smacked and knocked the book right out of Julie's hand. I gasped and the moderator looked shocked. Julie quietly stood up and said, "I don't think Maggie liked that book. I will get another one." When she got back with a new book, Maggie put her head on Julie's lap and she started reading. When Julie was finished, she looked at me and said, "Maggie liked that one a lot better." I smiled.

Action Needed—

Sometimes we have children at the Pleasanton Public Library who do not read or do not want to read. In those cases, Lucky and I fly into action. Together with the child, we read to Lucky or talk to him. Lucky and I try to make this a happy experience for the child. Once that happens, the door has been open for that child who now realizes that the library is a happy place to be and that reading is fun.

Reading Better—

A little boy came to our mat. We introduced ourselves to Jeremy, and he petted Dixie, my four-year-old, 80-pound Labradoodle. Jeremy said he was in first grade. We three got comfortable on the mat, and Jeremy read to us the book he had brought with him. Dixie had her head gently resting on his lap while he read, and then she closed her eyes and snoozed in pleasure.

When Jeremy finished that book, there was time for him to go up to the table and pick one of the books that the library always has in the ready for the children. He came back and read to us a story about a dog that goes to school and has many adventures. When he finished, Jeremy leaned into Dixie's face and said, "I read this book last week to that dog over there, but I think you liked it even better." When I asked him why, he just shrugged and said, "Maybe I read it better now."

When our time was up, I gave Jeremy the bookmark with a photo of Dixie. The library keeps dog treats at the desk, and, before his mother came to collect him, he went and got a treat for Dixie. It was a wonderful time for Dixie and me, and for Jeremy. This is why I volunteer for Paws to Read. We all gain!

Costume Time—

Bosco always took the opportunity to dress up in costume for various holidays. One Halloween, he showed up in his costume, carrying a plastic orange pumpkin with candy in it. The children enjoyed getting the candy, and, of course, Bosco was a big hit.

Nice Partnership—

I remember how delighted the children were to read to a dog at the Paws to Read program. Many of the children didn't or couldn't have pets of their own, so this was a great opportunity to share one. Buddy H used to love to go there to snuggle up with a child while being read to. It was truly an amazing sight to see a mutual understanding between a child and a dog. Buddy H would just calm right down, and the kids were eager to read for him. It was as though they worked so hard for each other.

A Fuzzy Chair—

Chex Mix was lying down, and Jane was sitting beside him, reading to Chex Mix. She leaned back over Chex Mix, and he was positioned like the back of a chair for her. Both Jane and Chex Mix were quite comfortable. It was no problem, as this was a form of attention for Chex Mix, and he loves attention of almost any kind.

Sisters, Sisters—

Two sisters were at the Paws to Read session one day. The older sister was in Mama mode, the younger one half in awe and half trying to impress us. The older one would read and then turn the book over to her younger sister, overseeing and correcting her. This kept up for a while. Finally the younger sister leaned over to Schnoz and quietly said, "You know I can do this."

Dog Makes a Difference—

On one occasion, a boy named Jake stopped at the end of one of the sessions to visit Buddy W. He explained that Buddy W was the first dog that he read to and said, "Now I read much more, and I come whenever my mom can get me into Paws to Read. Buddy is a cool dog."

It's sometimes difficult to measure the direct impact of Paws to Read and other reading programs but, from my perspective, if one child increases his interest in reading or is able to improve his skills, Buddy W and the other dogs are adding value.

Two Shy Brothers Open Up—

Two shy brothers, Ahmed and Jamal, for whom English is a second language, were recommended to our program by a local reading specialist. Their wonderful mother regularly brought the boys to Paws to Read, signing them up for every allotted space while also bringing them in on nights when they were not registered, hoping that a slot might open up. Ahmed and Jamal loved the dogs, especially the bigger ones, and they took pride in remembering and greeting each dog by name.

In time, not only did Ahmed and Jamal come out of their shells, but their reading improved so dramatically that their reading specialist made a point of letting us know when these boys no longer needed her services! Later, their mother told us that Paws to Read had made such a positive impact on her sons that she started paying their 13-year-old neighbor for an hour of her time after school each day, allowing her sons to read to her Golden Retriever!

Bookmarks Are So Special—

After each session, the children receive bookmarks with the dogs' pictures on them. One child told me that she would keep coming to the library until she had a bookmark for every dog there. The children would point to which dogs they had read to before. These dogs must mean something special to the children.

Winning Their Hearts—

Gunther would walk into the Rincon branch library each time as though he was running for mayor, wagging his tail and looking at everyone. The children loved him because he was fuzzy and snuggly. Although some new children were not quite sure about a big dog like Gunther, they warmed up to him quickly when he was brought near them. His calm, happy, and friendly manner won their hearts! Parents enjoyed taking Gunther's picture with their children, and Gunther loved the photo shots.

A Part of the Family—

A family from the Ukraine brought their shy, young daughter, Nadia, to Paws to Read, hoping to improve her English. When she first came to us, this timid little girl was so unsure of her English that she literally whispered her stories into the dogs' ears, as though sharing secrets with them.

In time, and with the loving acceptance of our dogs, Nadia's voice became more audible, and we all celebrated with her when she started winning prizes for her reading! She never missed a reading session and attended Paws to Read for years. The dogs were an audience of love for her. Every dog in the program became her dog, and Nadia became everyone's daughter.

Nadia developed an extraordinary relationship with a husband/wife team and their two pedigreed Yellow Labs, Ben and Scotty, both born in Scotland. Nadia's family and our wonderful therapy dog team couple also socialized together outside of the Paws to Read program as Nadia grew up. Only in Paws to Read could an American couple and two dogs from Scotland successfully mentor a lovely little girl from the Ukraine!

After a few years, Nadia's family carefully researched dogs and their care, and happily added a new canine family member. Paws to Read was truly life-altering for this little girl and her family.

Getting Closer—

Mojo and I were assigned a young boy named Tyler who was very cautious in walking up to Mojo. Since Mojo only has two-inch high legs and is a big cuddle bug, I knew there was more to this encounter than I saw. When Mojo has a child assigned to him, the first thing he does is give the child a big lick. Then he cuddles in the child's lap for his 25-minute nap while the child reads to him. Tyler asked me if Mojo wouldn't approach him and if he could lie down at the far end of the blanket. I assured Tyler that Mojo was extremely friendly, but he insisted on keeping a distance between them. Mojo was confused, but lay by me and watched as Tyler read the book.

After the 25 minutes were over, I asked Tyler if he could do one thing for me. He said, "Yes." I asked him to please tell Mojo that he was a good dog and to just pet his head. I explained to Tyler that Mojo thought he had done something wrong since he was not allowed to cuddle with him. With great caution, Tyler did as I asked, and, when his mother approached, she whispered to me that he had been bitten and was extremely afraid of dogs. She thanked me and hoped that her son would return again.

The following week, Tyler was there and asked for Mojo again. As he approached, I asked if Mojo could come a little closer this week. He allowed him to lie next to him. As the reading time continued, slowly Tyler reached over and petted Mojo's head, and Mojo gave him a big lick. This went on for the rest of the reading period. The boy's mother approached and asked Tyler if he wanted his picture taken with Mojo since he had talked about him that week. He said, "Of course!" Then he wrapped his arms around Mojo's neck and gave him a big hug. Both his mother and I had tears in our eyes.

The following week, Tyler came to Mojo and told him he was going to try another dog this week, but he loved him and gave him a hug. Words cannot express the joy in my heart. That is what this program is all about—helping in whatever way we can, whether it be fear of dogs, trouble reading aloud, interacting with strangers, or just sharing the experience of a dog with someone who has never owned one.

Initial Greeting—

Tioga greets each of his book-reading guests with a tentative sniffing of their face. If they retreat, he nuzzles their hand to reassure them that he is available. If, on the other hand, they talk, laugh, or move toward him, Tioga gives them a quick flick of the tongue across the tip of their nose, which he does so quickly and deftly that they usually laugh in surprise. Then it's time for reading.

A Long-Time Reading Partner—

During the break between the 25-minute reading sessions, Becky, a poised fifth-grade girl, came up to me. I recognized the look on her face that said, "May I pet your dog?" Instead, Becky looked down and smiled at Ella, who was wagging her tail and staring up at Becky. She told me she just wanted to thank me for bringing Ella and to say goodbye since this was her last night at Paws to Read.

Becky had read to all the dogs in the room at one time or another, but Ella was the *first* dog. That had been *four* years ago when she was in first grade. I was speechless that Becky would remember Ella. She gently petted Ella and quietly left. I never forgot that night because it reminds me that we never know how profound the influence of a dog on a child can be.

Paws on Halloween—

When we have Paws to Read sessions on Halloween, the dogs come in their costumes. Some of the owners had costumes that matched their dogs' costumes. The children loved it, and we all had a fun time.

Trading Cards—

Michael was the happiest, most polite little boy you could ever meet. He loved coming to Paws to Read with a rare passion. After his allotted reading session, he would beg his parents to wait and see if he could grab a vacant spot in the next one.

One of the handlers had started making trading cards with her dog's photo on it to give to the children who read to her dog. All the other handlers soon followed suit. With almost 50 dogs in the program, they became prized collector items for each child, especially Michael.

One night, a dog team came up to me and said, "Look what Michael gave us!" It was a small, business card-sized piece of paper with a blue border, printed on copy paper. It is shown below, misspellings and all. I still carry one of Michael's cards with me.

michael
reader

paws to read
It was nice meetting you tonight.
I hope I will see you again!
have a good night!

Seeking Permission—

Nicole had been reading to Bella one evening. At the end of the session, her brother Nathan came up to me. He asked, "May I pet Bella?" I responded affirmatively. He explained that he needed to ask first by saying, "I am not in the Paws to Read program. But my sister is, and she says Bella helps her to read better. I wanted to meet Bella and thank her."

Keeping the Dog Comfortable—

We did a session at the Livermore Civic Center Library during Autism Awareness Month. Mitsy seemed to know which children wouldn't mind her cuddling next to them and which children needed some space. Two young girls came to our mat to read. I told them they could sit next to Mitsy to read to her. They both answered almost in unison that it was okay, adding, "She looks so comfortable. We don't want to bother her." Mitsy just lay by me, and, at the end of the session, both young girls leaned over, gave her some nice hugs, and told her what a good girl she was.

Picking Out a Book—

My favorite moment was when a young boy named Jason couldn't pick out a book to read. He had picked out three books, but the choice of which one to read was just too much for him. So I suggested to Jason that he put the books on the floor and ask Kody to pick which one he would like him to read first.

Jason carefully spread out the books before Kody. Then he asked Kody which book he wanted to hear first. Kody took his paw and tapped on one of the books. Jason squealed in delight and got right to the business of reading that book. When he finished, he turned to Kody and asked him how he liked it. Kody rewarded Jason with a great big lick right up the side of his cheek. Kody has an uncanny way of understanding children and adults.

Grandmother Steps In to Help Grandson—

I received a call from a grandmother who wanted to schedule her young grandson for the second session of Paws to Read at 7:30 PM. Asking for a specific time was a rather unusual request, but this was one motivated grandmother.

One night, this quiet, elegant woman shared her story. She was tremendously concerned about her grandson Josh's reading disabilities and the limited resources in their area to help him. She actually lived in Escalon, 54 miles away, while Josh lived with his parents in Modesto.

Every Paws to Read night, this loving grandmother would drive from Escalon, pick up Josh in Modesto, and drive him to Pleasanton to read to the dogs, and then drive back home again. She said that making this effort would be worth it all if our dogs could only motivate Josh to read. Her devotion to her grandson, along with the joyful, loving attention of the therapy dogs, were rewarded with amazing, documented improvements in Josh's reading skills and comprehension.

Providing Delivery Service—

At a November session in the Castro Valley Library, Chex Mix did not participate in the reading. Instead, he was given a special task to do. Towards the end of each of the two sessions, he came in pulling his cart, which was filled with tiny pumpkins. He was the subject of a brief discussion of Newfoundlands and what they were bred to do. Then each child was invited to pick a pumpkin from the cart and take it home.

Understanding Any Language—

At the beginning of a session, Reneé Freidus announced to Rosita, "You've got Buddy." I raised my hand, and Rosita came our way, approaching very cautiously. She was very tiny, probably a first or second grader, and began to speak very quietly. She spoke some English, but with a noticeable accent. I explained that Buddy W was ready anytime and that she could begin to read one of the books that she brought. As I looked down, I noticed that the books were in Spanish. With her little voice, Rosita asked, "Will Buddy understand if I read in Spanish?" I was caught off guard, but said, "I think Buddy understands Spanish. Why don't you go ahead." She began reading in Spanish, and my eyes welled up while Buddy W and I listened intently.

What the Dogs Work For—

When my closet door opens on Wednesday nights, Mitsy dances with excitement. She knows it is library time and time for her to listen to the children read a story to her. Mitsy and several other therapy dogs attend the Paws to Read program, and it is amazing to see the interaction between the children and the dogs.

One particular night, Jennifer was doing a great job reading to Mitsy when Mitsy let out this big snore. Jennifer looked up at me and asked, "Am I reading to Mitsy or to you?" I responded, "Oh no, you're reading to Mitsy and she is so comfortable with you that she is resting, but she hears everything you are saying." I got a big smile, and Mitsy got a nice big hug from Jennifer. Mitsy works for hugs.

The Dog Wants to Read Too—

Marylou came into the session one evening. She is a small girl, but she was carrying a very big book. She sat down by Bella and started to read to her. Bella stayed next to her as she read. Halfway through the story, Bella stood up and put her nose into the book. Marylou asked me, "Is Bella reading too?" I wasn't sure if Bella was reading the story, but she sure seemed interested in it.

Mourning the Loss of a Dog—

Paws to Read quickly became more of a family activity than a working program. The most devastating event that could happen in our program was the loss of a Paws to Read dog. As painful as it was to lose a wonderful dog, we would often lose the presence of the handler, too, if s/he did not have another qualified dog. So these events were quite devastating for everyone.

Though we never announced these losses to the children, the regular participants would certainly notice the absence of a dog team. Some would ask questions outright and others, sensing the loss, didn't want to make it a reality by hearing the words.

One night, after we had lost a beautiful dog named Daisy just a few weeks earlier, a young girl named Madison came up to me after the program was over. She handed me a paper bag and said, "I want to give this to Daisy's mom. Maybe someday she can get a new Daisy and come back. I miss them."

Inside the bag was $26.88. I gently returned the bag to Madison and persuaded her to write a card that I then could pass along to the handler so the two of them could remember Daisy together and heal. The innocence and purity of Madison's kindness and the affection she had for this therapy dog team took my breath away.

Overcoming Bothersome Noise—

One evening, Ella and I were privileged to have the company of an extraordinary fifth-grade girl named Sarah, who wore large earphones to the session. The parent had explained to the staff that Sarah normally didn't go to public places because noise bothered her so much. However, because the girl so loved the Paws to Read experience, she found a way to block out bothersome noise with the earphones and attended frequently.

That night was Sarah's last night at Paws to Read due to her grade level. Instead of reading to Ella, she chose to fix her eyes on Ella, as she petted her head with the gentlest touch for 20 minutes nonstop. Sarah's face softened, and she paused the petting only to get a better view of Ella's face. When Sarah walked away, she turned around for one last look at Ella.

I often think about Sarah and wonder about the connection she had with Ella. Most children are wiggling and giddy with excitement while they stand in line to be admitted into the Paws to Read room. This quiet child had the most impact on me of all the children who have read to Ella over the years because of what she had to overcome to be there with the dogs she loved.

Loving the Children—

P.I.P. loves seeing the children come in for the Paws to Read session. He looks forward to spending 30 minutes with them, licking them, and trying to get them to pet him. After each session, P.I.P. does his many tricks for the children before they leave. Hopefully, he sends them home with happy memories and anxious to come back.

Knowing What to Do—

Mojo participated in the session for autistic/special needs children at the Livermore Civic Center Library. Although being a canine reading partner is very rewarding for Mojo, these children can be more challenging than those he usually works with at the Paws to Read sessions. But Mojo knew what to do. He remained calm and was very gentle with them. And they responded to Mojo by talking, hugging, and petting him. They are allowed to do whatever they are comfortable doing, as long as they don't hurt the dog. We have found that it is especially important to talk softly and to interact in a calm and non-threatening manner, just as the dogs do.

Oh, So Soft—

Christy started going to the Paws to Read program at the Rincon branch of the Livermore Public Library in the spring of 2011. She was quite popular with the children because, like the other therapy dogs, she is calm and likes to get pets and hugs. The children are all taken with the fact that, with her thick Norwegian Elkhound coat, she is so soft, much softer than most of the other dogs.

Dog Has Spirit, Even at 17—

After three years in the Paws to Read program, Shazam is winding down and preparing for retirement. At 17, she can barely see and cannot hear very well, but this doesn't bother the children. Shazam is very cute and has a great sense of smell, a tail that never stops wagging, and a contagious soul. It's this spirit that connects with each and every child that reads to her, and gives them the joy and confidence to continue reading. Shazam especially enjoys the dog treats after the kids finish reading to her, and she is rewarded for a job well done.

Dog Repositioning Himself—

As soon as Carl was settled in with a book, Tioga lay down respectfully and listened as Carl read the first few pages. Then, for reasons that were clear only to Tioga, he rolled over onto his back in the hopes that Carl would scratch his tummy. But Carl kept reading. Tioga realized he needed to try another method to get Carl's attention. Tioga tried putting his paw and then his head on the middle of the book that Carl was reading. Tioga was so pleased when Carl finally looked up from the book and scratched his head. In a perfect world, Tioga likes to hear a good bedtime story while someone strokes his head.

This Dog Means So Much to the Boy—

Chang came over to say hello to Chex Mix, and then he began to read to him. Chang read continuously for the entire time. As they announced that parents would be coming in shortly, we chatted a little about Chex Mix. He told me that he had a small dog, but Newfies were his favorite. His parents came into the room, and he stayed to pet Chex Mix some more. His parents asked if Chang had told me he had requested Chex Mix after meeting him last month. I said, "No, he didn't tell me that." His mother then said, "Since he met Chex Mix last month, he has written several stories for school about Chex Mix." Chang then told me that his dog has more energy than mine!

—Quotes—

- I like when I read to the dog. *(six-year-old child)*
- I had so much fun. I hope we meet again. *(child)*
- I liked it because I read to the dog and I played with him. *(six-year-old child)*
- Thank you so much for this program. I was so happy to see my son, who has reading problems, joyfully reading to a dog. Both the dogs and handlers were wonderful! *(parent of a reader)*
- I liked the dog because he was big and he was noisy and funny and he liked me and I like him and he was black. *(six-year-old child)*
- Thank you for being so sweet and loving. I had a great time. Thanks. *(child)*
- I had so much fun and thank you for the kiss. *(child)*
- This is the awesomest program ever. *(child)*
- I wish this was open for middle schoolers. *(parent of a reader)*
- I had so much fun reading to you. You are such a good dog. *(child)*
- You were a great listener. You rock. *(child)*
- Thanks for doing tricks and listening to me read. *(child)*
- I really like reading to you and you did a good job at listening. *(child)*
- Thank you for complementing me on my reading, Buddy. You are soooo cute! *(child)*

- You are so cute, Mitzy. I wish you were mine so I could love you. *(child)*
- I wish you were my dog. *(child)*
- I had an awesome time reading to you, Coral. I hope I get to see you again. I had so much fun. *(child)*
- I really liked reading to you, Miles, because you listen very atemply [sic]. I hope to read to you again next time I come. *(child)*
- Annie, I had so much fun reading to you tonight. You were very polite and attentive. I hope you enjoyed tonight as much as I did!!! *(child)*
- I loved reading to you, Buddy. You listened very well. Thanks for letting me pet you. *(child)*
- Thank you for letting me read to you, Bella. I thought you were very cute, and your roll-over trick was very good. Hope I can read to you again. *(child)*
- I had a wonderful time reading to you. Your [sic] awesome! *(child)*
- I love Paws for reading. *(child)*
- You are a great dog and a great listener. I hope you liked some of the books I read to you. *(child)*
- Paws to Read! Thank you for helping me be a better reader. *(child)*
- Tonight was the last time I will read to a dog in Paws to Read. I wish I could read eternally to these dogs. *(child)*
- I had so much fun reading to you. I had the best time reading *What Dogs Teach Us*. *(child)*
- Thank you for listening to me, Mitzi. *(child)*
- I think it is fun to read to a dog. *(child)*

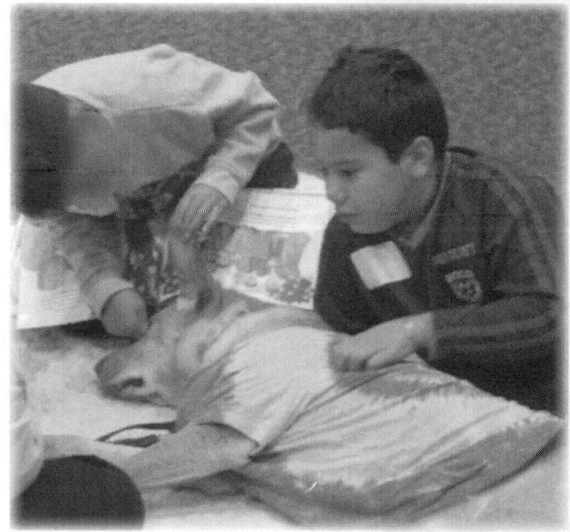

Dove

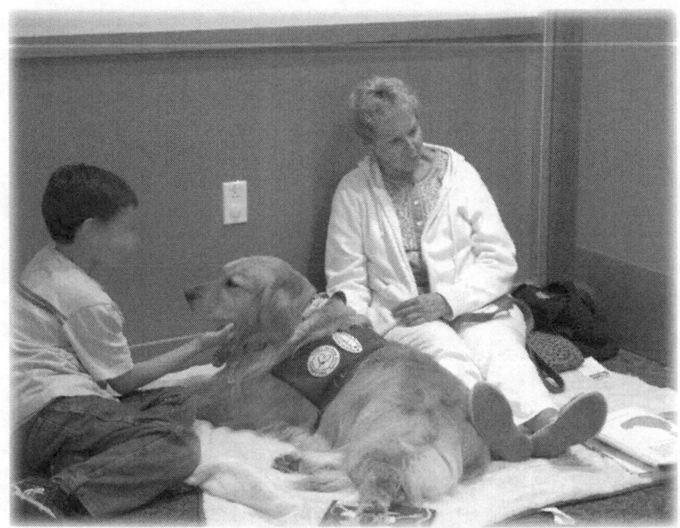

11

~CHAPTER 7~

livermore manor

Livermore Manor was an assisted living and Alzheimer's/dementia care facility in Livermore. Previously called Golden Manor, this facility provided residential services from 1962 until November 2011, when it closed. The building accommodated up to 20 patients in double rooms. It provided 24-hour care, every day of the year, with secure locks to keep patients from wandering. It had a large, fenced-in, park-like area for residents to use on sunny, warm days. There were several picnics held in this area each year as well as parties for birthdays and holidays inside the facility. Livermore Manor was located at 3356 East Avenue in Livermore.

Therapy dogs visited the residents at Livermore Manor every Friday morning for nine years. At the time of its closing, Lawrence and Mitsy were visiting people at Livermore Manor. Lawrence started in November 2002 and was there longer than anyone else, including staff, except for one resident. Lucy, a Toy Poodle, was there with Lawrence during the first few years until her passing. Sissy, an Australian Shepherd, came regularly in 2009, but had to retire when diagnosed with cancer. Mitsy started in the spring of 2010. Residents loved having both a large and a small dog, and they particularly enjoyed the days when both Lawrence and Mitsy were there. One resident always had newspaper and magazine articles as well as cartoons to share with the therapy dog handlers about animals, especially dogs.

—Testimonials—

I can't tell you how much I like the dogs because I care SO MUCH about them! I like them a lot. The dogs are a lot of company for us. They take our minds off of things. And I like reading about dogs too.

Sam Buranis, Resident

I like the dogs. They are 100% GOOD for both old and young persons. The doggies keep the people happy when you bring them here. I think you need to come more than once a week.

I have two dogs at home. When I come home from work, I am tired and stressed. My dogs are so wiggly and happy to see me. And I am so happy to see them.

Blanca Moreno, Caregiver

Lawrence seems to remember me. And he's on my toes. That's why I know he remembers me. I love him—from the top to my toes. He knows I love him.

Mitsy, here you are. Here is my sweet baby girl. I love you. You make sure your mom takes you with her everywhere she goes. Oh sweet little girl, come and let me pet your ears. They are so soft.

Patricia Morte, Resident

What Lawrence meant for my dad, Earl Raymer? Lawrence was my dad's therapy dog at Livermore Manor. He would come in on Friday morning with Pat, his handler. My dad had a stroke and dementia, so Lawrence was a big comfort to my dad when he was able to pet him. Growing up in Wisconsin, my dad always had a dog. I think seeing Lawrence brought back some memories of that time as well as comfort to him when he felt Lawrence's fur against his hand. My dad always had a smile when Lawrence came to see him.

At my request, Lawrence came to dad's memorial service. What an honor to dad. And a comforting presence to all of us at the service. It was a very hard day for me, and Lawrence helped me get through it.

Kristin Ramirez, Daughter of a resident

Having Lawrence and Mitsy both here to visit us makes someone like me who has been sick a long time have a new life. I want to caress them, and they are willing to be caressed. It eliminates the problem of loneliness.

Bert Robles, Resident

I like it when you bring the dogs. The residents are so happy. It's good because the residents can give their stress to the dog so they can relax. Having a dog helps us get our work done, like this morning when

I was combing someone's hair, and it was much easier as soon as the dog was there to see her.

Angelica Rosales, Caregiver

Prior to the passings of my wife and of my best friend, they were residents of Livermore Manor. They were given great care by the staff there. However, at this point in their lives, there were very few joys. But every Friday morning, we all looked forward to a visit from this great bundle of love in the form of a Black Labrador Retriever named "Lawrence, the Livermore Lab." I made it a point to be there to greet this dog and observe him make the rounds of the residents, pausing by each one to say hello in an individual way. It was a joy to see a sparkle return to many of their sometimes vacant eyes. He instinctively knew how to address each resident. He would rest his head in my wife's lap. She would smile and pat his head. It was a very special experience for her.

When I got a chance, I would also greet him and give him a pat and a quick rub-down. I think we made a connection of sorts. He knew how much I enjoyed and respected his vocation and efforts. He reciprocated with a wagging tail, a cold nose, and a lick of my hand.

At my wife's funeral, as I walked down the aisle to leave the church, who was there to greet me and offer condolences? No one else but Lawrence. I can still see him silhouetted against the open door of the church. His presence and greeting was very timely and welcomed. It created a good memory for me on an otherwise sad occasion.

I consider Lawrence a personal friend. He is a very special dog, and he deserves and has earned all the accolades we can give him.

Larry Sampson, Widower

Therapy dogs are excellent. Many patients have had pets and sorely miss them. Having a connection, even if brief or occasional, is valuable as it broadens the horizons of the incapacitated person.

Sometimes an incapacitated person is unable to converse with other persons, or they do not know how to converse with him or her. However, there is no such problem with an animal. It's a wonderful experience.

Marion Stearns, Wife of a resident

Animals are beautiful and sensitive beings, often imparting a wisdom that many humans are oblivious to on a conscious level. However, this special energy of an animal can be felt and enjoyed by all of us, no matter our physical or mental conditions. They provide whole other universes of connection and communication beyond the human realm. Thus, when people become in any way psychologically or physically "handicapped" for normal human social interactions, animals, such as these therapy dogs, can provide a particularly important role of helping these people to continue feeling some basic integration with their life and the world.

We humans are the "youngest" species to evolve on this planet. We are here on the backs of all the other creatures. We are very clever and this allows us to think we are somehow superior to other creatures. Nothing could be further from the truth. Let us wake up to how much we have to learn from all animals, and gratefully, respectfully cultivate their vital, comforting presence in our lives.

Hallie Whitcomb, Daughter of a resident

—Stories—

Below are stories for two dogs who went to Livermore Manor—Lawrence, a Black Labrador Retriever; and Mitsy, a Havanese/ Poodle mix.

Holding Tight—

Gus spent many days sitting in a recliner in the living room at Livermore Manor. His body was quite rigid, and he had trouble moving. But he always seemed to be able to reach out and touch Lawrence—it must have meant something real special to him.

One day, just before Lawrence and I were leaving, we were seeing Gus. He was stroking Lawrence and holding his leash. When I told Gus it was time for Lawrence and me to go and that we would see him next week, Gus suddenly grabbed Lawrence's collar and the leash. He was holding onto them so tightly that I couldn't get Lawrence away from Gus. Then Gus started to stand up from being almost fully laid back in the recliner. A visitor and a staff member tried to keep him from falling, while I continued trying to get the leash from him and have him let go of Lawrence's collar. How Gus did what he did, we'll never know. But he obviously wanted to keep Lawrence with him and was doing things we never expected him to be able to do.

Surprising Us—

Susan had been at Livermore Manor for several years, but never said a word. And that is the way it had been the many times Lawrence had come by to visit her. Then one day, to our surprise, when Lawrence rested his head on Susan's lap, she said, "You're a good dog. I like you, dog. I like you, dog." One of the staff members walking past in the hallway was so startled when she heard Susan talking that she dropped the binder she was carrying. I wonder why she talked to Lawrence, but no one else.

Teaching Lawrence a New Trick—

Geraldo walked up and down the hallway at Livermore Manor. He was quite bow-legged. One day, while Lawrence and I were walking up and down the hallway with him, Lawrence suddenly turned around and went between Geraldo's legs, turned around, and came back out. Geraldo called this "tunneling."

So now Lawrence had a new trick, "tunnel." If one stands with his legs spread apart and snaps his fingers between his knees, Lawrence walks through, turns around, and comes back. Geraldo taught Lawrence a new trick, one that he does to this day.

Changing Their Minds—

On one of our first visits to Livermore Manor, we went with Lawrence, Mitsy's Labrador buddy. We were introduced to the residents, and Mitsy was doing her little dance for them and looking for hugs. Two ladies in the living room didn't seem at all interested in Mitsy. I asked if they would like to pet her and their answers were "No," so we just continued to visit with the staff and other residents. But with each passing week, these ladies seemed to mellow and started to look forward to seeing and petting Mitsy and to calling her to them if she didn't see them right away. These dogs have that special gift of giving and asking nothing in return but a pat on the head.

Sharing Good Feelings—

Lawrence was making his weekly rounds to residents at Livermore Manor. He rested his head on the couch next to Lowell. He had been sound asleep when Lawrence approached him earlier in the hour, but now Lowell was awake. He scratched the top of Lawrence's head and rubbed his ear. But then Lawrence got tired, and settled down on the floor.

Lowell had his legs crossed, and Lawrence backed himself up to be under Lowell's higher foot. Lowell rested his foot, wearing only a sock, no shoe, on Lawrence's back. "This is nice and warm," Lowell said. Lawrence's body was moving slightly as he breathed, so I asked Lowell if Lawrence was also massaging his foot. "Oh yes. It feels good."

A few minutes later, Lowell started rubbing his fingers on the couch. Lawrence sensed that Lowell was ready to scratch him some more. So up came Lawrence, plopping his head on the couch next to Lowell. This time Lowell gave him even more rubbing and scratching. Lawrence's tail clearly said how much he enjoyed this. And presumably Lowell was enjoying this experience too.

My Pretty Baby—

Mitsy just started to visit at Livermore Manor in the spring of 2010. She loved visiting the residents and went from room to room and down the hall looking for folks to be with her. On one of our first visits, I watched as Emily greeted Mitsy, called her sweet baby girl, and just enjoyed sitting on the couch petting her.

Over the next few months, when Mitsy and I visited, we sadly watched a steady decline in Emily from walking, to using a walker, to not getting up at all. Later, when in bed most of the time, she still loved to hear us say, "Hello, Emily. Mitsy is here to visit with you." The staff would turn her toward us and she would reach up and weakly say, "There's my pretty baby," and give Mitsy a smile.

During one visit, her young son came in. I told him Mitsy and I would leave so he could visit with his mom, but he stopped us and asked if we would stay because his mom loved having the dogs visit. It warmed my heart to be able to visit with this nice young man and his mom, and to watch Emily smile at all of us and give Mitsy a little pat.

From Newspapers to Song—

Matthew liked to sit on the couch in the living room and read his newspapers. He enjoyed having the dogs come to visit. One day while visiting, Mitsy hopped up next to him and looked up with those beautiful black eyes of hers. Matthew put his paper down and broke into song, singing "How Much Is That Doggie in the Window" to her. Her tail was just wagging to the music. After his song, Mitsy just lay there awhile to receive her pets and then was off down the hall to find someone else whose day she could make a little brighter.

Not When Food's Around—

Lawrence was busy interacting with Bruce in the hallway. As he scratched Lawrence's back, Bruce asked Lawrence, "Whatcha doing, Buddy?" Lawrence was looking ahead, down the hallway, toward the front door, ears alert and tail wagging. There was no response from Lawrence, so I said, "Probably watching the cars go by." Then Lawrence moved to the next person.

Bruce kept calling his name, wanting Lawrence to come back. But now Bruce had a bowl with his morning snacks in it. He wanted to feed Lawrence, but I had to keep Lawrence back, and the staff member kept telling Bruce, "No people food for Lawrence, only doggie food." Eventually Lawrence was able to see Bruce once more that morning before heading out the door and on to other pursuits.

Helping When Needed—

Bernard was supposed to be sitting in a chair in the hallway, but he kept wanting to get up. Lawrence and I went to visit him. He sat back and rubbed Lawrence's shoulders. But Bernard kept easing toward the front of the chair while we kept encouraging him to sit back.

After a few minutes, we went back into the lounge to see other people. I peeked around the corner and saw that Bernard was crawling on the floor. Lawrence and I went down the hallway to get one of the caregivers. She came and instructed Bernard to crawl to the foot of the bed in a nearby room. Once there, she told him to stand up. Lawrence and I were next to them, and I added that Lawrence wanted him to stand up too and go back to the chair that he had been in so Lawrence could have his shoulders rubbed some more.

Bernard pulled himself up, turned around, and sat on the foot of the bed. The caregiver asked him to stand up. Bernard put one hand on the bed and the other on Lawrence's shoulders for support and stood up. We walked down the hallway to a couch and Bernard sat down. I told Bernard that Lawrence wanted him to stay there. Bernard said, "I don't care what the dog says. I want to know what the humans say!" Lawrence plopped down on Bernard's feet to keep him there for a while.

Teasing Lawrence—

Tim always enjoyed showing us articles and pictures of dogs. This morning, he showed a photo of a white dog wearing a decorative Santa hat. He said, "That's a picture of Lawrence after we dipped him in bleach." Then he showed us a picture of Michael Douglas on the cover of a magazine and commented, "That's Lawrence before his face transplant." Other residents in the room got a chuckle out of these statements.

Naptime or Dogtime?—

Geraldo was napping in his room when Lawrence peeked in. I said, "Lawrence is here and he wants to see you." Geraldo's eyes slowly opened, and he said, "I'm napping. What time is it?" When I said it's 10:20, mid-morning, Geraldo decided he should get up. He already had his shoes on, so he got up from his bed and started walking down the hallway to the lounge at the other end of the building.

On the way to the lounge, Geraldo told me buildings were designed like this in France to be an efficient way to house people and that these types of hallways were called "French tunnels." As soon as Lawrence heard the word "tunnel," he turned around and went between my legs and came back out again. This surprised both Geraldo and me, but Geraldo enjoyed seeing Lawrence do a tunnel, especially because this was in the same hallway where he had taught Lawrence to do this trick.

When Geraldo passed away, Lawrence stood by his bed for a while. He missed his good buddy who had taught him to tunnel.

—Quotes—

- I can't tell you what you mean to me. You are so nice. Look how you're putting your head against me. Look at your tail. You just love to be loved. *(resident)*
- You're a nice dog. I love you, dog. Yes, I do. *(resident)*
- You're a very special baby. *(resident)*
- It is so much easier to visit my husband when the dog is here. *(spouse)*
- I've never seen a dog that was so good and loved to be petted and talked to so much. *(resident)*
- You just do what you like to do. It's so much fun for you. *(resident)*

- Oh, how nice to see you here, my friend. It must be Friday. *(visitor)*
- I remember the first time I petted you. You just loved it. *(resident)*
- Such an affectionate animal. And he loves me. *(resident)*
- You are a very special dog. You are full of love. *(resident)*
- Come on. When you walk in, you're supposed to come see me. *(resident)*
- I'll make him happy. I'll pet him. *(resident)*
- It's so nice of you to come and cheer us up. *(staff)*
- Isn't he cute? Look at his face. *(resident)*
- Oh, you're so tired. You need to go to bed. *(resident)*
- With all that gray hair on your face, you need a make-up job. *(resident)*
- It's so sweet. He knows what to do and where to go. *(resident)*

~CHAPTER 8~

merrill gardens

Merrill Gardens is an assisted living facility in San Ramon. This site was established in 1996. There are about 50 Merrill Garden sites in nine states throughout the United States, 19 of these sites in California. The focus is to promote independent living rather than dependence on others.

The facility in San Ramon provides an apartment-style community in a homelike environment without the responsibilities of home maintenance. It can accommodate up to 81 residents in studio and one-bedroom apartment units. Services and amenities include anytime dining served restaurant style, 24-hour staffing, housekeeping and linen service, scheduled transportation, a library, social meeting areas, a salon and a barbershop, and a full activity program.

Merrill Gardens also has an Active Living Wellness Program, overseen by a medical doctor. It includes at least 30 minutes of activity daily for muscle strengthening, increased flexibility, and improved balance.

The setting includes landscaped grounds with walking paths and garden areas. It is located at 18888 Bollinger Canyon Road, San Ramon, California 94583. For more information, call 925-831-3964 or go to http://www.merrillgardens.com/assisted_living/San_Ramon_CA/zip_94583/merrill_.

Currently, Maggie, a Golden Retriever mix, visits the residents at Merrill Gardens twice a month on Monday afternoons. Nancy Rogers visited with her two Golden Retrievers. She went with Bear from 2001 to 2003 until he passed away in 2003 and with her dog Kane from 2003 to 2007 until he passed way. Other therapy dogs have visited once or twice a month in the past.

—Testimonials—

There are many kinds of therapy, but surely one of the best is a dog's therapy! A visit by Maggie, our dog therapist, is effective and fun.

A gentle pat from us brings a loving look from those big brown eyes. What is she thinking as she wags her tail and we all smile? She smiles as well. It is a happy moment.

Marjorie Christensen, Resident

I like to see the therapy dog, Maggie, come to visit us. It gives one a heartwarming feeling when you see a dog come toward you, with tail wagging, wanting to get to know you. No matter how you are dressed, how you feel, or how you act, Maggie comes to greet you. It makes you feel special to be given unconditional love.

Maggie is so well behaved. It is amazing. Maggie maintains an aura of peace and calm, and she makes those of us around her peaceful and calm. She is a good example to others about how pets can behave and benefit man. I would miss her if she didn't come to visit.

Gracie L. Dougherty, Resident

Maggie is a great companion during her one-hour visits with our residents. Just with Maggie's presence, she offers our residents her unconditional love and affection.

Norma A. Knowles, Active Living Director

The days that Maggie comes to visit us here are "red letter days," as everyone looks forward to patting her. Maggie is a Golden Retriever and since I, too, had a "Golden," her visits bring back so many happy memories. We all hope that Dusty will continue to share her "Golden" with us for a long time.

Marybell Loesel, Resident

—Stories—

Below are stories for three dogs that have gone to Merrill Gardens—Bear and Kane, both Golden Retrievers; and Maggie, a Golden Retriever mix.

Tennis Balls—

The first time Bear went to Merrill Gardens, he noticed the tennis balls on the walkers and realized this would be a fun place for him. Although he had to leave those tennis balls alone, he enjoyed walking around, seeing people, and carrying two tennis balls in his mouth at a time. Even though Bear was quite happy with tennis balls in his mouth, he had to be careful not to smile or he would drop them. But the residents were smiling at Bear, and Bear showed them how happy he was by wagging his tail.

Helping Someone Change His Mind—

When Maggie and I arrived one day, Brad said he didn't want to see Maggie. So we left him alone and visited other residents. As we moved around doing our visiting, Maggie seemed to sense that maybe Brad was now ready to see her. So she walked over to him and put her head on his lap. Brad smiled and said, "Thanks for you people coming here." Then he laughed and added, "How do you like that? Now I think she acts like a person! Actually she does!" Brad continued to pet Maggie and smile. I am glad Brad changed his mind about seeing Maggie and that they had some fun time together that day.

Ready for the Dog—

Jack and Bear were special friends. The caregiver where Jack lived said that Bear's visit was the reason that Jack was dressed and smiling. Jack loved Bear's white face and said that Bear looked old and dignified. It was like Jack looking in a mirror at himself. Jack told Bear that he didn't have any family and so Bear became his good friend. Jack would sit and talk to Bear and tell him his problems, all the while gently stroking Bear's head. Sometimes Jack was too tired to get out of bed. On those days, he liked to have Bear come to him and lie next to him. Jack said that Bear kept him warm and that he could relax and take little naps when Bear was there. Bear would just wag the end of his tail so that Jack knew Bear was happy too. That made Jack smile.

We Know We're Going—

Last Monday, our day for Merrill Gardens, I had the remains of a cold. I put Maggie's vest away and told her we weren't going to Merrill Gardens because we didn't want to make the residents ill. She lay down with her head between her paws and looked so sad.

The next day I was better, so off we went. She was so excited to know we were finally going. As usual, as we turned onto Bollinger Canyon Road, Maggie's tail started wagging since she knew she was getting close to seeing her friends! We arrived and she immediately went to the left to await her fan club. We didn't wait long. The residents started coming in after they finished their lunch, and lots of pats and tail wagging went on. Norma, the Active Living Director, came over to say, "Hi." Norma knelt down and told Maggie to give her a paw. Maggie placed a paw on each of Norma's knees, much to the delight of the residents standing by. Other residents came by. Maggie continued to walk around, and then lay on her back and put on a show while taking pats from all who were willing to give them.

Maggie and I look forward to our bi-weekly visits to Merrill Gardens, and I know she brings joy to many of the residents. There are conversations, smiles, and feelings of happiness each time we go.

Waiting for Her Friend—

Kane had a very special friend at Merrill Gardens. Ellie was 99 years old and had very few visitors. She waited each week in her room for us to arrive. When we got there, Kane would eagerly push into Ellie's room and rest his big head in her lap. Ellie was not well and was weak from age and the cancer invading her body. She was quite happy to just sit while stroking Kane as she sank peacefully into those big soft brown eyes. Ellie said she found rest and solace during those times together with Kane.

The Limo Driver—

Several months ago, I was going to San Francisco for a special occasion and had a limo service pick us up at the house. When I opened the door, the driver said, "I know you from someplace." We were going round and round trying to determine where our paths had crossed when Maggie walked up to the door. Suddenly, the gentleman looked at her and said, "I know where I know you from. You take your dog to Merrill Gardens." I said, "We do." He said his mother-in-law had been a resident of Merrill Gardens.

Though his mother-in-law had passed away, he indicated how much she enjoyed seeing the dogs. I thought it funny that he couldn't remember me or I him, but when Maggie appeared, it became clear. I think the visits the dogs make to residents are remembered, not only by the residents, but by those who visit them and love them.

—Quotes—

- I really like having Maggie visit us. *(resident)*
- It's a very important part of volunteer work to have the dogs here. *(resident)*
- I love having Blondie [her name for Maggie] here 'cause she is beautiful. *(resident)*
- It is very nice having Maggie here because we all miss our pets and it's comforting to us. *(resident)*
- Maggie is very friendly and swell. Animals are good for people. *(resident)*

~CHAPTER 9~

military and veteran events

In addition to the therapy dogs going to the VA in Livermore (see Chapter 13), the therapy dogs participate in other events honoring our veterans and military. These include Veterans Day ceremonies, Welcome Home Celebrations, parades, and concerts.

In the spring of 2010, the therapy dogs started participating in Welcome Home Celebrations for our troops. At many of the celebrations, there is at least one and up to three therapy dogs present to provide the kind of affectionate welcome home that only a dog can give. Therapy dogs have attended celebrations in Alamo, Antioch, Blackhawk, Brentwood, Camp Parks, Concord, Danville, Discovery Bay, Dublin, Livermore, Martinez, Oakley, Pleasanton, San Ramon, and Walnut Creek. Lawrence has attended more of these celebrations than any of the other therapy dogs and really enjoys being there. Now he gets excited in the back of the car whenever he sees more than one American flag or a fire truck, as there are often fire trucks at these events and many flags flying in the neighborhood. Other dogs that have attended these celebrations include Albert, Brooks, Chex Mix, Lady, Miles, Rivers, Sailor, and Thunder.

The therapy dogs have participated in other events. For example, Albert, Alfie, Belle, Buddy G, Lawrence, Miles, and Thunder have marched in the Veterans Day parades, either with veterans from the VA in Livermore or with the Pleasanton Military Families. Lawrence and Thunder have attended Veterans Day ceremonies and a program at a local firehouse honoring our first responders on 9-11. Albert went to the dedication of a bench for two young Fallen Heroes.

—Testimonials—

I recently had the joy of meeting a therapy dog called Lawrence. It was at my soldier son's Welcome Home and Purple Heart Ceremony.

Anyone who has had an experience with this kind of dog can say for sure what a blessing they can be.

Everyone loves dogs, and these dogs are specially picked for their love and concern for the frail and injured and sick. They have that certain something that makes you melt when you look in their eyes. I have seen these dogs in hospitals with wounded soldiers and in children's hospitals. The way they relate to the sick and wounded is amazing. You can't help but touch them when they are near you. They bring comfort to those in distress. How they just seem to know who needs them is a mystery—just an internal awareness that takes them right to the person who needs them at that moment. I think they all have old loving souls.

As I watched Lawrence, a ten-year-old Lab, come forward among the crowd at my son's Welcome Home Celebration, I noticed that hands went out all up and down the aisle. Everyone wanted to touch him. What a wonderful gift he and others like him are to mankind. I am thrilled when I see soldiers' families bringing dogs from the war zone who have befriended their sons and daughters. Lawrence added a lot to our son's homecoming because our son loves dogs.

Thank you Lawrence. You truly are therapeutic!

Mrs. Rose Adams, Mother of a soldier at his Welcome Home Celebration

Therapy Dogs have become an integral part of our Welcome Home Celebrations for returning military in the Tri-Valley. Many of our service members return home after serving dangerous and difficult missions. Having a friendly "Lawrence, the Livermore Lab" or one of his affectionate, well-behaved dog pals there to greet them clearly brings joy to all who have the privilege of encountering these endearing animals.

Candace Andersen, Mayor of Danville, 2008 and 2012

I have served with Lawrence in several parades honoring our veterans and have seen his caring support of our ailing and injured veterans at the Veterans Hospital in Livermore. He never asked for anything but the chance to serve. He has helped to teach me that service comes in many forms and circumstances. Those that serve share one thing—a great heart—and are in their own right, heroes. Whether our heroes use two legs or four legs or none at all, their hearts are the only badges they need—hearts of courage, honor, and generosity.

Marilyn Carter, Livermore Veterans Foundation

For the past several years, the Diablo Valley Flag Brigade has had the privilege to include Pat Wheeler and her beautiful therapy dogs, Lawrence, the Livermore Lab, and Albert, join us in Operation Welcome Home, honoring returning service members.

These welcome homes include presentations and proclamations from Congressmen, State Senate and Assembly representatives, mayors, city council members, high school cheerleaders, Boy and Girl Scout Troops, and many veterans and Veteran Support Organizations.

But we know that we have truly succeeded when we say "Mission Accomplished" because Pat has presented a "bookmark" with the pictures of eight therapy dogs on it to these returning service members so they can "bookmark this day in their lives" and remember that the entire community cares enough about them and what they represent to take time out of their lives to show their respect.

We look forward to each and every Welcome Home knowing that Pat and her faithful four-legged companions will always be there for these beautiful events.

Duane and Sharon Ferrell, Co-Founders, Diablo Valley Flag Brigade

I have had the pleasure of meeting several of the therapy dogs and their owners. They always bring a smile to my face! We appreciate their presence at the homecomings that we do for our returning military and other military-related events. I love the "ranks" the dogs have received for their hours of service.

I would also like to thank the owners of these therapy dogs for their hours of training, their service of smiles and of visiting with patients, and the commitment to their dogs and the community for getting the pups to all the places they take them to brighten someone's day! You are Sergeants of Smiles for sure.

Patrice Frizzell, Pleasanton Military Families

When you see Pat introduce the dogs to our homecoming soldiers, you can see how it relaxes them completely. The soldier will be talking or just standing there, and they will be the featured speaker, and yet you will see them reach down with their hand and pet the dog. When Pat presents the bookmark to the soldier, it provides another opportunity for the soldier to say thank you, but they always reach down to the dog and acknowledge it with another pet on the dog. It always brings a smile on their face as soon as Pat is introduced, and she appears with a dog. Then the dog takes over the show. The soldiers automatically will direct their attention to the dog with a large smile and a friendly petting of them. Enough can't be said about the program and the response Pat gets from our returning troops. The emotions that Pat and her volunteers bring to our troops cannot be measured. It is simply great. Thank you, Pat, and the other therapy dog volunteers.

Richard Ghera, Adjutant, American Legion Post 237, Pleasanton

Pets seem to have a way of making people smile, relax, and be friendly. Their uncanny ability to love unconditionally is amazing. I have lived my whole life with dogs. I have laughed with them and cried with them. They listen without judgment, and they respond by snuggling up next to you and somehow make you smile, even when you are down.

These things are what make the therapy dogs valuable to all they come in contact with. They are gentle creatures, and they know that the people they touch need them. They seem to sense that those they come in contact with are hurting and need the love they have to give.

I have seen these dogs in action at many events such as Veterans Day ceremonies, parades, and Welcome Homes. I see the smiles they put on the faces of the people who come up to pet them. They draw a crowd, you can be certain. But they also know when they are to take a back seat to that soldier coming home or the veteran that is being honored. They patiently wait their turns to come up and pay tribute to those who have sacrificed more than any of us. These dogs are indeed valuable, and they have a mission just as our troops do. They serve honorably and courageously. Lawrence, Sailor, Miles, Thunder, and Albert—Thank You for Your Service!

Tami Jenkins, Founder, Livermore Military Families

Thank you for bringing Thunder and Lawrence to the Tri-Valley Veterans Day Program in Danville. Those wonderful animals are a big hit with veterans and the public at large wherever they go. I see them at many Welcome Home Celebrations, and they always bring a smile to the returning warrior's face. They are extremely well-behaved animals, which is a testament to the care and training that they receive from their handlers. Their appearance at veterans-related events is always welcome.

Raymond F. LaRochelle, Director of Events, Viet Nam Veterans of Diablo Valley

Thank you for bringing Lawrence to the Welcome Homes. He is a great addition and a favorite among many of us. It's good to remember the veterans who are in the hospital and important to know that the therapy dog program exists.

Pat Levy, Blue Star Moms Chapter #101

When a therapy dog handler comes up to welcome the honorees, their hands automatically find their way to the dogs, usually Lawrence, the Livermore Lab, and they find themselves petting the dog while they listen. Sometimes it seems as if they don't even know they're doing it. Always, it brings a smile and visible relaxation to the honoree. The therapy dogs seem to know just the right things to do at the right time to make a connection, and it's a connection that opens the doors to ease other connections. It makes me wish I could have them join all of the career coaching workshops I do for veterans. I think they'd be more effective.

Joy Montgomery, Director, ReBoot Camp

I joined the Pleasanton Military Families group shortly after my son, First Lieutenant Thomas Murphy, left for his tour of duty in Afghanistan. The support that all of the members give to the troops overseas and the families back home is great and was an important part of my life during my son's deployment in Afghanistan.

I attended a number of the Welcome Home Celebrations for our returning troops prior to the return of Thomas, and I saw Lawrence, the Livermore Lab, at most of them. I thought he was a very special part of each celebration, and he always brought additional smiles and laughter to the events. He is always quick to make new best friends. I looked forward to seeing him again at each of the celebrations, and my husband and I were very happy to see that he could be at our son's celebration as well. Our son loves dogs, and it was heartwarming to see his reaction when Lawrence, the Livermore Lab, was introduced to him.

Pat and Lawrence are now two of my favorite members of the Military Support Families, and I want to thank them for all they do for our returning heroes.

Jenny Murphy, Mother of returning troop member;
Member, Pleasanton Military Families

The night of my Welcome Home Celebration was a great surprise and has filled my mind with very special memories. From the time I was picked up at the restaurant and escorted by the veterans on Harleys to my home, I was shocked and honored to have so many friends, family, neighbors, the Mayor of Pleasanton, veterans of several wars, and people whom I did not even know there to greet me and welcome me home from Afghanistan.

There were many people there representing different groups to present gifts and express their thoughts and appreciation for my service.

Out of the many new faces, during the presentations, there came a most unexpected face walking up to me, looking up at with me with a wagging tail. He was introduced as Lawrence, the Livermore Lab. He gave me a warm welcome and added a special smile to my face. His owner, Pat Wheeler, explained that he goes to most of the Welcome Home Celebrations and visits hospitalized vets as well. He is definitely part of my special memories of that night, and I think he is doing a great job for all of the veterans that he visits.

The troops in my Company would love to have adopted some of the local dogs during our tour in Afghanistan, but it was against regulations. I know all of them would have enjoyed a welcome home from Lawrence, the Livermore Lab. I too hope to have a dog of my own once I get permanently settled and a dog like Lawrence, the Livermore Lab, would be great!

First Lieutenant Thomas O. Murphy, Commanding Officer, 649th Engineer Company, U.S. Army, California National Guard

As part of the Tri-Valley patriot community, I attend many Welcome Home events for our military. Some of them are coming home for good while others are coming home for a brief break from combat. Reconnecting can be a challenge when people have changed significantly. The greetings from representatives of many local support groups can go on for quite a while. It's friendly and includes both serious and humorous exchanges.

It has been a wonderful experience meeting Lawrence at the homecomings. I remember the first time I met "Rear Admiral" Lawrence and Pat. It is nice of Pat to bring Lawrence to the homecomings. I like seeing how Lawrence reacts to the men and women returning home. I realized what a wonderful addition Lawrence is to these celebrations.

After watching the presentation of certificates, coins and such, Lawrence and Pat came forward with a gift also—a bookmark with Lawrence's picture on it so our returning hero can bookmark this day in his or her life. The reactions to Lawrence are ones of caring and of spending a few minutes petting and giving him a hug. You could see the happiness Lawrence brought to each one of our heroes.

This bit of happiness will be remembered by each of the men and women being honored, as well as by all of us attending. We all look forward to seeing Pat and Lawrence, as their appearance brings love and happiness to all of us attending the homecomings.

Thank you for the great work you do.

Joyce Oxsen, Veterans of Foreign War Auxiliary to Post 6298, Pleasanton

Therapy dogs. What a blessing! I am a member of the Blue Star Moms of the East Bay Chapter #101 and have been to many Welcome Home Celebrations for our military servicemen and women. The addition of therapy dogs adds so much to our events. For one thing, we want as many groups, individuals, and "animals" as possible in order to show, with greater impact, how much our service personnel are appreciated by their community and fellow Americans. We want to get across to our troops that they are definitely not forgotten and that there are those of us on the home-front supporting them in all their efforts to defend our freedoms.

That said, the therapy dogs are such great icebreakers, not only for our service personnel, but the group as a whole. They provide a bridge for people to connect to one another that might not otherwise happen. During our presentations, I have seen many times the overwhelmed, deer-in-the-headlights look, of "our guest of honor," and then they reach down to touch whichever therapy dog is there and all is well. "Our hero," thereafter, is more relaxed and in the moment. Many thanks go out to these "Petting Officers" and their handlers for participating in our *so very important* Welcome Home Celebrations for our service personnel.

Georganne Seavey, Blue Star Moms Chapter #101

Lawrence and Thunder brought such emotional appeal to our 2011 Veterans Day ceremony in Danville. At our countless Welcome Home Celebrations for our amazing military officers and troop members, the soldier's family is part of an intense ceremony. Lawrence brings a lighter sense of pride—especially to the youth who are learning how and why we honor these soldiers.

Karen G. Stepper, Member, Danville Town Council;
Mayor of Danville, 2006 and 2011

I have seen Lawrence at many of our Welcome Home Celebrations. He is such a joy to be around. Every time he is there, we get to take our picture together while he is sitting with us. We all just pet him. It is so soothing and therapeutic that it just makes you want to be around him all the time. I really enjoy being around Lawrence. I hope to get to see him more often.

Trevor Stoneham, Chaplain, Warriors' Watch Riders

It's with great community spirit and sense of pride that I support the work of Pat Wheeler. Pat unselfishly spends her time in our community with Lawrence, the Livermore Lab, attending Welcome Home Celebrations for our young military men and women. This terrific duo stimulates such emotions from the community at these events. We are very proud of Pat, Lawrence, and all the therapy dog teams. Keep up the great work!

Robert Storer, Member, Danville Town Council

I know that animal-assisted therapy has been around for a long time, but I have never had any personal contact with a therapy animal until Lawrence and other therapy dogs began coming to Welcome Home Celebrations for Pleasanton's returning military personnel. These animals have given me a greater appreciation for the stories I have heard about their therapeutic value. I now fully understand how they can have a calming effect on patients and are able to "cheer up" a patient that might be "down in the dumps." I sincerely hope that the use of these animals in our VA hospitals and elsewhere will continue to be supported.

Jerry T. Thorne, Councilmember, Pleasanton City Council

The Diablo Valley Flag Brigade (DVFB) was founded on September 12, 2001, by a small group of community members. I joined shortly after 9-11. The DVFB displays patriotic banners on appropriate holidays and honors residents in the area who are currently on duty with any branch of the U.S. military, including the Guard and Reserves. The DVFB is dedicated to the remembrance of 9-11 and devoted to the support of our troops.

In 2005, the DVFB started coordinating Welcome Home Celebrations. On Christmas Eve 2005, I attended the Welcome Home Celebration in Moraga for six service members. I found it to be such a beautiful event that I have been devoting much time to the DVFB's Welcome Home Program ever since. It gives me a real sense of doing the right thing, as a civilian giving back to those who serve our country through military service. Now I coordinate and emcee the Welcome Home Celebrations for troops coming back from Afghanistan, Iraq, and other tours of duty. In 2010, the DVFB presented 145 9-11 flags to military personnel during numerous Welcome Home Celebrations.

It is so beneficial to have the "four-legged helpers" involved in our Welcome Home Celebrations. I feel it is very important to show all service members that there is a wide array of communality supporting their sacrifices to serve our country, from the local politicians, to the Girl Scouts, and all the like-minded folks in the community. Dogs have a very special presence for most people, with their unselfish love for their masters. I have seen first hand how their presence can heal a depressed soul with amazing results.

Our mission is to show those service members we are welcoming home that all of us in the community are here to support their decision to serve and to be 100% behind them when they return home and re-enter civilian life. Lawrence and his therapy dog crew are a big part of that process. Thanks for all you do!

Bryan Welden, President, Diablo Valley Flag Brigade; Organizer and Emcee for Welcome Home Celebrations

At my son's Welcome Home Celebration, there were many surprises in store for him, but I think the biggest smile on his face came when Lawrence, the Livermore Lab, was introduced. The crowd had quite a reaction to him as well, especially when Pat announced his name!

A few weeks later, my son was at the Livermore VA hospital to take care of some paperwork, and Pat and Lawrence were also there. Lawrence apparently recognized my son and ran past several other people there to greet him. What a special dog Lawrence is. Thank you for sharing him.

Marcia Wright, Mother of a U.S. Marine Corps Corporal

—Stories—

Below are stories for some of the therapy dogs that have attended the Welcome Home Celebrations and participated in other military and veteran events—Albert, a Border Collie/Black Lab mix; Brooks, a Pointer/Lab mix; Chex Mix, a Newfoundland; Lawrence, a Black Labrador Retriever; Miles, a Golden Retriever; Rivers, a Queensland Heeler mix; and Sailor, a Portuguese Water Dog.

First Meeting with a Real Petty Officer—

Lawrence was very excited going to the Welcome Home Celebration for a Coast Guard Petty Officer returning from a special duty assignment tour in Afghanistan. He had yet to meet a non-canine Petty ("Petting") Officer close up. When we arrived, Lawrence did his usual walking around, introducing himself to everyone.

As the motorcycle escort with the California Warriors' Watch Riders was getting closer to PO Jared's home, ten dignitaries lined up along the street to shake Jared's hand and welcome him home. Lawrence and I stood behind them on the other side of the sidewalk. But after four of these dignitaries had shaken Jared's hand, Lawrence suddenly barged through the line and had Jared on the ground with him in a flash. The fifth dignitary in line commented, "Well, we've been upstaged by Lawrence." Jared and Lawrence thoroughly enjoyed meeting each other, and Lawrence stayed around well after the end of the celebration to spend more precious time with Jared and his wife.

Dogs Are So Special—

Staff Sergeant Francis was returning home just before Christmas and a tour of duty in Afghanistan following four tours in Iraq. What a hero! Sailor and Lawrence were there to welcome him back with all the love and comforting Francis was willing to receive. After all the groups had welcomed Francis home, including therapy dogs Sailor and Lawrence, people started heading home. Francis looked down at Sailor and Lawrence, and started petting them. He said they reminded him of when he was having a very bad day in Afghanistan. Then a dog came up to him, and he petted that dog. "It turned my day around. I love dogs." That's what therapy dogs try to do—not let any of us have a bad day, especially those sacrificing so much for our country.

What His Rank Means to Lawrence—

I was talking about Lawrence and the work he does at the VA in Livermore. When I mentioned at one of the Welcome Home Celebrations that he was now a "Rear Admiral" for 1,000 hours of tail wagging at the VA for our veterans, Lawrence turned his rear end toward the audience and wagged his tail rapidly. Apparently, he is proud of his accomplishments.

Basic Training and Uniform—

Chex Mix attended his first Welcome Home Celebration in April 2012. Lawrence was there to oversee his basic training on how to welcome home a troop member. Chex Mix did a great job of meeting people before the honoree arrived. As usual, he enjoyed greeting everyone and getting attention, even when lying on the pavement in the shade, trying to stay cool.

When we went up to thank Marine Corps Lance Corporal Johnson, the emcee said, "I'm glad I don't have a coat on!" as he looked at Chex Mix's long flowing fur. He then asked, "Does anyone need some hair? I'm sure Chex Mix will donate some to you." After chuckles from the audience, Chex Mix approached Lcpl. Johnson to get some pets from him and give him some bookmarks with his picture on them. But Chex Mix was eyeing the ice at the side, in a container with cold drinks. Even though it was a warm day, Chex Mix informed me later that he would be glad to continue attending these events to honor these special people who have served our country.

Group Photo Time—

At the end of each Welcome Home Celebration, a group photo is taken with the honoree, his or her family, and all military members and veterans present plus firefighters, police officers, and family members of military personnel. Of course the therapy dogs are invited to participate as well since they are "Petting Officers." It takes a few minutes to get everyone lined up, as there is usually quite a crowd at these events.

At one Welcome Home Celebration, both Brooks and Rivers were still interested in interacting with people, and we were unable to get them to turn around and face the camera. So we have a photo with their happy tails instead of their smiling faces. At least their tails provided a gentle breeze on a warm day.

Always a Devil Dog for the Marines—

Whenever Lawrence and Chex Mix attend a Welcome Home Celebration for a Marine, they wear their devil horns so they can be considered Marine Corps Devil Dogs. People really enjoy seeing them as a Devil Dogs, especially the Marines being welcomed back.

Sharing Lawrence with His Wife—

A Vietnam Army veteran came up to me before a Welcome Home Celebration and told me how much he loves seeing Lawrence at these celebrations. He said he had told his wife about Lawrence and that she wanted to know what Lawrence looked like. So he downloaded a photo of Lawrence from the slideshow of one of the Welcome Home Celebrations and now uses it as the screensaver on his computer. That way he not only can show his wife what Lawrence looks like, but also can see Lawrence in between celebrations. He said his wife and he like to read and wanted bookmarks with Lawrence's picture on them for themselves. Of course I gave the bookmarks to them. This veteran sure is a Lawrence fan.

The Good Life—

When welcoming home an Air Force member, I mentioned that Lawrence oversees a crew of "Petting Officers" at the VA in Livermore and that the Navy veterans there promoted him to "Rear Admiral" last year for 1,000 hours of tail-wagging. I said to the young man, because of what you do, Lawrence doesn't have to worry about being able to eat, having a place to sleep, or getting lots of attention. A member of the audience piped in, "Of course not. Lawrence is in the military."

The Bookmark Is Special—

We present a bookmark with pictures of the therapy dogs on it to the returning troop members at the Welcome Home Celebrations. One evening, Albert presented a bookmark to the Army National Guard Sergeant returning from a year in Iraq. I told him, "Albert wants you to bookmark this day in your life." As I handed him the bookmark, he looked at it and said, "This is awesome!"

His four children were by him, each one holding one the items given to him. He let one of his daughters hold the bookmark. She leaned over to Albert, and, pointing to his picture, said, "See Albert, you're on here!" She then went to other people in the room showing them Albert's picture. Hopefully, this made it a memorable evening for the entire family.

Thanking a Service Dog—

At one of the Welcome Home Celebrations, a woman who was a friend of the honoree came with her working service dog who was trained to help her with balance issues. Since her dog was working, he was not allowed to interact with people. But she was hoping he could meet Lawrence since he rarely has an opportunity to interact with other dogs. Lawrence, of course, was pleased to oblige.

The dogs sniffed each other and then sat down close to each other. Lawrence seemed to know that he was a service dog and was not to interact with people other than the woman he was working for. So whenever people came over to us and wanted to pet both dogs, Lawrence would let them pet him, but blocked their way of reaching this dog. Lawrence clearly knew what job each dog was to perform.

Supply of Photos—

Ross, a member of the Warriors' Watch Riders, saw Chex Mix for the first time at a Welcome Home Celebration, though it wasn't Chex Mix's first one. Ross came over and started taking pictures of Chex Mix. Lawrence looked at Ross as if he was being ignored. Ross said, "I already have lots of pictures of you, Lawrence, in the photo album on my computer. I need to get some of this new dog."

Two Hands Needed—

We take both Brooks and Rivers to the Welcome Home Celebrations. If we leave one at home, that dog gets quite upset with us! And when it was our time to go up front and thank the honoree for his service to our country, both Brooks and Rivers want to be with him. Good thing he had two hands so he could pet both dogs at the same time. I just had to be careful not to get knocked over by Brooks' tail!

A Big Hit in the Group Photo—

One afternoon, Peggy, a member of the Warriors' Watch Riders, took Chex Mix from me for the group photo. After the photographer and others had taken several pictures, Peggy returned Chex Mix to me. She exclaimed, "I may have to tell my husband he has been replaced!"

Winding Down from the Celebration—

On his first time as the only therapy dog at a Welcome Home Celebration, Chex Mix made himself very special to Garrett, the young man coming back from a year in Iraq. After the celebration was over and the group photo taken, Garrett saw Chex Mix lying down on the driveway. Chex Mix looked so comfortable that Garrett lay down on the driveway next to Chex Mix. Both needed to unwind from a busy time celebrating Garrett's welcome home, and Garrett seemed to know that Chex Mix had found the best way to do it. Apparently, Garrett really liked Chex Mix, and, of course, Chex Mix didn't mind at all.

Leading the Parade—

Lawrence and I were working at a booth for Valley Humane Society at the First Wednesday Street event in Pleasanton in early July. This is an opportunity for not-for-profit organizations to make the public aware of their services and encourage support, as well as for local vendors to sell their products. Lawrence was dressed with a military hat and a flag bandanna since it was close to the Fourth of July. Our shift was to end at 6:00 PM. But then someone told me that the 91st Division Army Band would be coming down Main Street at 6:30 PM. I knew people in that band and decided to wait until they passed our booth.

I made myself comfortable in a chair near the VHS booth with Lawrence resting on the pavement in front of me. About 6:35 PM, we heard the band coming. Suddenly Lawrence was up and moving forward to the street. The street was filled with people wandering around. Lawrence knew the band needed someone to clear the way. He stepped out in front of the drum major, made a sharp left turn, and paraded down the street in front of the band all the way to the Veterans' Building where the band was presenting a sit-down concert and featuring its bagpipers.

Lawrence marched to the tempo of the music, staring straight ahead the entire way. I had to ask only one man to move out of the way. Otherwise, Lawrence cleared the way for the band. But even when the band came to the end of the parade, Lawrence didn't leave them. I was concerned since a specialty pet shop had a booth there selling gourmet dog treats, and Lawrence being a Lab, well . . . I was afraid their entire table would be turned over by him and he would inhale the treats. But no, Lawrence wanted to be with the band. He even stood next to the bagpipers when they played. The band's commanding officer thanked us afterwards. How often does a dog come to the rescue of the Army?

Marching in the Rain—

The Pleasanton Military Families asked that a therapy dog march in the Veterans Day Parade in Pleasanton with them. It was raining, but Miles didn't mind doing this important job because he got lots of love from all the veterans and children in the parade. Also, everyone was looking at him, so he didn't let the rain upset him. He was a real trooper and enjoyed by all the veterans and people in the parade. I enjoyed the experience too.

Bench Dedication to Two Fallen Heroes—

On Veterans Day in 2011, Albert and I attended the dedication of a bench to two young Fallen Heroes from Livermore—Private First Class Ethan James Hockman, 1985-2006, and Sergeant Ryan Jeffrey Hopkins, 1988-2010. This was a cooperative effort of the Livermore Area Recreation and Park Department (LAPRD) and the Livermore Veterans Foundation (LVF). The young men had been neighbors and boyhood friends. Both served in the U.S. Army, and Sgt. Hopkins had been deployed to Iraq.

As youth, the soldiers played in Maitland Park, a favorite place of Albert's for his walks. The bench overlooks the playground where the two of them used to play. Albert was at the dedication ceremony to comfort their parents. He was also attentive to what was going on during the ceremony, paying his respects, in his own way, to these two Fallen Heroes. A sad occasion, but also a special one, never to be forgotten. Albert hasn't forgotten them. When we take walks in that park now, he stands quietly by the bench, not distracted by other dogs in the park, honoring these two young heroes.

—Quotes—

- I can't believe how his eyes lit up when he saw Lawrence. *(neighbor)*
- The bookmarks are such a nice gift. Other groups give them books, so they can use these bookmarks. *(presenter)*
- I like your saying they should "bookmark this day in their lives." They will remember this special day every time they look at the bookmarks. *(veteran)*

- Thank you so much for bringing Lawrence. We love having him here. And my puppy loves Lawrence's smell when I get home. *(presenter)*
- Lawrence is working overtime. Must be drudgery for him, but then look at his tail going. *(veteran)*
- Are you and the dogs going up there? If he doesn't call you, I'll raise my hand. *(attendee)*
- You dogs did a great job! *(veteran)*
- Thank you for what you do. You are such sweet dogs. *(attendee)*

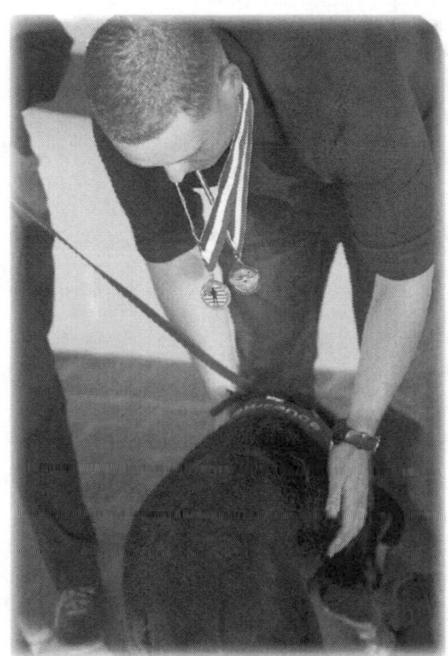

OUR COUNTRY

COME HOME

LAFAYETTE
SUPPORT

Thanks
Therapy
Dogs

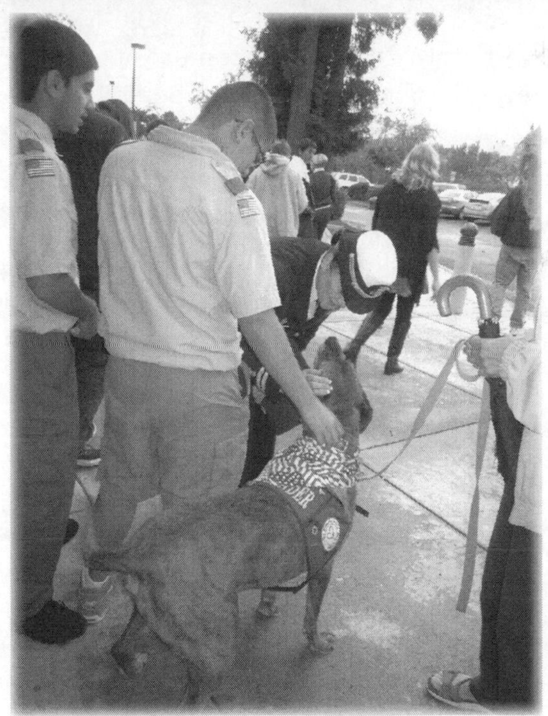

~CHAPTER 10~

the parkview

The Parkview is an assisted living and memory care facility for seniors in Pleasanton. It offers a vibrant, elegant lifestyle for seniors who need some assistance and yet want to remain as independent as possible. The residents enjoy social, recreational, and leisure activities with new friends as well as deliciously prepared meals served in a beautiful dining room.

Housekeeping, laundry services, beautician and manicurist services, and transportation to churches and medical appointments are some of the many amenities provided to help the residents maintain independence as long as possible. Two fully licensed LVN nurses are available on a daily basis to oversee care needs and answer any questions residents or families may have about health issues.

The Parkview has 86 apartments for seniors who desire assisted living services and 19 private apartments for those who need more intensive services due to memory loss. There are studio and one- and two-bedroom apartments. Common areas include a community dining area, a living room, a library, a wellness center, and some multipurpose rooms. Outside there are walkways and courtyards.

The Parkview is located adjacent to the Pleasanton Senior Center and Centennial Park and near a shopping center. The address is 100 Valley Avenue, Pleasanton, California 94566. For more information, call 925-461-3042 or go to http://www.eskaton.org/parkview.html.

Several therapy dog teams have visited the residents at The Parkview since 2007. They see residents in both the assisted living area and the memory care unit. The therapy dogs are at The Parkview two or three days each week.

—Testimonials—

I have witnessed many wonderful interactions between our residents and the therapy dogs that come to visit our assisted living community.

Most of our residents beam with delight when their furry friends stop by for loving strokes on their heads. These dogs are so patient. Even when our residents have lost the ability to interact with one another, they light up when these beautiful animals approach them.

I also give credit to the handlers for devoting the time it takes to accomplish this level of good behavior by the dogs and for bringing so much joy to others. I will be forever grateful.

Jolynn Abernathy, LVN, Resident Wellness Nurse

I would like to share what I know and what I have seen with my two dogs, Baby and Harley (Bichon Frisés). I have seen, with my visits, the joy, the laughter, and the great smiles that the residents have. They just laugh and laugh because my dogs just follow me; they stay right behind my heels, never leaving my side. The residents get a kick out of this. I take them over to the residents. The huge smiles and laughter that the dogs bring to the residents just make my day. They talk about how they had pets and how they miss them and how happy they are that The Parkview has these pet visits. They can't wait for the next visit.

The residents are thrilled when The Parkview has its Pet Parade with all kinds of dogs, in different shapes and colors. Some dogs come dressed up. We have it on the patio, and the residents sit on the patio waiting for the dogs to come. They are so happy when the dogs arrive. It just makes their day.

We have therapy dogs come as well as dogs of family members and friends. We have Bella, Benji, Cabo, Caper, and Shasta. These therapy dogs love going to the memory care unit. I feel our dog visits reduce anxiety and blood pressure, improve physical and mental health, and just make everyone feel good—the residents, the staff, the dogs, and the handlers. We have different families come in with their own dogs too, and they take the time for the residents to pet their dogs and to talk to the residents. They all love the conversations!

Patricia Rawlings, Activity Director

The animal therapy visits provided by volunteers to The Parkview Memory Care Unit are a true blessing to those seniors suffering from dementia or Alzheimer's disease. I have witnessed residents who are agitated calm down and residents who are withdrawn start to interact with their surroundings and become connected again to the world around them. Often, these residents will react to the animals and not much else.

Animals will decrease their anxiety and agitation, and increase a feeling of calmness, security, and wellbeing. The positive exchange of affection between the animals and the seniors not only provides mental stimulation, but helps them to recall distant happy memories with their own pets. Just the feeling of petting the soft fur of a dog can open a window, if only for a brief moment, of a long ago memory of a loved pet. Families and staff appreciate the positive experience that the volunteers and their animals provide to our beloved residents.

As a family member of a loved one at The Parkview as well as the Administrator, I am slowly losing my father to this dreaded disease. Although he will often not remember the visits he has from his family members, he always remembers when he has had a visit from Cabo, the dog. My father has always loved dogs . . . our earliest known picture of him is at the young age of three in Mexico with his dog. His faithful companion while he was still in his home was Molly, his Beagle. How he loved that dog! Animal visits to any resident in the progressive stages of Alzheimer's are a true blessing.

Sylvia Zaininger, Administrator and daughter of a resident

I have seen the pet therapy dogs here at The Parkview. Each time, I see the joy the dogs bring to my mom and the other residents. They are all so happy to pet the dogs. They bring a smile to my mom's face, which I haven't seen in a long time.

Daughter of a resident

—Stories—

There are stories in this chapter for seven dogs—Bella, a Shetland Sheepdog; Benji, a Collie/Labrador Retriever mix; Cabo, a Yellow Labrador Retriever; Caper, a Golden Retriever; Ella, a King Charles Cavalier Spaniel; Gandalf II, a Chihuahua/Schipperke mix; and Shasta, a Border Collie/Beagle mix.

Great Memories—

Caper's favorite place to visit is the Memory Care Unit of The Parkview. It is the first place she visits after walking through the main doors of The Parkview building. She leads me down the hall and around the corner and down another hall. Caper checks periodically to make sure that I am following right behind her. When we come to the special doors for the Memory Care Unit, she sits and waits patiently for me to unlock them. Then she is ready to go!

One of her favorite people, Carol, is no longer there. But when she was, Caper would find her room, and Carol would greet Caper with a hug and then take the leash and walk Caper around the halls. Carol used to have a dog. She missed her dog very much, but being with Caper seemed to make her feel better. One day, Carol couldn't go walking any more, but Caper didn't care. Caper would visit Carol in her room, and sometimes Carol would recognize her and even smile at Caper. Caper would put her front paws on Carol's bed and nuzzle her hand. Carol seemed to enjoy those special times.

Winning Over People—

Our first visit was to the Memory Care Unit. It always warms my heart to watch how excited and gentle Benji is with each person. He has won over so many people this way and is quite content to just sit and let them pet him for as long as they want. For a little excitement, he shows off his tricks, including rolling over and the popular "High Five." Of course, in the Memory Care Unit, there are challenges, but Benji is not fazed by any of them.

How Dogs Strut—

Cabo attends many of the holiday events at The Parkview. And he has an outfit for each holiday. From Easter to Halloween to Christmas, Cabo shows up, strutting his costume throughout the facility and getting lots of looks and laughs from residents.

Bringing Back Happy Memories—

When I mentioned to one of my close friends that Shasta was recently accepted into the therapy dog program, she asked if I would stop in and visit her mom the next time I was at The Parkview. She explained how much her mom loved dogs and how much she had missed having her own dog. It seems that this is a very familiar story with so many of the people we were visiting. I can't imagine what it would feel like to not have the companionship and love of an animal.

With that in mind, it wasn't long before Shasta and I met up with Rita. She was so sweet and soft-spoken that I think Shasta took an instant liking to her that very first day. Rita could not see very well, and she told us that if we didn't see her out and about, that she was probably in her room. She said, "Stop by any time."

After a couple weeks, I realized we hadn't visited with Rita lately. She had made sure several times to show me exactly where her room was. Shasta and I knocked softly on the door. "Come in," Rita called out to us. As we walked in, I told her Shasta is here to visit. Rita broke out with a huge smile. I knew she couldn't see Shasta yet, but I guided her hand to the top of Shasta's head and we began talking.

As I looked around the room, I noticed a large framed picture of a tiny Toy Poodle displayed proudly on a table. "Oh, that's my little dog, Lily," she said. Shasta had settled by her feet, and Rita was reaching down, petting her on the back. She told me Lily had passed away a while ago, and that otherwise she never would have considered moving without her. It seemed that touching Shasta brought her closer to her memories and the love and happiness that she felt with her precious friend.

Loving Kisses—

Ella had favorites at this facility. She especially liked the elderly woman, Matilda, who beamed when Ella approached her wheelchair in the hall. I held Ella up to her, and she asked if Ella would kiss her on the cheek. Ella granted her wish and Matilda would continuously exclaim, "I just *love* dogs!" Then she thanked me for bringing Ella to visit her.

How Dogs Talk—

When Cabo arrives at The Parkview, he is ready to see his friends there. He goes in and sits by a resident who is in a corner, away from others. Cabo doesn't want anyone to feel lonely. He goes up to them, wagging his tail, as if to say, "Everything's okay. I am here to bring you love, joy, and comfort. Please pet me, and please feel free to get a dog treat from my mommy and give it to me." Cabo is always prepared, though, because he carries dog treats in his therapy dog vest so residents can give treats to him.

Cabo has learned a trick. The residents place a treat on his nose, Cabo flips it in the air, and catches it sometimes. But Cabo seems to purposely miss it sometimes, hoping the residents will give him more treats.

Treats for Her Friend—

Shasta and I had been visiting The Parkview residents on a weekly basis for quite awhile. It seemed as though certain people were actually anticipating our arrival. It was heartwarming to see their whole demeanor change as they saw her wagging tail.

When Shasta and I come through the front door, we would normally run into several people preparing to go out with family or friends. If people weren't in too much of a hurry, there would be time for a quick hello before we headed down the hallways in search of people to spend some time with. An open door was an opportunity to say hello.

Shasta had a good friend named Lola. She was always so cheerful and smiling as she reached out her hand to pet Shasta. Lola adored dogs. In fact, she loved all animals. She really looked forward to spending time with Shasta and the other therapy dogs as well. I'm sure these experiences greatly enhanced her quality of life. I imagine Shasta picked up on this unspoken message.

Whenever we made our visits, I always brought with me what I refer to as *high value treats* for the residents to give to Shasta. These were special goodies that were only given on special occasions. Lola seemed to enjoy these moments almost as much as Shasta did! Lola did not just hand over the treat. Before she would give Shasta her treat, she would ask Shasta to do something for it. Sometimes it was a paw shake or a sit and wait. They both seemed to enjoy this type of interaction so much. At times, it was like I wasn't even there. It was just Lola and Shasta having a good time together.

A Win-Win Situation—

Gandalf II loves getting attention, and he is more than ready to give attention to the residents at The Parkview. Being small, he can lie in people's laps and next to them on the couch. This makes it easier to pet him than some of the larger dogs. It's a win for him and a win for the residents. And all seem so comfortable.

Letting People Know He Has Arrived—

Benji and I visit once a week, and we both get so much joy from interacting with the residents. I'm pretty sure Benji could do it alone and has figured out the routine, but then I would be robbed of the rewarding experience. Benji is quite the talker and usually announces his arrival at The Parkview. This brings huge smiles to the people in the main foyer at the time.

Doing Special Work—

Bella was sitting in the hallway in front of Joanne, who was in a wheelchair. She was looking directly at Joanne, with her loving eyes. Margie, another resident, came by and asked me, "Are you with a church?" I replied, "No. We are with the therapy dog program." Margie said, "Well, you are doing God's work!"

Substitute Dog—

Rick was a very special friend of Shasta's. He had given up his own dog just two weeks before moving into The Parkview. All he could think about was how much he missed the dog. He enjoyed the feeling of being nuzzled and the comfort of the large, warm body under his hand as he gently petted Shasta's back.

Rick's dog, Max, had been his constant companion for the last ten years. As Rick's hearing got worse, Max had begun to bark when the phone rang. This turned out to be a great help, and Rick decided then and there that Max should have a prominent role in regards to the phone. He practiced with her for weeks until he could get her to bark when he told her to. The dog's voice was the first thing you heard when his answering machine came on! He assured me that his voice did follow with the typical "Please leave a message at the beep."

As Rick related this cute story to Shasta and me, his voice cracked as he told us that during the move, the battery must have been low in his answering machine because when he turned it back on in his new home, Max's message was gone! The machine was sitting on the table. He had not even bothered to hook it up again. He said he felt so sad and that he didn't feel like doing much.

He seemed a little brighter as he petted Shasta while she licked his other hand. I had recently trained Shasta to bark on command and now I had an idea. I quickly explained to Rick that Shasta might be able to assist him in recording a new message for his answering machine. This seemed to perk him up quite a bit, and he began deciding what the new message would say. I must say she did an excellent job of recording a greeting message. Rick seemed just a little bit more accepting of his new situation.

To do something so seemingly small with Shasta that produced something so meaningful to someone else became the highlight of my day. I am so thankful to work together with my dog. Just being a *team* greatly enhances the bond between the two of us.

A Special Touch—

One of Ella's favorite people at The Parkview was Alice, a sweet woman in Memory Care. The woman was in a wheelchair and could neither speak nor use her hands. However, that did not stop her from enjoying Ella's touch. I lifted Ella up to her and brushed Ella's long soft ears on her cheeks and hands. Alice would close her eyes as her face lit up with a smile from ear to ear. She leaned her face into Ella's fur, and her eyes expressed her appreciation and joy at the sublime healing touch of a dog.

Getting Extra Attention—

Benji and I visit the common areas around The Parkview, where, each time, we meet old and new friends. Of course, there are some that like to sneak him a piece of cracker or cookie, and so consequently those residents get a little extra attention.

We have seen residents come and go, and we have listened to the stories of many that had to give up their pets. A visit from a therapy dog like Benji often makes their day and brings back fond memories. I love listening to their stories and watching them sneak treats to Benji as their way of thanking him for bringing back some memories of their pets.

Therapy Dogs in The Parkview Pet Parade—

The Parkview Pet Parade is held annually. It is a time for all the therapy dogs plus dogs of friends and family, as well as dogs from our community, to come and assemble together for some meet-and-greet time. Shasta's black and white coat was shining under the purple therapy dog vest. It was an especially wonderful day because it was Shasta's fifth birthday. This was also our first time to take part in the event.

I brought some tasty treats and Shasta's most coveted toy named "Skunky." The main room at The Parkview was full of people and dogs. Shasta and I sat together on the floor, waiting as each dog had a turn to go to the middle of the room to be introduced and to show off a bit. I could tell by the shining faces and smiles that this was truly a very popular celebration.

I heard some voices saying, "Hi, Shasta," as it was our turn in the spotlight. We were presented to everyone, and I spoke a bit about Shasta and how we decided to participate in the therapy dog program.

I put Shasta in a sit, told her to stay, and tossed her "Skunky" about 20 feet. She patiently waited until she heard me say, "OK!" There was a round of applause to which Shasta joined in with a few woof-woofs. Next we began with her down on the ground as I placed several treats right in front of her. I gave her a special hand signal and told her to wait. The seconds ticked by as the room went still. Shasta had the small pile of treats locked in her gaze. Again, when I said, "OK," she gobbled them up.

When we were all through, there was an opportunity to take Shasta around to visit with friends we already knew as well as meet some new friends. There were refreshments for all. Even the dogs got a little party bag of goodies. It was a great time, and there was no doubt that everyone really enjoyed all the festivities.

How Dogs Sing—

The Parkview has special events going on throughout the year, and Cabo has participated in many of them. A singer was entertaining some of the residents in the multi-purpose room. Cabo entered and sat down next to the singer, in the front of the room where everyone could see him. Cabo barked along to the song, "How Much Is That Doggie in the Window." The residents laughed and clapped, which only encouraged Cabo to keep singing with the performer.

Good Pals—

One of our regular stops has been to visit Carlos in his room. Carlos loves Benji and thoroughly looks forward to this one-on-one time. Unlike many of the residents in the Memory Care Unit, a visit from Benji draws some good conversation out of Carlos. Even though Benji is a fairly big dog, Carlos loves to have him rest on his lap. It is so sweet to see the interaction, both Carlos and Benji smiling the entire time. Carlos has often commented that Benji should live there with him, and he always makes me promise to come again.

Thinking During Playtime—

It was obvious to me that Shasta liked to incorporate a bit of *thinking* into her playtime. It all started with the basic commands like sit, down, stay, and come. I could tell that, after awhile, she would kind of glaze over and loose interest. Just for fun, I took "Skunky" (Shasta's most coveted toy) and a teddy bear and laid them both on the floor in front of her. "Get Skunky," I said, and she did!

We developed more interesting, as well as complicated, ways of learning and having fun. It was during this time that I created her most favorite game, which was something similar to hide and seek. The difference was I hid "Skunky," and she would seek for it until she found the toy.

Shasta did very well with this game, and we really loved playing together. Frequently, I would bring "Skunky" so Shasta could dazzle her friends with her exceptional tracking behaviors. One morning, we found several ladies chatting together in the library. We knew Jenny and Maria, but there were three new people who wanted to watch.

Everything started out with my explanation on how she learned to seek out "Skunky," how much more she could do with the games at home, and how much she enjoyed playing the games. The ladies were sitting near the fireplace towards the front of the room. I told Shasta to sit and wait in front of the couch with the ladies as I walked off towards the computers in the back of the room. I jumped at first when I heard what sounded like all five women shouting together, "She's looking, she's looking!" I just couldn't help myself. I had to laugh. That made them laugh too. It was a very successful morning indeed.

Scheduling Her Time—

When Caper arrives at The Parkview, she proceeds to go into the large living room area directly ahead of the entrance. She visits each person individually, even if they are sitting in a group. She seems to know how to allocate her time and moves on to the next person so that she will be able to spend time with all the residents in the living room that day. Some residents want Caper to spend more time with them, but she gently lets them know that she must see other people. Caper seems to have a way of assuring them that she will be back to see them in the future.

—Quotes—

- My parents love dogs and I am so glad The Parkview is allowing the therapy dogs to come in. *(daughter of two residents)*
- My dad sits on the patio and watches the dogs play. He says that makes it feel like home. *(daughter of a resident)*
- Therapy dogs are one of the greatest assets to humans. I'm so glad that The Parkview is animal-friendly. *(son and nephew of two residents)*

~CHAPTER 11~

school programs

The therapy dogs visit schools in the Bay Area. Some are one-time visits (see Chapter 14 for stories on some of those visits). In other cases, therapy dogs go to schools on a regular basis. They participate in reading and tutoring programs and visit special day classes. Programs at four schools are covered below—Alisal School in Pleasanton, Las Perales Elementary School in Moraga, and Marylin Avenue Elementary School and Emma C. Smith Elementary School in Livermore.

Alisal Elementary School—

Through the Paws to Read program at the Pleasanton Public Library, arrangements were made to have a therapy dog team visit a special education classroom each week at Alisal Elementary School in the Pleasanton Unified School District. The school has an enrollment of about 660 students in grades K-5. The student body is about 55% white, 21% Asian, and 13% Hispanic or Latino. About 14% of the students are English language learners, 11% qualify for free or reduced lunch, and 14% receive special education services.

It is located just down the road from Amador Valley High School and the historic Main Street area of Pleasanton, at 1454 Santa Rita Road, Pleasanton, California 94566. For more information, contact 925-426-4200 or go to www.pleasanton.k12.ca.us/alisal/.

Starting in the 2009-10 school year, therapy dog teams visit a special day class (SDC) for first and second graders that have mild to moderate learning handicaps or cognitive impairments. Three therapy dog teams visit the class one day each week for one hour. Under the supervision of the teacher, Christine Fitzsimmons, the dogs, with their gentle presence, encourage students to talk and to listen.

—Testimonial—

In the fall of 2009, I had begun my second year of working in Pleasanton Unified School District (PUSD), in a special day class (SDC) for students with learning handicaps and/or language impairments. A flyer was emailed out to share with families at our school, inviting families to attend a local library program called Paws to Read. I was new to the area and interested in what this program was all about. As I scrolled down the information, I thought to myself, this program sounds AMAZING!! But surely they couldn't intend to include only students who read, could they?

My class was the perfect example of students who were eager to learn, needing soft and cuddly encouragement, with a wagging tail, but would not be candidates for reading to the dogs. While we're a very smart bunch, not all of my young, elementary-aged students were able to read. So I wrote a quick email to the leader of the program at the library.

Her response was phenomenal! Not only was she interested in talking to me more about my students and their specific needs, but she was offering to set up a meeting between me and a few local dog owners who might be a good fit for working with my students. I didn't know what would come of it, but was willing to give it a try. After meeting with the dog owners and their fabulous fuzzy friends, I was hopeful that this could be a good experience for us all! I had no idea what I was in for!

We decided to have the dogs visit us in our classroom, as our program would be different than that of the library. All the students in my class were working on individual goals, and all were working on language skills. I began to refer to our therapy dogs as "our talking dogs" and it's been the most appropriate term! :) On a weekly basis, the dog owners visited with their therapy dogs for a one-hour session. During that time, the students rotated around stations in the room to work in groups of three or four students on each task.

On Dog Day, our dogs would visit and become one of the stations that students visited. While with the dogs, the students reviewed vocabulary and rehearsed terms we had been using in school that week. We encouraged the use of appropriate social skills such as turning towards the person or dog that you are speaking to, and, with the dog owners, modeling conversational turn-taking and speaking in complete sentences.

I had invited the "talking dogs" with the hope that we would gain an extra hour per week of a different style of rehearsal for the same language goals that we spent the entire week on, but after only the first few sessions, I was STUNNED at the difference a dog made! It was immediately clear, based on the students' energy levels, ability and stamina of focus, length of utterance, quality of voice, and their simple smiles, that this program was a hit!

As students bonded with the dogs and their owners, the responses that we saw in our students only increased. On each morning of Dog Day, the students were THRILLED to hear that their friends were returning to our classroom, and the excitement level of the day increased. But there were side-effects of bringing this program to Alisal that I had not anticipated: better attendance on Dog Days, better attitude than on non-Dog Days, and, the most important one, to me, was the excitement of the entire school campus to welcome our dog program each Dog Day.

Our classroom is located on the back hallway of the school, requiring our dog volunteers to check in through the office and walk all the way through campus (past the library, lunch room, and most of the classrooms) before finding our welcoming rainbow rug, where they meet with our students. As you can imagine, when I walk through the school with a friendly dog, the school day STOPS for any student who happens to be in the hallway. It takes us several minutes to make what should be a two-minute walk, because our dog friends are so friendly and simply LOVE kids. They happily greet any six-year-old who happens to be walking to the library, and each week, that lucky six-year-old (or line of 25 six-year olds) is happy to stop and say HI! As I began to have my students "escort" the dogs to the office, I realized the positive "face time" this gives them on campus. They are proud to walk around campus with such a special, fuzzy friend, and are even more well received by our general education peers because of that positive exposure.

I can't find words to explain the magic that happens when our dog friends come to visit kids who don't want to talk or can't find their words. It's a humbling thing to watch, having attended years of college and having logged in more than a decade of running my own classroom. After all of this training, who would have thought that I'm just not equipped with the tools to be an expert? A wagging tail and a wet nose. Thankfully, for my class, I have found, in our local dog volunteers, exactly what I was missing.

Christine Fitzsimmons, Special Day Class Teacher

—Stories—

Below are stories for the three therapy dogs that have visited the SDC students at Alisal—Buddy W, a Golden Retriever/Yellow Labrador Retriever mix; Ella, a King Charles Cavalier Spaniel; and Lucky, a Golden Retriever.

Helping the Children Open Up—

Lucky and I visit this classroom every Tuesday. We work with children who need more help with talking and listening. Lucky is great at this job since he is such a good listener. The students talk to Lucky about things they have learned in school, everything from penguins to space travel. They share stories with Lucky. The teacher says even the quietest students, some of whom were afraid of dogs when they first met Lucky, light up and talk with Lucky. In 2011, the students gave Lucky the "You Make a Difference Award." Apparently he does for these students.

The Magic of Soft Fur—

Once in a while, there will be a child who is afraid of dogs. During our first visit to this classroom, where the students needed encouragement to speak, one seven-year-old girl from a different culture couldn't say hello to Ella. Ming crouched in the back of the group of children, watching Ella cautiously out of the corner of her eye. As each of the children eagerly took turns petting Ella, she watched and waited.

When our time in the class was nearly over, I invited her up to see how soft Ella's fur was. Since Ella is small, I held her in my arm at my side with her head behind my elbow and her tail facing forward. Ming came forward slowly, and I gently guided her hand to Ella's back. She touched the fur and quickly withdrew her hand. We practiced this once more, and I congratulated Ming for trying.

During our visit the following week, Ming wanted to try again to pet Ella's back. She succeeded and giggled with pleasure, and she was surprised at her accomplishment. At this point, I turned Ella around and asked Ming to look into Ella's eyes and say hello. That was the moment that Ming realized she wasn't afraid of this dog. She became one of Ella's most ardent fans. Subsequently, the teacher noticed how Ming relaxed in class, grew in confidence, and became more talkative.

Teacher Very Pleased—

During one of our first visits to Alisal, we met the students, and Buddy W was well received, as had been his predecessors, Lucky and Ella. At the first gathering when Buddy W and I participated, I did show-and-tell with Buddy W and shared information about his history. Shortly after that, I received an email from the teacher reading, "I was STUNNED by language development at the rainbow rug with you and Buddy!! :) Amazing!!! Garth typically talks in class, but NEVER the amt. that we saw today!! And introducing all of his friends to you?!? Phenomenal . . ."

Questions for the Dog—

Ella and I had come to assist with the language arts class in the SDC at Alisal. Our job was to visit, and, with the guidance of the aide, encourage the children to ask questions of Ella. Since the children had difficulty forming questions, speaking with more than short phrases, or speaking at all, it was hoped that the dog would arouse their curiosity.

I'll never forget Lucas who spoke very little, seemed to be in his own world, and had a hard time staying focused. One day, after a few visits to the classroom, I asked Lucas if he had a question for Ella. Instead of holding a blank stare, Lucas bent down and looked at Ella for a while. Then he asked her if she had fish at home like he did. It was quite a moment, as we were stunned and teary-eyed that he asked a question. From that day on, Lucas smiled when he saw Ella walk into the classroom, wagging her tail, and he always reached down to pet her.

—Quotes—

- The therapy dog teams are truly amazing in the classroom and deserve fame and attention!!! *(staff)*
- I asked my mom if Ella could be my birthday present. *(student)*

Bingo

Los Perales Elementary School—

Los Perales Elementary School, one of three public elementary schools in Moraga, is located at 22 Wakefield Drive, Moraga, California 94556. It serves approximately 350 students in grades K-5. Almost 60% of the students are white, about 20% are Asian, and 7% are Hispanic or Latino. About 6% are English language learners and 8% have disabilities. Students are grouped heterogeneously by classroom, and combination classes are formed when enrollment requires them. To meet individual needs, Differentiated Instruction is found within all classrooms. For more information, go to www.lpes-msd-ca.schooloop.com/.

The school hosts a team of therapy dogs on an almost monthly basis after school. The Paws to Read program at the nearby Orinda Library was brought to the campus by an interested parent who was looking to support and augment literacy efforts for this school through a new PTA-sponsored program called LP Reads. The result was a program called All Ears. In addition to hosting the therapy dog reading teams, the LP Reads program creates additional touch points for students with books and reading through author visits, grade-level book bags, and a read-aloud program that brings in community members to read to children in the lower grades.

LP Reads funds these activities via grant writing and participation in the Amazon Affiliates program, which can be reached through the Amazon link located on the LP Reads Children's Literature Blog (http://lpreads.blogspot.com/), a resource that LP Reads created to help parents in selecting books for their young readers.

As in the public libraries, the number of dogs and readers participating in the LP Reads All Ears program can vary, as can the day of the week. However, the sessions generally include from one to five dogs, and each child has 20 minutes with one dog per session.

—Testimonials—

The love of books is something that I hope each child finds. However, I know that, in the elementary grades, reading can be anything but joyful for a lot of children. When I heard about the UC Davis study on the impact that reading to dogs can have on children in terms of reducing anxiety and building fluency, I knew we had to get it started at our school.

The children who come to the program seem to light up, and, judging from the number of dogs who fall asleep and the kids who can be found lounging (sometimes snuggled right in with their canine companions), it is clear that the program creates a calm and relaxing environment. I believe the program works and I am so thankful for the volunteer teams (including Amy Berryhill and Hunter) that make it happen for our kids.

Dustie Robeson, LP parent and LP Reads Co-Founder

I just wanted to say thanks for your sponsorship of this program—my kids can't stop talking about how cool it was, and they've actually wanted to READ before bed at night the last two nights. They both have their little card from the dog, Hunter, on their nightstands—cute! For a mom who has struggled with the reading thing for quite awhile now, it's like a miracle. Great work!

Mother of an LPES student

—Stories—

Stories for Hunter, a Black Labrador Retriever, are provided below.

Excited to Go to Work—

When we arrive at Los Perales for the LP Reads All Ears program, Hunter is still his typical Lab puppy self. He happily leads me toward the school library. When we enter the room, he wiggles with excitement to play with all the other dogs in the room. When I remind him that we are here for work, not play, he settles right down into his alter ego and assumes the position of therapy dog.

Watching the Dog's Magical Work—

Hunter absolutely loves children and has to contain his excitement when he sees one of the students approach him with a book in hand. If invited, Hunter will shower them with kisses. If not, he is on his best behavior and relaxes into position while a young boy or girl builds his/her confidence by reading to him. He watches and listens without judgment. He relaxes and enjoys the story. He's 100% in the moment. It's amazing to watch the magic unfold as a child who normally struggles to read becomes more self-assured and reads with enthusiasm. It makes my eyes water to see the mother's joy in knowing that her child has a new inspiration for reading.

—Quotes—

- This is a wonderful program. Thank you for providing this service. *(mother of LPES student)*
- I like to read to the dogs because they listen and don't bark. I want a dog, and this is like having a pet sometimes. *(seven-year-old student)*

Marylin Avenue Elementary School—

Marylin Avenue Elementary School is a public school serving students in grades K-5. Student enrollment is close to 500, three-quarters of whom are Hispanic or Latino. Over 80% of the students come from socio-economically disadvantaged families, two-thirds are English language learners, and over 10% of the students have disabilities.

The school has two programs that involve the therapy dogs, the annual Read-a-Thon and the weekly BELIEVES program. Marylin Avenue School students also attend the Friday afternoon Paws to Read program at the nearby Rincon branch library (see Chapter 6 on Library Programs). The school is located at 800 Marylin Avenue, Livermore, California 94551. Its website is www.marylin.schoolloop.com.

Read-a-Thon—The Read-a-Thon program started at Marylin Avenue School in 2002 as an annual celebration each March of Dr. Seuss' birthday and as part of National Turn Off Your TV Week. Each classroom sets a reading goal for itself, and the students and teachers read as much as they can during the two-week period set aside for the annual Read-a-Thon.

One day of Read-a-Thon is designated as a Read With Us Day. Community members, school district personnel, and special friends of the school are invited to come and share their love of reading and a favorite book with the classrooms. The special friends include the therapy dogs who come to listen to the children read in the school library where the staff has set up blankets for the handler/dog teams all over the school library. Children come, class by class, to visit the dogs and to read favorite books to them. Over 200 children participate during the two 90-minute sessions.

BELIEVES Program—Livermore's **B**roadens & **E**nriches **L**ives, **I**nstills **E**ducational **V**alues, **E**ncourages **S**tudents—the BELIEVES program began in 2006 with an After-School Education and Safety grant from the State of California, funded through Proposition 49. The Livermore Valley Joint Unified School District received funding for two elementary school sites, one of them Marylin Avenue Elementary School.

The BELIEVES program serves about 90 students daily at the school. The program is free to families at Marylin Avenue School and is open every day that school is in session. It is offered from school dismissal until 6:00 PM. Program goals include social development, physical activity, educational enrichment, and supporting students' academic progress.

Starting in February 2012, one of the ways that BELIEVES supports academics is through the Paws to Read program. Therapy dog teams participate every Thursday afternoon during the school year in the BELIEVES program. The dogs and their handlers offer a Paws to Read program to students who need to work on their reading skills. Up to nine therapy dog teams participate in this program.

—Testimonials—

When I was the reading specialist at Marylin Avenue Elementary School, I always was looking for ideas to celebrate literacy with our students as a way of honoring the work they are doing to become proficient readers and writers. The Read-a-Thon has become one of the ways to promote students' reading skills and love of books. On days that the therapy dogs were present, I visited the library as often as I could.

The therapy dogs participate in our BELIEVES program every Thursday after school. This includes the Paws to Read program in which a child reads aloud to a dog. Having the therapy dogs involved provides another opportunity for children to have positive emotional connections to books and to reading. As I work to improve our literacy instruction at Marylin, this is a welcomed opportunity to help our students with their reading skills and interest in reading. Having the therapy dogs present also provides a calmer environment in which students can work on their homework and receive tutorial services from our staff and volunteers.

I've since retired from my reading specialist role at Marylin Avenue School, but the therapy dogs remain a treasured memory with a treasured message I'll never forget—*Be steady, be there, don't give up!*

Sharon Draggoo, Reading Specialist (retired) and Literacy Coach, Marylin Avenue Elementary School

Therapy dogs offer students a non-threatening audience to practice oral reading skills. The dogs do not offer critical feedback, which allows students to practice in a safe environment. We know that the more time students spend reading, the more fluent they become with their reading. Students learn to self-correct themselves while reading to the therapy dogs, which will help them become better independent readers.

The program is too new to document gains in reading. But the increased desire to read while the dogs are on campus and the concentration students exhibit while doing their reading make me confident that reading skills will be improved as a result of the therapy dogs working with BELIEVES students.

Kim Farrand, Teacher on Special Assignment, Livermore BELIEVES Coordinator, Livermore Valley Joint Unified School District

Paws to Read is more than just a reading program to the students in BELIEVES. We have children with a wide range of literacy strengths and weaknesses sit together and fearlessly open books and read with enthusiasm. Whether it is one of their favorites or new material, the energy the kids bring to their canine audience is something we have yet to replicate in other areas of our after-school day. After spending time with the dogs, students leave sharing stories about their favorite partner and the books they read. The interaction leaves our students feeling good about the reading process and good about themselves, and they are more confident in practicing their language skills.

Derrick Psaros, BELIEVES Site Coordinator

When I first met the handler/therapy dog teams from Paws to Read and witnessed their generosity and love, my heart soared. The handlers, more often then not, spend a lot of time preparing their dogs for this valuable work. The time enhances the dogs' already sweet temperament.

The Marylin Avenue School project started in February 2012 when a core of five teams expressed a desire to help improve literacy in the schools. These five teams were: John Flotten and Miles, a Golden Retriever; Paula Huertig and Christy, a Norwegian Elkhound; Sue Lesure and Princess, a Golden Retriever; Sharron Lindsey and Fiori, a Yellow Lab; and Nancy Menise and Schnoz, a Standard Schnauzer. Others with an equal interest in helping kids in schools have joined up so that now we have additional teams: Darlene Austin and Rico, a Chihuahua/Terrier mix; Judy Butterly and Mitsy, a Havanese/Poodle mix; Sharon Fogarty and Cricket, a Chihuahua; Frances Hewitt and Cabo, a Yellow Labrador Retriever; Jocelyn Lewis and Dave, a Golden Retriever; Nancy Rogers and Caper, a Golden Retriever; Liz Stewart and Angel, a Rhodesian Ridgeback; and Cherie Stueve and Miss Maybelle, a Golden Retriever.

To watch these teams wind their way into the hearts and minds of the children at Marylin is to witness an idea whose time had come. I'm sure I speak for all children, parents, educators, and facility managers when I say we are so very grateful that these handler/dog teams, throughout the kingdom, give us the magic of their gift.

Gail Turner, Therapy Dog Volunteer Coordinator

During their Paws to Read time, students are thoroughly engaged in their reading. The only sound is the readers sharing their story with their friends, both canines and classmates. In this setting, reading becomes an enjoyable activity of student choice rather than a required part of the school day. It is okay to enjoy reading. I am pleased that the Marylin Avenue School community has provided this opportunity for our students.

Anne White, Member, Board of Education,
Livermore Valley Joint Unified School District

—Stories—

Stories for three therapy dogs that participate in the programs at Marylin Avenue Elementary School are provided below. They include—Cabo, a Yellow Labrador Retriever; Christy, a Norwegian Elkhound; and Schnoz, a Standard Schnauzer.

Teaching Me Lessons—

Upon one visit when a first grade classroom was in the library for its turn with the dogs, I saw a young boy, Brian, for whom reading did not come easily. He held a special place in the part of my heart reserved for students. The teachers and specialists who had puzzled over his slow skill development were many, and his progress was slow. That day, he was nestled next to a therapy dog, listening in as a first-grade friend read a book, but Brian's eyes were intent on the dog by his side. This is an image I still hold in my teacher's mind.

Brian sat for the full half hour that his class was assigned to join the dogs, listening to friends read aloud, and never leaving the dog's side. Reading for Brian, on that day, was the engaging, relaxing, and comfortable activity that we teachers strive to give each student. I can't recall the dog's name who became Brian's reading pal that day, but I do remember the dog's patient, enduring eyes as she listened to story after story with seemingly rapt attention, Brian's hand on her neck. That steadfast dog gave a special reading lesson to Brian. That steadfast dog also gave a lesson to me—be steady, be there, don't give up.

Why Do You Need a Dog?—

Schnoz and I arrived one afternoon at Marylin Avenue School. A new girl came up to me and asked, "Can you see okay?" I replied affirmatively, to which she replied, "Why do you need a dog?" Most people wonder if Schnoz can see okay, since he is a Schnauzer and has long eyebrows hanging over his eyes. So her questions surprised me.

Teachers Love Dogs, Too—

In the fall of 2011, Christy joined the new Paws to Read program at Marylin Avenue School. Students in grades two to five come to the school library to read to the therapy dogs. Christy is a favorite of both the students and the teachers. They both like the fact that she is so soft and huggable. Every week, one of the teachers tells me, "I really love this dog!"

Fans of the Dog—

Afternoon in the school library is where Cabo spends an hour each Thursday. In the new BELIEVES reading program, Cabo has become a popular dog to read to. Children recognize him and can't wait to sit next to him and practice their reading skills.

Andrew, a regular in the program, loves to talk to Cabo as if Cabo understands him, and, at times, I believe he does. I watch the children come in with smiles on their faces and their eyes open wide, wondering, "Which dog should I read to today? There are nine in the room. So many choices!" However, Cabo has his fans. These children love that they can sit against Cabo and read, and Cabo enjoys the attention.

Becoming Good Friends—

Two third-grade boys came into the library together to read to the therapy dogs. Brett has lived in Livermore all his life and José has only been in this country for four months. Both were sitting by Schnoz so they could read to him. Since Brett had a better command of English, he patiently helped his friend, José, out while José was reading to Schnoz. I am willing to bet that these two boys will remain friends all their lives.

Finally Time with Christy—

Mason had been trying very hard to get to read to Christy for three weeks. The fourth week, this second grader hurried over to Christy when he saw her and sat down with his book. He exclaimed, "I finally get to read to this dog!" Both Christy and Mason were so happy to have a special reading time together.

—Quotes—

- I look forward all day long to coming to read to my dog, Christy. *(student)*
- The kids are very serious in their reading, and some even go so far as to be sure the dogs are able to see the pictures while they read or when they finish a page. This is so cute to watch. *(staff)*

Emma C. Smith Elementary School—

Emma C. Smith Elementary School covers kindergarten to grade five. It is located at 391 Ontario Drive, Livermore, California 94550. For information on the school, go to www.smithelementary.org.

The school has approximately 680 students, about 60% of them white. Other major groups at the school include Hispanic/ Latino (10%), Asian (6%), and Filipino (4%). About 10% are considered socio-economically disadvantaged, 9% are English language learners, and about 11% have disabilities.

The school's Counseling Enriched Special Day Classroom is a specialized program designed to educate and support children with emotional disturbances and other moderate to severe behavioral issues that impede their ability to be successful at school.

One of the incentives for this program is having the therapy dog, Cabo, visit the classroom on Fridays. He has been coming each week since 2009.

—Testimonials—

Cabo comes to our classroom and we take him out to the field and play catch. He loves coming to visit the kids, and the kids love having him visit. Every week I rotate responsibilities. So, for example, I choose one student to walk Cabo out to the field and another one to walk him back. Someone gets to fill his water bowl for when we get back from the field and someone gets to hold the Chuckit! ®, a plastic stick for throwing tennis balls. This is an earned activity, and, if a student has not had a good week or day, they might not be allowed to join us for our "Cabo" time. The students never tire of having Cabo come on Fridays. They get so excited when he arrives, and Cabo gets just as excited to see the kids.

Cabo is in the yearbook, and we actually took a photo for my class picture. We love Cabo and probably will have to hold him back in fifth grade indefinitely because we don't ever want him moving on to middle school!

Michelle Holbrook, Third Grade Teacher

Cabo has been in our classroom since 2009. He is a great addition to our class. The students look forward to his visits every Friday. Cabo has his own school supplies, toys, and water bowl. He has a "CABO WALL" with pictures of him through the years. Cabo is in our class picture in the school yearbook. He is wearing a tuxedo and has a perfect smile.

Cabo teaches the students sharing and patience by taking turns, walking him, throwing his ball, and getting his water. We all look forward to more years of Cabo with us.

Sally Holmes, Special Education Aide

What I like about Cabo is he is intelligent, smart, and awesome. He is the best dog I ever met! He is funny because he runs around the whole classroom and licks us a lot.

Student

The thing I like most about Cabo is he is a good doggy sport in the classroom. Once he went to the softball field and I threw the ball and he went past the ball and didn't find it. He's a funny dog.

Student

What I like about Cabo is he doesn't do dumpy on the little lawn. I like when he puts his nose in the bucket in the classroom to get his ball!

Student

—Story—

Below is a story for Cabo, a Yellow Lab, who visits Emma C. Smith School.

A Fun Game with the Students—

Cabo's middle name should have been "Playtime," because playing is what he LOVES to do when he is visiting the students. Cabo is the only dog with permission to visit the school campus and play ball, with a Chuckit! ®, on the field.

When we arrive, the students immediately drop what that are doing and run up to him. Kayla asks me, "Can I walk Cabo out to the field today?" And Sean asks, "Let me carry the ball and Chuckit! ® for Cabo, please!!!" So off we go every Friday for a half hour to play ball on the field. The students line up and take turns at throwing the ball with the Chuckit! ®. Cabo enjoys doing this and so do the students. Everyone wins at this game.

—Quotes—

- Cabo is a cool and amazing dog. *(student)*
- Cabo is funny. He always gets his ball in the classroom. *(student)*

~CHAPTER 12~

shepherd's gate

Shepherd's Gate is an agency whose mission is to meet the practical, spiritual, and emotional needs of battered and homeless women and children. It has provided services and housing to over 10,000 women and children since it was founded in 1984. There are two campuses in Northern California—Livermore and Brentwood. The Livermore site is located at 1660 Portola Avenue, Livermore, California 94551, 925-443-4283, www.shepherdsgate.org.

Many of the women and children are homeless because of abusive relationships, addictions, loss of financial support, and other reasons. Although the mothers and children can stay at Shepherd's Gate, no pets are allowed. Services provided include education, job skills training, counseling, anger management/conflict resolution courses, parenting classes, GED studies, Bible studies, 12-Step Recovery programs, assistance with financial management and budgeting, medical services, and volunteer opportunities and Mission trips. Shepherd's Gate provides childcare four days a week so mothers can go to school, attend classes at Shepherd's Gate, look for employment, and go to appointments.

Shepherd's Gate won a grocery store gift card in a raffle held by an educators' group to which Pat Wheeler belongs. So one day, Pat went into the office at Shepherd's Gate to find out which grocery store as well as the name of the staff member to whom the gift card should be sent. Pat brought her dog, Lawrence, with her. Staff members were concerned about Lawrence being in there and said, "No dogs allowed." So Pat whisked him out as soon as she had the answers.

When Pat went back two weeks later with the gift card, Albert was with her, proudly wearing his therapy dog vest. One of the staff members saw Albert and fell in love with him. That staff member pursued her wish of allowing a therapy dog on site to visit the children.

After approval by the board, Albert started in May 2006. He usually goes once a week, weather permitting, for 30-60 minutes.

The purposes of Albert's visits started as follows—(1) to get the children over their fear of dogs; (2) for the children to learn how to handle dogs safely; and (3) to teach the children about unconditional love. We have added a fourth goal over the years, to teach the children responsibility. We give the children the opportunity to take Albert for walks while holding onto the leash (handler also has a hand on the leash and ultimately controls Albert), monitoring Albert's behavior to make sure he is behaving himself, and making sure we clean up after Albert.

Albert used to run up the slide, wait at the top while the kids lined up behind him, and then would slide down and wait for the kids at the bottom. But he had to stop doing this when he developed bad arthritis in his back legs. He still sits by the children on the bench, lets the children pet him, plays soccer with the kids by stopping the ball they kick towards him, watches the kids on swings, plays hide-and-seek with them, goes into the playhouse when invited by the kids, listens to the children read to him, and lets the children take him for walks. He also does tricks for the children and obeys their commands when they tell him to Sit, Halt, Forward, Circle, Tunnel, About Turn, Left, Right, and Down.

—Testimonials—

I met Albert in 2009 when I started volunteering at Shepherd's Gate. He stops by the office with Pat, on his way to play with the children. Always gentle and friendly, Albert would greet me, wait patiently while I petted him, and then turn toward the door ready to begin his day. He knows that he is going to play and he is ready for it.

He is gone for about an hour, and, if I have to run an errand back at the house, I see him with the children. They are walking him, talking to him, and just playing, like children do with pets. It always seems so comfortable and easy. The "normalness" of this strikes me as so amazing, because so much of what these children have experienced is not normal.

Albert will check back into the office on his way out. Pat leaves a treat when she arrives, so Albert has something to look for when he is done with the children. He comes barreling through the door and right up to my side, knowing the treat is waiting. I can almost imagine a smile on his face as he devours the treat. I truly feel Albert enjoys his time with us as much as we enjoy our time with him. He is truly a blessing to us.

Terry Higuera, Office Manager

Having Albert come to Shepherd's Gate each week to see the kids helps the children in many ways. Firstly, a lot of the kids who move in here are terrified of dogs. When I mention to new kids that we are going outside to see a dog named Albert, you can see the fear in their eyes. But after a couple weeks, they are excited to hear that Albert is coming and they come over to pet him.

Secondly, through Albert we are able to teach the kids how to behave around dogs. We teach them to ask the owner if they can pet the dog. We show them how to approach the dog and how to pet him. We teach them not to run up to Albert, screaming, because it might scare him. We also teach them to hold the leash and help walk Albert. When they are done walking him, they hand their part of the leash back to Pat. We tell them not to drop the leash.

Lastly, pets are not allowed at Shepherd's Gate. Some kids who moved in had pets before and they miss them. Having Albert to play with helps them adjust to their new home.

Jenifer Leigh, Childcare Coordinator

I can't begin to thank you for faithfully bringing Albert to Shepherd's Gate! God created many animals like Albert to bring joy and pleasure and comfort to his children. Albert has brought joy and new discoveries to hundreds of children and their moms since 2006! We are extremely grateful for the therapeutic value he brings to these hurting kids and their mothers.

I remember one day there were two desperate women waiting in our office for help, wondering if they would see a better life. At that moment, God sent Albert into the room! He seemed to sense that these women were in need of a little joy. I was amazed as he walked up and snuggled between them. In no time their spirits were lifted as they interacted with Albert and then the other people around them.

Albert enters a room and instantly everyone is drawn to him. He creates a common bond that makes adults and children alike able to share and laugh and to leave their troubles behind for a time. I think he just gives unconditional love which is representative of the unconditional love that God offers to everyone through his Son, Jesus.

Thank you for being a catalyst for much joy at Shepherd's Gate for so many years.

God bless you.

Steve McRee, CEO/Executive Director

The joy on the children's faces when they see Albert is radiant. They love to pet Albert and see him wag his tail. Many of these children have not had animals. They receive unconditional love from Albert and give love to him.

Kris Rascon, Childcare Volunteer

The biggest advantage of the volunteer dog is helping the children learn how to approach dogs and how to pet them. Some of the children are afraid of dogs and don't ever spend time with Albert. Other children overcome their fears and spend a little time with him. The children who spend the most time are those who love animals or are especially sensitive to emotions. Albert gives these children a chance to express that side of themselves.

Marie Urabe, Childcare Teacher

I love therapy dogs. They truly are amazing! I love to see my daughter with Albert! He always brightens her day.

Mother

My two-year-old daughter loves it when Albert, the dog, comes to visit us at Shepherd's Gate. We love animals, and, because we live at a shelter for women and children, we do not have the option of owning a pet of our own.

It is an instant joy to see Albert's tail wag when he sees our children and us approach him. It is wonderful to see how excited the children get when they are able to help walk the dog and play with him.

It always melts my heart to hear my daughter burst out in words when she sees Albert, "Mommy! Look! Puppy!" Later, "Bye Puppy!" It's a feeling every mother enjoys.

I believe therapy canines should be able to grow in population throughout all facilities and programs that treat broken, recovering, and healing persons—men, women, and children.

Thank you for your services!

Mother

This dog—Albert, the therapy dog—makes my girls happy. When they see him, they get so happy. They run up to him and pet him gently. That's new for them because they used to be afraid of dogs.

Mother

Albert is my friend. I like him to come in the [play] house. I like to play doctor and make him all better. I like sliding and walking with him.

Four-year-old child

—Stories—

All the stories below are for Albert, a Black Lab/Border Collie mix, since he is the only therapy dog that has gone to Shepherd's Gate.

Overcoming Her Fear—

One girl at Shepherd's Gate was very scared of dogs since she had been bitten on the ear by a dog when she was one year old. She was afraid to go near dogs and to pet them. Albert helped her get over her fear of dogs. Slowly, she learned to come over to Albert and pet him. She soon looked forward to Albert coming. From Albert, she learned to pet other dogs. She no longer lives at Shepherd's Gate, but she has a large dog of her own now. Thanks to Albert, she was able to overcome her fear of dogs.

A Fun Reunion—

When not working at Shepherd's Gate, Albert likes to go to public parks with playgrounds where he can see more children and go for a walk. One day, at a park in Livermore, three children suddenly ran off the playground towards Albert. Their mothers were concerned, seeing them run off toward a dog they didn't recognize at first. One of the girls turned around and exclaimed, "It's okay, mommy. This is Albert and he loves us!" Albert thoroughly enjoyed this reunion with three of his good buddies from Shepherd's Gate, and so did the girls.

Albert to the Rescue—

One two-year-old boy had brand new socks on under his sandals. The socks kept slipping out of the sandals. And the Childcare Coordinator kept pulling them back on. But all of a sudden we noticed one sock was gone. She and I kept looking around the areas where he had been playing and walking. Surely a bright white sock would show up on the dark woodchips on the playground, the sidewalk, or the green grass. But after about ten minutes, we gave up. Then the Childcare Coordinator told Albert, "Find sock." He immediately went around to the back of a piece of playground equipment and pointed to the sock with his front paw. Albert saved the day, and the sock.

Game Time with Albert—

Albert likes playing Hide-n-Seek with the children. The kids hide on the playground, behind equipment, under the slide, in the tunnel, or in the playhouse. They count to ten and then instruct Albert to find them. His nose to the ground, he tracks them all down. And the children get a good laugh out of watching him do this.

Squirrel Patrol—

When at Shepherd's Gate, and everywhere else, Albert is always on squirrel patrol. There are several squirrels in the area around the playground—on the roofs of the buildings, running along the fence, jumping from tree to tree.

One day Albert was particularly intrigued by something. He was staring intently through the fence toward an area of bushes. Next thing we knew, four toddlers (two on either side of Albert) were hanging onto the fence and staring at the same area as Albert. They wanted to see what he saw. They were there on the fence for about three or four minutes, until Albert decided to do something else. It takes a dog to get these young toddlers to focus on something for more than 30 seconds.

Christmas Time with Albert—

Every Christmas, Albert gives educational gifts to all the children at Shepherd's Gate. These include books, games, and puzzles. One year, a couple days after Christmas, Albert made his weekly visit to Shepherd's Gate. Upon arrival, several youngsters were immediately on him, hugging him and thanking him. I could barely see Albert with all the kids on him, but his tail was happily wagging, so I knew all was well.

First Time Meeting a Dog—

A new infant, Meghan, was at Shepherd's Gate one day. Albert sat on the bench in the playground area, watching Meghan enjoy her time on the swing as she watched him with a twinkle in her eyes and a smile on her face. Then she was moved to her stroller. Albert went over to introduce himself, approaching Meghan slowly and then touching her hand with his nose. They made eye-to-eye contact, as each met a new friend. A short time later, Meghan was reaching out and petting Albert on the head. Both have a new friend and, hopefully, she has learned about dogs.

Thank You, Albert—

Albert was heading back to the office one day so we could sign out. A mother opened the side door of a building as we walked past. She was thrilled to see Albert. She said she was under so much stress because she had recently stopped smoking after 20 years of smoking. She kneeled down, and petted and hugged Albert. She said, "This makes me feel so much better. I wish you were here every day. Thank you, Albert."

Water for Albert—

It was a cool and cloudy morning, but with all the running around he had done, Gary was thirsty. So Miss Johnson went to get some cups and a jug of drinking water. Gary quickly gulped his cup of water down. Other children came over to get a drink of water.

After Gary had drunk three cups, he decided to offer some water to Albert. So Gary held a cup of water in front of Albert, and Albert quickly lapped it up, his tail wagging happily. Next thing we knew, several children were lined up in front of Albert, each with some water in a cup to give Albert a drink. Albert thoroughly enjoyed all of the cups of water.

Learning Good Manners—

Kathy was so excited to see Albert. Sometimes she is the only child in childcare, on the days that Albert comes, who isn't ill or napping. So she gets lots of one-on-one time with Albert. It was a cloudy, gray day, with rain in the forecast and light sprinkles starting. But Kathy wanted to take Albert for a walk. So she took Albert's leash, and we walked around the building, keeping an eye out for squirrels.

When we turned left to head to the fountain, a woman approached us and said, "Hi. My name is Brenda. What is your name?" Kathy immediately replied, "I am Kathy and this is Albert." Pointing to me, she said, "This is Pat." And then she turned and introduced Brenda to her teacher, who was also walking with us. Kathy told Brenda about Albert and said that he is her friend.

Then we headed to the fountain, where Albert always steps in the water and then on the dry bricks to show off his pawprints. So Kathy stepped in the water and then on the bricks to show Albert her footprints. The teacher was so pleased seeing Kathy politely introducing all of us to Brenda and also showing interest in pawprints and footprints because usually Kathy is very quiet, and she needs to learn good manners.

A Flower for Albert—

After missing a couple weeks because of rainy weather, Albert and I were finally able to go to Shepherd's Gate. Bobby and his little sister, Molly, were so happy to see Albert there, and, of course, Albert was so excited to be back at Shepherd's Gate after a long break.

Albert enjoyed the petting and attention the children gave him, constantly wagging his tail. But then it was time for Bobby to go with his mother and meet his bus for school. As we walked back toward the office to sign out, Bobby came running toward me with a dandelion he had picked for me. He thanked me for bringing Albert. He turned around and headed back to where his mother was so they could wait for the bus.

Suddenly, Bobby yelled out, "Wait! I need to give Albert a flower too!" He came running towards us with a dandelion for Albert and gave him a nice good-bye pat for the day. Albert wanted to eat the dandelion, but I had to keep him from doing that. I did let him sniff it, though.

—Quotes—

- Oh Albert, you're so pretty. No, no. I mean handsome. *(resident)*
- Albert, I'm so glad to see you. I missed you last week. *(child)*
- I think I love Albert more than my kids do. I miss my dog so much. It is wonderful having Albert here. *(resident)*
- You are so pretty, Albert. Can your eyes see how pretty you are? *(child)*
- Mommy, that's Albert. He's my friend. *(child)*

- Thank you so much for bringing Albert. The kids always have a good time with him. *(resident)*
- I really appreciate your coming here, Albert. There is nothing better than animal therapy. *(resident)*
- Thank you so much for bringing Albert here. It is always such a joy to have him here. *(staff)*
- Albert is so alert. He is so interested in everything. It must be nice to have Albert here. *(visitor)*
- This is Albert. We love having him come here every week. I wish he could stay here all the time. *(staff member introducing Albert to visitor)*
- Oh Albert, you're so soft. I want you to cuddle with me when things are stressful. *(resident)*

~CHAPTER 13~

veterans affairs palo alto health care system livermore division

The VA Palo Alto Health Care System (VAPAHCS) is part of VA Sierra Pacific Network (VISN 21), which includes facilities in California, Nevada, and Hawaii. VAPAHCS consists of three inpatient divisions located at Palo Alto, Menlo Park, and Livermore in addition to seven Community Based Out-patient Clinics (CBOC) in San Jose, serving Santa Clara County; in Capitola, serving Santa Cruz County; in Monterey, serving Monterey and San Benito Counties; in Stockton, serving San Joaquin County; in Modesto, serving Stanislaus County; in Sonora, serving Calaveras and Tuolumne Counties; and in Fremont, serving Alameda County. Additionally, there are four Vet Centers located in Redwood City, Santa Cruz, Modesto, and San Jose.

VAPAHCS is a teaching hospital, providing a full range of patient care services, with state-of-the-art technology as well as education and research. Comprehensive health care is provided through primary, tertiary, and long-term care in areas of medicine, surgery, psychiatry, physical medicine and rehabilitation, neurology, oncology, dentistry, geriatrics, and extended care.

VAPAHCS has 833 operating beds, including three community living centers and a 100-bed homeless domiciliary on the Menlo Park campus. VAPAHCS is home to a variety of regional treatment centers, including a Spinal Cord Injury Center, a Polytrauma Rehabilitation Center, the Western Blind Rehabilitation Center, a Geriatric Research, Educational and Clinical Center, a Homeless Veterans Rehabilitation program, and the Men's and Women's Trauma Recovery Programs. In 2011, VAPAHCS provided care to more than 62,000 veterans.

VAPAHCS maintains one of the top three research programs in the VA with extensive research centers in geriatrics, mental health, Alzheimer's disease, spinal cord regeneration, schizophrenia,

Rehabilitation Research and Development Center, HIV research, and a Health Economics Resource Center.

An affiliation with the Stanford University School of Medicine provides a rich academic environment including medical training for physicians in virtually all specialties and subspecialties. Over 1,300 University residents, interns, and students are trained each year.

The Livermore Division (LVD) has a Community Living Center (CLC), formerly known as the Nursing Home Care Unit (NHCU). It has beds for up to about 100 patients. The CLC provides occupational, physical, and recreational therapy services in addition to having chaplain, medical, nursing, psychology, and social work staff. Patients also receive services from the audiology, dental, optical, and speech pathology staff and from an art therapist.

The Animal-Assisted Activities/Therapy (AAA/T) program falls under Recreation Therapy Service. Animal-Assisted Activities (AAA) consists primarily of visiting patients in their rooms, in waiting areas, and at various events. Animal-Assisted Therapy (AAT) involves closer work with a VA staff member on helping patients attain certain goals (e.g., walking greater distances, trying new words, getting out of their room and participating in special programs).

—Chapter Foreword—

I was asked to present the awards that recognized the contributions of the therapy dogs who have dedicated thousands of hours of service to our veterans at the Livermore VA Community Living Center and have heard first-hand from the veterans themselves what these dogs mean to them.

The therapy dogs help us to see something other than just the world around us. They help all of us to see that, in this world, there is a gentler side. They help our veterans to navigate the dark landscapes, which are the memories that followed our service men and women home.

These therapy dogs offer a world of uncompromising acceptance and affection, a silent understanding when someone looks into those big tender eyes. I have seen men and women who have come back from combat zones and who could not tell their story to another human being. But they could open up and tell their stories, their lives, and their pain to a four-legged friend who would never judge them, but would only listen and love.

The testimonials and stories in this chapter tell about what the therapy dogs do at the VA for the men and women who have served in our Armed Forces and what they mean for our veterans. The work of the VA therapy dogs and their owners, or, perhaps, I should say, their partners for their hours of commitment, is very important for these men and women. Without their partners, the dogs couldn't drive to the VA on their own. But I think that somehow these therapy dogs would still find their way to the VA because they understand the importance of what they do for our veterans.

John Marchand, Mayor, City of Livermore

—Animal-Assisted Activities/Therapy Program at the VAPAHCS LVD—

The Animal-Assisted Activities/Therapy (AAA/T) program at the VAPAHCS in Livermore provides at least one therapy dog visiting the CLC almost every day of the week. The dog goes from room to room, visiting any veterans who want to see the dog. The dog also visits people in hallways and group activity rooms, and on the patio areas. Sometimes they are in the dining room area, when food is not being served, for special events such as concerts, Protestant services, memorial services, and games. The dogs usually stay two to three hours.

The screening process at the VA is more complex than for the therapy dog teams at other sites. It starts with having the potential handler shadow an experienced handler with his/her dog for two hours at the CLC. This provides an opportunity for some initial training about and orientation to the VA, for the potential handler to ascertain if he or she feels comfortable at the VA, and for the experienced handler and VA staff to determine if this individual's personality is appropriate for this setting.

The next step, after all the veterinarian paperwork is completed for a dog, is an off-site evaluation of the potential handler/dog team by an experienced handler from the VA. This is usually done at a local shopping center since that provides a busy and noisy setting with lots of people and distractions. This evaluation covers the dog's temperament, basic obedience (similar to what is on the AKC Canine Good Citizen test), and special items needed for a therapy dog team at the VA. Concurrently, the potential handler must go through the application processes and orientations with both Valley Humane Society (VHS) and VA Voluntary Service (VAVS) if they haven't done so already.

Once these are completed and the team has passed the evaluation described above, the team is ready for the last part of the evaluation, which is on-site at the VA. The experienced handler with his/her dog goes around the CLC with the new handler/dog team. As with the first visit to the VA, this is one more opportunity for both parties and VA staff to ascertain if this team is appropriate for this setting, and also a chance for more orientation and training as well as meeting key staff and veterans. If the team doesn't work out for the VA, they are referred to VHS and VAVS for other possible assignments.

—Therapy Dog Awards Ceremonies—

In the summer of 2006, one of the veterans was reading about the upcoming "Make A Difference Day." He pointed out to other veterans that, "These dogs make a difference. We need to honor them." The first Therapy Dogs Awards Ceremony was held in October 2006 on Make A Difference Day. Since then, it has become an annual event, conducted by the veterans for the dogs. Therapy dogs receive VA Voluntary Service pins for the hours they have served (50, 100, 150, 300, 500, 750, 1000). They also receive Navy Petty Officer pins for various levels of service.

Why are all these dogs Navy dogs? In June 2005, the VA did not have enough staff available for the Livermore Rodeo weekend to take some of the veterans downtown to participate in the parade. So the Residents' Council asked if Lawrence could march in the parade for them. His tail gave a very positive response. So he was listed as representing the VA in the parade. But then KKIQ, the local radio station, called to find out which branch of the service Lawrence was in and what his rank was. His owner, Pat Wheeler, didn't know what to tell them. So she went to the VA to find out. Upon arrival, there were two veterans in the lobby of the NHCU. She posed the question to them. The Marine Corps veteran said, "Oh, he's a Master Sergeant in the Marine Corps!" The Navy veteran quietly responded, "Oh no, he's the Chief Petting Officer." Now all the therapy dogs are Navy dogs and have "Petting Officer" ranks until they exceed 750 hours when they become a "Captain," and, at 1,000 hours, a "Rear Admiral" for

1,000 hours of tail wagging. A new dog starts with a PO2 pin, though we were told by the veterans to call that dog a "Petting Officer" since "none of these dogs are second class."

Even though these dogs have Navy ranks, they fit well into all branches of the military. When the handler gets out the therapy dog vest, the dog is Semper Paratus, always ready to go (Coast Guard). As soon as they arrive at the VA, they march right in, ready to do what needs to be done (Army). When the dog enters a veteran's room, there is a feeling of great uplift as spirits soar (Air Force). After a busy afternoon, when it is time to go home, Anchors Aweigh (Navy), home for a rest from the busy day. And we all know that dogs are Semper Fi (Marines).

Although the veterans are the ones who present the awards to the dogs eligible for them each year, often there are political officials and dignitaries present. They have included Congressman Jerry McNernery, Livermore Vice Mayor John Marchand, and Fred "Spike" Schau, the Northern California State Coordinator of the Warriors' Watch Riders and an American Legion Rider. At each ceremony, a VA staff member has spoken about the value of the therapy dogs at the VA.

—Testimonials from Veterans—

I think that the therapy dogs are great to relax with. You can display affection for a dog where it might not be readily accepted by a human being. And it's very gratifying to see the dogs actually learn who you are and respond to your petting with affection. Not having them here would leave quite a gap in our lives. When the dogs come around, the rest of my day is more relaxed and tolerable. All of us in here have things we have to tolerate. The therapy dogs make it easier to cope with being in an institution like this. It is a pleasure to have them here. Now how do we get the therapy dogs' opinions?

Robert Alvis, U.S. Air Force, 1941-66

The dogs run the show here [in physical therapy]. They make sure we do our exercises.

John Berroteran, U.S. Navy, 1963-65

I know some of these dogs very well and they know me too. The dogs like getting attention, and I know they like me. These dogs are very important to us, and they always make us feel better. They are curious about things too. I have been here four or five years and I've enjoyed all the dogs. I even made paintings of some of them. It means something to me when they come to see me.

Lawrence, the Livermore Lab, is special to me. He is a pretty good dog. He's always there, wanting to get petted. He likes it, and we like it too. He's more inclined to help than hinder.

Michael Brown, U.S. Navy, 1964-65

The patients and families look forward to the dog visits. When I get out of here, I want to steal one of these dogs. While here, I want one of these dogs in my room, 24/7. He couldn't leave my room to go see other people. They would have to make appointments to come see him.

Emil Burch, U.S. Army, 1944-47

The dogs are fantastic! They keep us moving. Everybody here loves a friendly dog. The dogs help us keep a healthy attitude. Their happiness reflects on us. Almost everybody here has had a dog. They all have some good memories of their own dog. Petting a therapy dog brings back those happy memories.

Jon Bussey, U.S. Coast Guard, 1974-78

I first saw the dogs in December of 2008 and it was a heart-warming experience to see that the veterans were all delighted to see them. They really look forward to seeing them!! In my opinion, the dogs brought joy to the veterans, especially the bedridden and the veterans who only have visits from the dogs!!

Paul Cashion, U.S. Navy, 1960-69

The therapy dogs make me very happy at a moment's notice. You can always guarantee that they'll give you the same reaction. I like feeling them. They can deliver sincere happiness. When I get home, I want to buy a dog because of this program.

Gabriel Corral, U.S. Navy, 1987-90

The dogs elevate our morale and attitudes. Most of us are sad and not at our peak of feelings being in a hospital. So seeing, rubbing, and petting the dogs makes us happy. They appreciate us. We need our morale boosted. There is much negative conversation here. But when the dogs come, no negative things go on. It is good to have the positive things from the dogs. And they seem so well disciplined.

Edward Cunningham, U.S. Army, 1959-62

The therapy dogs take our minds off of ourselves and help us reflect on the past when life was better. Plus, I think that just touching and petting them makes you feel like you're part of something else besides the dilemma that you are in at the particular time. If you love animals, it gives you that energy you get from loving something or someone.

Paul Dalmau, U.S. Coast Guard, 1959-63

The therapy dogs give us a sense of calm. They are especially needed here when we are having a bad time. The dogs can get through to people when other people can't. The dogs make a very important connection, one that takes a person out of a bad place and makes them feel different.

Many of us miss the pets we had, and seeing these dogs help us. They give us shut-ins a connection to the outside world and remind us of our younger days which were happier, especially when we got a new puppy.

These animals bring us out of our depression. I'm glad I am here where they let therapy dogs come in. More places should do it.

Louise Darnell, U.S. Air Force, 1951-53

The dogs make my therapy time go by in nothing flat. My time in physical therapy goes faster with Albert here. He brightens up my day. And I have less pain too.

Mary Louise Dorr, U.S. Army, 1949-73

Every time I see one of the therapy dogs, they remind me of our two dogs at home. I can see in the therapy dogs' faces that they know they have a job to do. I just imagine what might be going through their heads, knowing that everyone they see is sick. I see a concert with the handler coming in without any regret of how much time is spent here. As the dog and the handler march to a tune only they hear, they proudly find as many people as they can to give them that moment of joy. The new dogs have the face of a rookie. But one day you know they will be as seasoned as Lawrence and Albert. Hip-hip hooray and tally-ho for the therapy dogs!

Ron Dubbs, U.S. Navy, 1980-98

We can do so much more [in physical therapy] with a dog than without one. Albert, I'm complimenting you and all the other dogs.

Allison Gibbs, U.S. Army, 1962-66

Note: Mr. Gibbs worked with the Lions Club on programs for training guide and helper dogs.

I think the therapy dogs bring a lot of relaxation to the patients and enjoyment also. What's nice about them is the fact they are just so loving and so docile. No matter where you pet them, they enjoy it.

Paul Groves, U.S. Navy, 1968-74

The therapy animals make me smile. They make me happy and let me pet them. I look forward to seeing the animals when I know they will be here.

Jason Hiatt, U.S. Air Force, 2003-06

The dogs are natural friends of human beings. They make great companions and are attentive. They give us love unconditionally. You can't say that for humans!

I feel that the therapy dogs are especially good for older people who are lonely and need good companionship. I love the dogs that come here and share their love with me. I have a high respect for these dogs. They give a lot of themselves. And they love getting attention back.

David Jorden, U.S. Army, 1961-74

While my professional healthcare providers and the various therapists have and continue to provide me with excellent care, they cannot equal the therapy given to me by the therapy dogs. Both Sherry (my wife) and I have greatly enjoyed the visitations of the therapy dogs. We grew particularly fond of PATCH, "Chief Petting Officer," who unfortunately passed away on September 11, 2009.

Aside from being a beautiful, smiling, happy-faced, and very friendly Golden Retriever, Sherry and I remember PATCH as having a unique appetite for bananas. Believe it or not, he consumed a whole big banana. What a dog! What a dog! Whenever he came to visit, he went in the direction of the drawers where the bananas were stored—PATCH was my match when it came to bananas! I was always happy to share and watch him swallow up my favorite fruit. Bananas always reminded us of PATCH—our "BANANA DOG." Thank you, Salomé, for bringing PATCH to us.

K. Lambert Kirk, U.S. Army, 1942-48

Dogs are the best example of love that there is. Their love is unconditional. They don't care if you are short or tall, ugly or good looking, skinny or fat. They just don't care; they'll love you anyways. We need to discover what true love is, and we should learn that from the dogs. As long as you treat them with respect, they'll love you. They'll give their life without hesitation for you. Dogs are the best animals we could ever have.

Jay Lyons, U.S. Army, 1944-46

Don't these dogs just love us and their masters too! They love us twice as much as people do and without condition. Love is such a big part of them. And they let you dismiss anger. [Buzzer goes off in his room while the dog is visiting.] Look, the dog is calm. He is not in a defensive mode. He knows it's not serious. Dogs are so smart. They stand by confidently to protect you. To me, you can't get a greater love than that of a dog. They are made of love.

They are a big part of us. Most people don't know how big a part of us they are. They have every emotion we have.

Michael Manzer, U.S. Army, 1970-71

The therapy dogs at the VA are very loving dogs. They were all loving and good companions to me. They made me smile and made me think of happy thoughts. They helped to keep me calm. They let me take the focus off myself when I thought about how they were feeling. I asked myself what I could do to help them feel happier. That way, they could help me better. Whether they were happy or not, they let you know if something was okay or not.

Mariela Meylan, U.S. Army, 1999-2004

When the therapy dogs come around, I never gave them cookies because they aren't supposed to eat cookies.

There is a big dog that comes around, and someday I'm gonna ride him. His name is Rio. He reminds me of a St. Bernard dog. We have several smaller dogs, but the dog I miss is Jiffy and her owner, Doug.

It is a pleasure to have the dogs around with the tails wagging and all. Sometimes the tail is wagging the dog. And the dogs just look happy, and they are very well mannered.

Tony Miranda, U.S. Marine Corps, 1942-78

It means so much to have all the dogs come and visit. It makes my day. All the guys talk about them after they visit. It means a lot to all of us, not just me. I've never heard anyone say they didn't enjoy the dogs being here. I miss my dog so much. But when the therapy dogs come to visit, I feel the satisfaction of being with a dog. The therapy dogs' responses are so unconditional. All they ask for is a pet, and you've made a new friend.

Mark Mosegaard, U.S. Navy, 1973-77

It's great having these visitors come by. They're good for the patients. A lot of us don't have anyone to visit. It's good for morale. It's always good to get a visit, and it gives the dogs a chance to make friends with patients. A lot of people are interested in the canine world and like seeing these dogs almost every day.

Paul Penke, U.S. Marine Corps, 1982-85

I think God knew in the beginning that we needed companionship, and canines were one of the best choices. They're a lot like us. They need companionship too.

The therapy dogs do what they were intended to do—provide good therapy for us. And the owners aren't too shabby either. In fact, they're doggone nice people. These dogs are a valuable asset to us.

Yes, the dogs are wonderful. I watch all the programs about dogs and cats too. They're fascinating and interesting, and dogs are so smart.

Michael Quinn, U.S. Navy, 1954-58

Being a patient at the VA for six-and-a-half years, I looked forward to the dogs coming. It was comforting to pet them and to see them. They were very healing.

Lee Roland, U.S. Navy, 1960-64

These dogs are so important here. It's nice to have a dog that wants to be touched. These dogs like to be petted and scratched. They remind me of my puppy. I miss my dog, Hank, his brown eyes and cold nose. These dogs cheer you up inside. When you're stuck in your room, it's nice to see the dogs. It gives me hope that some day I'll go home and see my puppy again.

Greg Schullerts, U.S. Navy, 1971-75; Vietnam Veteran

I have always had a dog—a Maltese. I love dogs. They're the best companion you can have and I miss mine. Dogs always have love for me. I love the therapy dog program. The therapy dogs make me homesick for my dog. But I love having these dogs come see me. It makes my day. They're always faithful to me.

John Schultheis, U.S. Marine Corps, 1941-45

I've been here off and on for a couple years. Last year, I was really sick and every time a dog came in, it was really uplifting. The therapy dogs bring me a lot of joy, comfort, and healing. They're like a breath of sunshine that comes into the room and puts a smile on your face.

John Soria, U.S. Air Force, 1966-74

I always enjoy seeing the therapy dogs and the people that bring them. But I enjoy the dogs more than the people. They exhibit a freedom of life that, in a way, I don't have, but I enjoy things they don't have.

All the therapy dogs have their own personalities, which I really enjoy and respect. But at the same time, their affection and love for the handlers is great to see. All of the people and dogs are extremely well kept up, and the dogs have a very enjoyable life as joy-givers, or bringers of joy and love and affection. It just makes my day to see them come into my room, and I feel a little sorrow to see them walk out.

Michael Sturdivan, U.S. Air Force, 1965-70

I like the dogs visiting. I've always liked dogs and grew up with dogs. I grew up with a beautiful boxer. The handlers are great; the therapy dogs are great. They have all got their own personalities. There are some you get more attached to than others, and that is the way it should be. You have a dog you recognize, and it's nice to see him. There is one dog in particular that I always feed some Cheetos to, and, every time he sees me, he starts to salivate. He just looks at me, and his mouth starts drooling. It's great. He nuzzles me. He would jump up in bed with me if I weren't in the chair. I used to sleep with my dog.

One lady brings around a white and a black dog. She comes around all the time, and her dogs are as cute as can be. I think the large one with short hair that comes around is a mixed breed with a long face and a really good personality. None of the dogs you can be afraid of because they are all so awesomely gentle! It's just great. I know there are a lot of other fellow veterans that really like them too.

Mark Thompson, U.S. Air Force, 1966-70

The therapy dogs allow life to continue happily. Without them, we'd be rather unhappy and not very cheerful with other people. We have fun with life because there are the dogs making us happy. I wouldn't be happy to be here without the dogs. They make me glad to be alive. I love to see them coming. It's important that they come. They make us all happy. It wouldn't be okay without them. I can't imagine them not being here. I'd love to have them live here. They have to go home—but why? When they're here, they bring love. They make life worth living.

I love these animals. They don't hurt us. They love us. I can't imagine anyone not loving them. They lie down on the floor and love us and make all of us relax. Even if you feel bad, you don't feel bad when the dogs come.

Lillian Wagner, U.S. Army, 1951-73

The therapy dog program here is a wonderful motivator for the patients. These days are like a best friend coming to visit. I love all the visiting therapy dogs, but one in particular, Belle, I am especially fond of her. I had an opportunity to present Belle with a "Chief Petting Officer" pin for completing 100 hours of service at the awards ceremony for the therapy dogs. This ceremony was held on January 10, 2010. Then there is Buddy G, Belle's canine companion at home with Lou and Joan (their human companions). Buddy G is a new recruit, and is learning quickly that he is loved and accepted. All of the therapy dogs have a guardian angel pin on their vest that they wear each time they visit, as this is something I can give them in return for their unconditional love.

I love my canine friends and look forward to the visits when I am up to it. When I am in a lot of pain and having a bad day, I cannot tolerate even the slightest touch or movement.

The therapy dog program is overseen by Recreation Therapy. This program has the highest number of animals and people volunteering throughout the VA. There are 24 therapy dogs currently and 28 volunteers with more "waiting in the wings." The Livermore program is coordinated by Pat Wheeler. Pat and her special dogs have put on an outstanding program that has excited and enticed many people (along with their canine counterparts) to participate in the program.

I was a Voluntary Service Officer and a VA volunteer for over 20 years here at the Livermore VA Hospital. My best friend and companion at the time was my dog, Tosha. She wore her vest and visited her beloved veterans before the program was what it is today. She is now in Doggy Heaven after many years of service.

I have had many canine companions in my many years. My first was Shotgun, a German Shorthair breed. Then there were Greta and Gretchen, German Shepherd mixes. And then Tosha, and now Tara, a Beagle, who lives with my good friend Ying-Yang "Yankee." His nationality is Taiwanese, and he is a chicken rancher and family member in California and a real estate investor in Taiwan. Yankee visits me often and brings me some goodies as well as home-made, home-cooked goods. Sometimes he is able to bring Tara with him to visit as well. Tara is able to visit me on a special Pet Pass for family companion animals that entitles her to visit only me. She knows right away when they get off the elevator on the second floor that she is there to see me, and she comes straight to my room.

I could go on and on talking about the therapy animals, but I choose to stop here to allow others that are writing for this book to share their experiences.

Ray Walton, U.S. Army, 1947-53; Korean War Veteran

The dogs are nice. They make me feel happy. I like playing with them. They're fun. I had a Cocker Spaniel. These dogs bring back happy memories of my dog. I had kitty cats and birds longer though. The therapy dogs are my good buddies, even if they are not cats.

Jesse Welch, U.S. Navy, 1971-72

The therapy dogs have the ability and a way of making you relax and taking the stress off so the pain is not so noticeable. Then we can do more in physical therapy. The dogs don't have to do anything, just be there. If you're feeling depressed and one of these dogs comes up to you, you feel so much better that you forget what was making you sad. The dogs put a smile on your face, and you can't be depressed and happy at the same time. The dogs take the hurt out of our being alone. You feel better just because they come to visit you.

Gary Wickett, U.S. Navy and Merchant Marines, 1978-84

Dazzle means brightness and joy. Our Dazzle sparkles with friendship for all of us.

Rose Wilson, U.S. Navy, 1946-51

I think the therapy dogs are very nice. They are especially nice for those patients who don't have a family. The dogs make them very happy. They get all excited when the dogs come, especially those patients who have nobody that comes to see them. I'm lucky. My mom and dad came to see me when I was in the VA. But I still loved seeing the dogs.

Joe Zammit, U.S. Navy, 1969-70

I like the way the dogs come to me when I call them. I taught Albert to wag his tail on command. Now he will do it for his owner as well as me and other people too. I like Schnoz. He and I both have a grey beard. We compare our beards when he comes to see me.

Carl Zepada, U.S. Army, 1951-54

All these dogs are my babies. I love them very much. They mean a lot to me. They keep my mind high. Otherwise, I'd get lonely.

Veteran, U.S. Navy, 1980-94

I can't say enough about [the therapy dog program]. I've got to have these dogs here every day. I've liked dogs all my life. These dogs bring back good memories for me—believe me!

Veteran, U.S. Navy, 1950-62; U.S. Army, 1992-93

—Testimonials from Staff—

Our four-legged volunteers are special treats to the residents of our Nursing Home Care Unit. They bring warmth and compassion, and stimulate memories of past friendships that many of our residents had with their former pets.

William Ball, Chief, Voluntary Service

Oh, our therapy dogs! Where would our vets be without them in a world where the vets are limited on what they can do. A visit from these special friends puts a light in our eyes and a smile on our face—the vets and the employees also! The therapy dogs give us something to look forward to in our everyday life. Thank you for bringing us these special friends.

Suzanne Beasley, Pharmacy Tech

I actually enjoy having a therapy dog come to the facility. This puts a smile on my face and brings joy to me as a person. I also feel that touching and playing with animals lowers my stress level. I noticed that when the therapy dogs arrive, it is a welcome event for the residents. They all gather around the therapy dog and start petting and touching the dog. The therapy dog provides them company and much needed smiles. The visits from the therapy dogs are a welcome break from the everyday routine for all involved.

Ali Bleibel, RN, BSN, Clinical Nurse Manager

The therapy dogs are good for our patients because they make our patients' lives a bit happier. They put a smile on their faces that nurses can't. Sometimes it almost makes their pain go away. The therapy dogs make patients smile, and one thing leads to another. Then laughter—that's the best medicine even doctors can't prescribe. I feel this program is very beneficial to our patients, and the dedication and commitment of those involved are very much appreciated.

Jeff Bohn, LVN, Licensed Vocational Nurse, Nursing Home Care Unit

I find the therapy dogs very useful and comforting towards the vets. Their presence is nourishing to the care of the vets.

Ismael R. Briseno, CAN, Certified Nursing Assistant, Short Stay Unit

Therapy dogs are best for people, especially people who are in a hospital or nursing care facility. Therapy dogs make patients feel more at home and relaxed.

Lincoln Bui, Pharmacy Tech; U.S. Army Reserves, 1991-99

Animals have long been recognized as being a positive force in the healing process. Dogs have a calming and therapeutic effect. Bearing this in mind is something I would like to share with you, the readers. I have been a police officer since the early 1970s, in several states and the District of Columbia, and currently am a Federal Officer for the Department of Veterans Affairs. During my tenure in law enforcement, I have had the pleasure and agony of witnessing many things that will have a lifetime effect on how I view the life of others as well as myself.

In 2007, I was diagnosed with Acute Myeloid Leukemia (AML), which is a cancer of the Myeloid line of blood cells, characterized by rapid growth of abnormal white blood cells that accumulate in the bone marrow and interfere with the production of normal blood cells. AML accounts for approximately 1.2 percent of cancer deaths in the United States. AML progresses rapidly and is typically fatal within weeks or months if left untreated.

After having been diagnosed with this disease, I decided to follow the advice of my oncologist/hematologist to treat this disease as aggressively as possible, initially with chemotherapy in two phases—induction and consolidation therapy—with hopes of bringing about remission.

This leads me to the area for which this short story is all about. We have a Poodle/Chow mix named Sarah, aka Shorty, aka Stinky. She has been with us since she was a six-week-old pup. She's all black and has a blue tongue. During my time in and out of the hospital and treatment center she was in her eighties in dog years. This being a trying time for me and my family, I always looked forward to my "Sarah" standing outside of the hospital or treatment center and looking up to my window and barking until she got my attention. Then she wagged her tail with total delight, and we both conversed with each other at a distance.

This was something I looked forward to either two or three times a week, or however often my spouse bought her by. Sarah was a godsend to me as she has always been soothing and calming. She would easily take my mind off the bad things going on in my life and make me realize how blessed I really am. Even during my lowest point, she would lick my hands and let me know that everything was going to be fine.

Having worked in the law enforcement field for many years, I have witnessed the overall effect that therapy dogs have on everyone that comes into contact with them. They assist us in law enforcement by calming patients when they are upset, and, with some, they become a pal and more than a companion with patients that need compassion and comfort. They play an intricate role in the entire healthcare industry, and, as a trained professional law enforcement officer, they help make our jobs easier with their lasting effect on the lives of patients, staff, and visitors.

Elliott Carter, Police Officer

I have been working here at the Livermore Division of the VA for the past six years. I have had the opportunity to care for hundreds of veterans and watch as they settle into the Community Living Center (CLC), either for short- or long-term stays. The VA has tremendous resources and programs for helping our veterans acclimate to the CLC and smooth their transition to a group setting. Our therapy dog program is a vital component of this process.

For our veterans who are known pet lovers and the many that have been converted, our dogs are a wonderful sight as they walk down the hallways, greeting everyone with a wag of their tail or a perk of their ears. Whether it be a bed-bound vet or ambulatory vet, all seem to brighten up and respond equally with affection and a smile. It may take only a little pat or a good scratch, but the veterans really appreciate the dog's visit as it brightens their day.

For many of our veterans, the loss of independence is difficult to overcome and having therapy dogs available provides an escape and a simple pleasure to help them cope with their difficulties. Therapy dogs are an invaluable resource to our veterans (and staff). I only wish there could be more visits!

John F. Cesca, MD, VA Staff Physician, Extended Care Service

The therapy dogs are one of the most cherished services greatly appreciated at the VA. We have had the good fortune to be comforted by the loving and gentle therapy dogs that often visit and enlighten the veterans with joy and friendliness. The magical touch of the therapy dogs often makes people smile.

Veterans who are adored by the therapy dogs often find it peaceful and relaxing to have such therapeutic interactions that potentially distract them from possible physical and emotional discomfort at the moment. It is truly special to have the friendly connection with the therapy dogs with trust, comfort, and a peaceful mind. With the power of touch, the therapy dogs have a positive impact on veterans, family, and staff at the VA. Thank you so much! It is great to have them!

Joanne Chien, Nurse Practitioner

During my five years at the VA, I have seen several therapy dogs come by here. It is a pleasure to see them. I always get a big smile on my face when I see them. I believe if I, as a civilian, can get that much pleasure out of seeing the dogs, they must do wonders for the veterans. There have been times when I would go to get a patient, and Lawrence would come around the corner. So we just let the X-rays wait a moment longer so the veteran has some quality time with Lawrence. These dogs give the veterans love and affection, and put smiles on their faces. Smiles are always a good thing.

Rachael Craft, RT(R), Radiologic Technologist, Radiology Department Service

The therapy dog program at the VA in Livermore is a tremendous success. The dogs are varied in size and temperament (they are all gentle), so that there is a good match for each of the participating patients (and staff!). They are clean and well groomed.

The handlers are respectful of the special needs of this population. They are diligent in the observation of needed infection control measures, of those who are fearful and those who may have allergy problems. They keep the visits to a tolerable level for each individual. The handlers also report what may be potential physical or emotional health problems that they observe to the staff.

Best of all, the therapy dogs bring a great deal of comfort to the patients. With their quiet, gentle ways, their unconditional love, their wonderful sense of what precisely is needed (extra attention or just a quiet presence), the patients who are agitated are calmed, those who are withdrawn are drawn out, those who need love but don't know how to ask are loved completely.

In the atmosphere created during a therapy dog visit, no one is judged, controlled, ignored, or scolded. There is only the freedom to be oneself, to ask for what one needs, to give and receive love, to share the sorrows and frustrations, the joys and the little triumphs that no one else cares about or understands.

As a physician assistant, I have seen some remarkable responses. Residents who have not responded to anyone or to any outside stimulus reach out to touch, usually tentatively at first, then with increasing interest and enthusiasm. Individuals smiling and laughing when there has been only anger or sadness, and sometimes the therapeutic shedding of tears long overdue. Feelings being shared by those who have remained silent. The obvious comfort of a patient as he or she enters the last days or moments of their lives. There are many subtle responses, all of them promoting healing and a sense of wellbeing.

The VA in Livermore is indeed fortunate to have such an active program. A debt of gratitude is owed to the organizers, the handlers, and most of all to the therapy dogs who bring love and joy to so many hearts.

C. Winn Crannell, PA-C, Physician Assistant

The majority of veterans assigned to me as their social worker are not capable of participating in many types of social contacts with others for various reasons. But when the therapy dogs visit these particular veterans, you can visibly see them react by smiling and petting the dogs. Although the therapy dogs positively affect all of the veterans who are patients at the Nursing Home Care Unit, certain patients greatly benefit from their presence.

There are also many veterans who are here for long-term care and have had to leave their pets behind. The therapy dogs bring great delight to these veterans and will evoke memories of their own pets, and they will share their stories about them.

I do have one story to share about how the program has helped a veteran. This veteran would not come out of his room and staff tried everything to get him out over a very long period of time. I remember coming out of my office one afternoon to see this veteran standing at the nurses' station with one of the therapy dogs. I did not recognize him initially because I had only met him in his room. When I did realize it was him, I was just amazed. He told me he was walking the dog.

Social Work staff has a memorial service twice a year for veterans who have passed away at the Livermore Community Living Center. This is a very somber time when families gather to honor their loved ones. They come together to share stories and pictures with other veterans and staff who attend the service. There is usually at least one therapy dog in attendance. The dog provides comfort to the families, as this gathering can be an emotional and tearful experience. I have witnessed how families will seek out the therapy dog, and this brings a smile, even though they are crying, as grief emotes many different emotions simultaneously.

This program is so wonderful and beneficial. Not only do these precious dogs help the veterans, they also bring joy to the staff who work very hard caring for our veterans. I thank the therapy dogs for all they do for our veterans.

Sandra du Pont, MSW, Licensed Clinical Social Worker

When I walk into the nursing home, usually on a Friday, I sometimes see the dogs and their owner-handlers making the rounds and offering the gift of companionship to our veterans. The dogs are also "veterans," as they have logged many hours of loyal service to the sick and infirmed, the disabled, and the lonely among our patients. I have witnessed spirits uplifted by our tail-wagging friends, as they unselfishly approach a patient and offer the medicine of friendship. The owners and their dogs create a positive kinship, a bonding, and, more importantly, a laugh and a smile from our patients. We can all learn from these canine friends, as they serve our veterans.

Alan Field, Carpenter, Engineering (now at VA Martinez)

I have been a registered nurse since 1996. Currently, I work at the Veterans Community Living Center in Livermore where therapy dogs are utilized as a useful tool in patient care. When I was first introduced to this novel technique, I must say that I was a bit apprehensive, even as a long-time canine owner. But now that I have seen the idea in action and the excellent results it produces, I can state confidently that I am a firm supporter of canine therapy.

Through a volunteer program, dog-owners bring their companions to the hospital at scheduled times throughout the week. Our patients always look forward to these visits. When the dogs arrive, they greet the patients with unconditional love and affection. The time spent with their furry friends has a calming effect on the patients, and the psychological benefits of this interaction are very valuable. I have personally seen terminal patients with symptoms of cognitive and emotional impairment benefit hugely from canine therapy. They begin to feel more relaxed and appreciated. This type of calming effect can only be achieved with a dog. The dogs' wide grins and big eyes can melt away anyone's heart, but their unconditional love is a beautiful, natural way to help a patient through a difficult time.

To help us provide the best patient care possible, medical laws and practices must continue to reflect the benefits of canine therapy. I am proud to say that in Livermore, our country's veterans are not missing out on this.

Bozena Gunderson, RN, Registered Nurse, Extended Care Service

For several years now, our Community Living Center (CLC) residents have been visited by Thunder, Belle, Lawrence, Albert, Rio, and several other therapy dogs. These faithful canines provide almost daily coverage, visiting bedridden patients, veterans who lack human visitors, and those who are separated from their own pets. The dogs and their owners undergo extensive training (and grooming) to insure that they remain calm and friendly during their regular rounds.

Our four-legged therapists offer a head to rub or a smooth coat to pet, bringing a smile to even the most curmudgeonly of our veterans. The residents (and staff) look forward to the visits, greeting each hairy therapist by its name (and sneaking treats to some of them). Our therapy dogs serve as an essential component in our efforts to provide a homelike environment for our residents.

Donna Heinle, MD, MPH, Medical Director, Extended Care Service

When the volunteer dogs come to visit the VA Livermore Community Living Center, it's a very special time indeed. To the dogs, everyone is a special friend, and they lavish their love and attention on as many patients and visitors as they can. And as far as the patients are concerned, they love to pet, hug, smile, and laugh with the dogs. The dogs bring a smile to everyone's face, and their tails never stop wagging. I think it's safe to say they're as happy to be with us as we are to have them here.

They come in all sizes, ready to spend time with anyone who needs them. Their handlers do a wonderful job of bathing and grooming them before they come to visit. Thank you to all who take time out of your busy lives to share your dogs with the hospitalized veterans. A special thanks to Albert, Lawrence, and Rio. You make the patients' days so much brighter.

Michael Hyatt, Housekeeper, Environmental Management Services;
U.S. Navy, 1965-69

Therapy dogs visit the Community Living Center several times a week to interact with the veterans at the Center. Experience has shown that these canine visits are highly therapeutic for the veterans. The staff also enjoys the visits and the effect the dogs have on the veterans.

When the dogs arrive, they immediately have a calming and favorable effect on the residents. Veterans who may be angry, anxious, stressed, lonely, or depressed immediately gravitate toward the dogs and begin paying attention to the dogs.

The veterans pet and play with the dogs, and one can see a calming effect on the veterans just by the dogs' presence. Because the dogs love the attention and are not demanding of the veterans, they seem to provide a certain amount of emotional support. The dogs are not judgmental and simply provide love and attention to all the veterans. In some cases, bonds have developed between individual veterans and specific dogs, which relieves the veteran's anxiety and brightens the veteran's day. The dogs also have a positive effect on the staff, which takes pleasure in observing the veterans' enjoyment.

Holland Jordan, LMSW, Social Worker,
Community Living Center; U.S. Army, 1986-99

The Animal-Assisted Activity (AAA) program is a valuable part of recreational programming in the Livermore Community Living Center (CLC). This program is implemented by VA Palo Alto Health Care System Recreation Therapy Service (RTS) and in partnership with Valley Humane Society. Trained dogs and their handlers visit the veterans in the CLC seven days per week. It is a casual meet-and-greet visit program with a focus to enhance the quality of life of the CLC veterans by providing opportunities for sensory, social, and mental stimulation, as well as rapport building.

Staff and volunteers observe veterans enjoying the visits from AAA dogs and volunteers daily. Although individual responses to these dogs vary, they all share one outcome at the end of each visit; that is, every one of them is stimulated in a special way. Some appreciate just the social interaction with the handler, while others enjoy petting the dog and reminisce about their past pets. Some even keep a schedule of days that their favorite dog visits and look forward to it. For a few, the AAA visits are the only accepted recreational intervention, and, in some cases, a rapport building tool between veterans and staff to get them to engage in other recreational programs. Recreation Therapy Service values this partnership with Valley Humane Society and what they offer to our veterans at the Livermore CLC as it tremendously contributes to our wellness program and the overall psychosocial wellbeing of our veterans.

Livermore Recreation Therapy Team—
Nafisa Kakar, CTRS, Certified Therapeutic
Recreation Specialist; Rishoo Tyagi, RTC,
Recreation Therapist Certified

I'm very proud that I work in a place where dogs are made available for visits with patients every day of the week throughout the year. Visitation of nursing home residents by therapy dogs has been shown in a number of studies to have documented positive effects on patients' wellbeing, mood, and stress indicators (e.g., blood pressure). Anecdotally, the fact that patients here get to see these dogs on a regular basis is a critical component to their recovery and care. For some patients, while they may not be able to look forward to visits from family or friends, they can look forward to visits from a canine friend who may, over time, get to know them well.

Dogs have a sophisticated ability to be attuned to the verbal and nonverbal signs that humans put out. They know when you're happy, when you're sad, when you're anxious, and when you're sick. In some ways, they're as attuned to these signals as other humans, and, in other ways, more so. In addition, a skilled canine "therapist" has the ability to ladle out large quantities of what I consider bona-fide supportive therapy techniques that are part and parcel of the Humanistic Psychology tradition—dogs are experts at giving people "unconditional positive regard." In other words, they love you without precondition, pretense, or ulterior motive (unless they happen to be a little hungry). This is a powerful therapeutic stance that human therapists often require years of training to develop, but appears to come naturally to the therapy dogs.

I have witnessed with my own eyes the benefits of therapy dog visitations with the residents. They become more relaxed and engaged when they are interacting with these animals. I have witnessed a resident becoming unusually engaged and motivated to do his restorative therapy (walking) when the therapy dogs were integrated into his activity. I have seen an agitated and demented veteran who generally is inconsolable (and consequently yells throughout much of the day) become quiet and peaceful when given access to a therapy dog.

An interesting development over the few years or so at the VA is that nursing homes are no longer called nursing homes; instead, we refer to them as "community living centers." The idea is that an important part of our job is to provide our residents and patients with a "homelike environment" as much as is humanly possible, in order to safeguard their wellbeing and satisfaction with life. What better way to provide a "homelike environment" than to provide them with the dogs?

These therapy dogs reach humans in a primal way—through nonverbal, deeply emotional routes that are with us when we are born and exist long after awareness and higher-order cognitive functioning sometimes fail us in late life. That is why these dogs are so powerful.

Geoffrey W. Lane, PhD, Geropsychologist, Psychology Service

I want to express how much the veterans enjoy the therapy dogs. Their eyes light up so much with joy when the handlers bring the dogs in. They love to pet the dogs, and it makes them feel like they are at home with their own pets. So please continue to bring the dogs in.

I also want to thank their handlers. They also play a large part in making our veterans happy.

Barbra Lao, Health Technician, Community Living Center

The therapy dog program is vital to the healthcare industry. It's the best medicine ever prescribed. I am a police officer at the Department of Veterans Affairs and have had the opportunity to observe these dogs. The dogs that I am most familiar with are two Black Labs named Albert and Lawrence. They are owned by Pat Wheeler, who coordinates the program.

The dogs are always well groomed and disciplined. If they meet other dogs, they don't bark or react to what the other dogs might do. When they enter a patient's room, they don't run and jump up on the patient. They walk calmly to the wheelchair or bed and wait for the patient to respond.

I recall one incident when I was called to the Nursing Home to assist staff with a patient who was very upset. He refused to take his meds or comply with any of the directions from staff. The dogs were in the area and, when they entered the room, the patient's whole attitude changed. He calmed down and took his meds. When I arrived everything was under control and my presence wasn't needed. There was another incident when Albert assisted in finding a patient who had wandered off.

One of the nurses credits the dogs with helping to lower patients' blood pressure. The presence of the dog has a calming and soothing effect, and, just by rubbing the dogs, the patients' blood pressure goes down.

For a few of these patients, the dogs are the only family they have or visits they get. The visits allow the patients to forget about the hospital environment for a while.

It seems that sometimes health professionals have forgotten how important such care is to the patients' treatment. Thanks to the therapy dog program, such special care has been reintroduced to the healthcare profession.

Ron A. Leisure, Police Officer; U.S. Army, 1968-80

I see patients on the patio areas when I am working. When I see the people come out to the VA with their dogs, it really surprises me how much the patients like to see the dogs. Some of the patients reach out to touch the dogs and really seem to enjoy that. I enjoy seeing the dogs out there myself. It is good for all of us to see and pet the dogs.

Del Lewis, Groundskeeper; U.S. Army, 1971-72

Many times I have heard the expression, "I never thought I'd be in here," from a patient or resident in a nursing home or extended care facility. Being away from home with its comfortable surroundings, especially when one is ill, can be a daunting feeling. A patient will ask, "How long am I going to be here?" or "Do I get to go home?" Often there are no easy answers from a medical team.

Visitors come and go, often posing questions to the patient who either doesn't know or really doesn't always want to talk about their illness, especially if it is terminal.

One thing that will bring comfort and a smile time and time again is when the "quiet visitor" and his handler enter the patient's room.

Whether a pure bred or a mixed breed, from the wag of their tail to the occasional paw given at bedside, the therapy dog seems to be saying, "I'm here to offer a moment of comfort; if you want to talk to me, scratch behind my ears, pat my head, that's great; but if you cannot, that's ok too! I might just quietly lie down next to the bed for a while."

No words are needed, no questions to answer. The patient may later reflect on a pet they once had, but most of the time they just give a smile of appreciation that says, "Thanks for the visit. Glad you stopped by to see me. Come again soon."

Geri Mauthe, LCSW, Licensed Clinical Social Worker (retired),
Nursing Home Care Unit

How can a beautiful, gentle, warm, fuzzy animal not make you happy? These therapy dogs bring such joy to the immediate environment it is unbelievable. I have had the pleasure of being visited by Jiffy, Lawrence, Albert, and Poli. Jiffy was my love. She and I would sometimes end up on the floor, and it just made my day better. I can't imagine what the animals do for the patients that can't get outside or even out of their rooms. These animals calm you and leave you in a better disposition than before they arrived. I have been in the most chaotic of days and they seem to take all that away. I always look forward to Tuesdays now because Lawrence has been integrated into one of our groups, and I have never seen him livelier! Lawrence loves going to the group!

Jane Mazurczak, Program Support Assistant, Mental Health

Canine heroes—how many are there? There are the pups that sit so proudly on the fire trucks next to brave and selfless firefighters. There are the police canines that stand ever ready to protect the officer at their side and uphold the law. There are the military dogs that go into battle to preserve our military and fight for our freedom. There are our pets—loved, cared for, and caring. Then there are our therapy dogs.

Canine therapy visits are a gift to our patients at the Livermore VA. The patients look forward to and so enjoy the time they share with the dogs that visit. The visits have a calming and healing effect on most patients. Additionally, there is an enhanced level of pain relief by either decreasing a patient's need for pain medication or offering better management of their pain from the medications they do receive. Each dog is unique and a welcome and vital part of our patients' treatment.

A therapy dog has been identified as a caregiver. So much is written about the impact that these dogs have on the recovery of our clients. There is another impact that these dogs have—the impact of their love and devotion to the caregiver. Caregivers bond with these dogs, getting to know and understand them individually. Their eagerness, willingness to undertake the task at hand, gentleness, obedience, and unique personalities bring a sense of fun and grace to the caregiver. There is a renewed energy among the staff after a canine visit. To these canine heroes in the healthcare field, a heartfelt gratitude for all they bring to each of us.

Barbara Militano, RN, Registered Nurse, Short Stay Unit

As a federal employee with the VA for over two decades, I have seen first hand the benefits of the therapy dogs for those patients and staff that welcome visits on a regular basis. Sometimes, these therapy dogs are the only visitors a patient might receive in the course of weeks.

A relationship develops between patients and the dogs. The dogs are quite friendly to everyone, and very smart. The dogs remember which patients gave them good back scratches or snacks on their last visit. These dogs remind patients of home. They bring happiness to the patient. A good "WELL DONE" to these therapy dogs and their handlers for caring about the VA patients!

These dogs also make a difference for staff. I work at three VA sites—here in Livermore and in Palo Alto and Menlo Park. I see dogs almost every day I am working in Livermore. I only see a dog two or three times a year at the other sites. The dogs can really make your day at work. Yesterday, when I walked in, there were two people on the housekeeping staff petting Zito. I went up to meet Zito. It's a really nice deal for all of us. Dogs put us in a good mood. One day I arrived in a really bad mood. The dog put me in a good mood and made me relax. They make this a special place to work.

Rodger W. Nelson, Linen Handler, Environmental Management Services; U.S. Navy, Vietnam War Veteran

The visits to the Community Living Center by the therapy dogs have benefited veteran patients during Occupational Therapy (OT) treatment. Increasing range of motion, muscle strength and coordination, and normalizing tactile sensation are some of the goals we work on in OT in order to improve a person's function and ability to care for himself. Veterans can experience these physical benefits while stroking and petting the dogs. Lowering blood pressure and anxiety, and reducing perception of pain are physiologic functions that can benefit them. Residents who find it difficult to interact with other folks because of isolation, difficulty with speech or communication, or other reasons sometimes relate to the dogs in ways that no other approach can achieve.

In Occupational Therapy, the dogs visit residents and staff. There is always time to break from the activity at hand to greet and interact with the dogs. Taking cues from the residents, handlers either allow the dogs to approach or grant a wider berth. One veteran, who regularly interacted with Schnoz during OT, was frequently able to extend his participation in treatment sessions; his visit with Schnoz gave him the psychosocial "break" he needed to complete the treatment sessions. Another veteran enjoyed visits from the dogs during OT; it allowed him to reminisce about his long-lost dog companions and happy times with his family. Another veteran enjoyed regular visits from Jiffy while participating in OT treatment sessions for painful joints that interfered with his mobility and ability to care for himself. He always had pleasant interactions with Jiffy, despite the significant pain he experienced.

It can be challenging to re-create the environment of home in the hospital. The sight of therapy dogs in the halls of the Community Living Center can give the impression of a homelike environment to residents, which benefits quality of life and improves the overall experience.

Keri Ojeda, OTR/L, Occupational Therapist, Extended Care and Out-patient Services

Our volunteer dogs have made a new impact here at the VA. Our patients seem to be responding very well to them. Patients tend to be healed and not judged through the dog's unconditional love.

Jammu Owens, Voluntary Service Staff

When the dogs are present on our floor, the patients are calmer and more relaxed. Then I can get better and more typical responses during their pulmonary function testing. The patients follow my instructions better too. And Lawrence is a big-time employee. He's a whole lot better than all of us put together!

Fernando Palumpon, Respiratory Therapist

As an employee of the VA since 2002, I have seen the therapy dogs that come in and brighten up the lives and days of both staff and residents. I see residents light up at the sight and touch of their favorite therapy dog. I see the memories, which might have been forgotten, resurface when they come into contact with the many therapy dogs that inhabit their space, even if it is only for a short time. As for the staff, I get to see nurses and doctors smile fondly as they walk by or stop beside their favorite dogs to hand out well-deserved pets.

And lastly, being a dog lover and owner of two very wonderful, but aging canines myself, the therapy dogs that I see and encounter occasionally make me miss my two so much more as I watch these dogs' faces and eyes look up at me with the hope that I may have something really special and tasty hidden in one of our food carts as I walk by. These therapy dogs are a very welcome and needed respite from the day-to-day life for everyone.

Patricia Remmell, Food Service Worker, Nutrition and Food Service

I would like to say how the therapy dog program at the Livermore VA has been a welcomed addition. I see it every time the dogs come in for a visit. There are smiles on the faces of the veterans. The patients may not have family that visit or have infrequent visits. Some are withdrawn from others, but will respond to the dogs. Patients that are in pain tend to forget or overlook that they are having pain.

The staff also enjoys having the dogs come and say hello. They make our day brighter. My hat's off to Thunder, Lawrence, Rio, and Albert, just to name a few. Thanks.

Pam Robinson, LVN, Nursing, Short Stay Unit

Communication—What is it, how does it work, and why are therapy dogs so good at it? Communication involves relating and sharing. In human communication, we recognize several rule-governed subsystems which let us talk about talking more easily; i.e., what is communication and how does it work? But there is so much more than the noises we make with our mouths. There is verbal and nonverbal communication. Nonverbal communication accounts for 80-90%, depending on whose statistics you like. All of this holds true for animal communication as well. To study communication, we use a model which includes the message sender, the message, and the message receiver.

Words have meaning (semantics), and they are organized into sentences and paragraphs (morphology, syntax). We have learned that we are more successful if we are polite than nasty (pragmatics) and speak clearly so we can be understood (phonology). We know it's important to speak loud enough to be heard and use a pleasant tone of voice (prosody). And we know we should listen attentively so as not to miss the point. Good eye contact helps. When we are young, we learn to pay attention to touch, position/spatial relationships (proxemics), movement (kinesics), and cultural rules. We become sensitive to facial expression, tone of voice, and gesture. Human infants recognize their own mothers long before they begin to speak. As we mature, we are able to appreciate subtleties when communication is produced in different modalities or formats: reading, writing, art, music, dance, aroma/scent. We have codes for all kinds of messages.

Animals demonstrate understanding of these subsystems and have highly developed skills. They utilize the nuances in effective communication with members of their own species and with us. In many ways, they are better at it because they ignore the extraneous distractions, do not succumb to dishonesty, and do not engage with phonies.

Dogs who are successful therapy dogs display a gentle kindness with unique appropriateness in relating and sharing. They are not misled by facial expressions (scowling) or words ("go away, leave me alone"). The overture of friendship they extend (a wet nose, nudge, rub, or lick) is appropriate to the needs of the adult/child being approached. They are nurturing, which requires sensitivity to the recipient's needs. One is often impressed by the dignity and respect demonstrated by the therapy dogs to those who are ill, aged, or handicapped while the same "therapist" can be encouraging, playful, and even mischievous with those who are younger, shyer, or otherwise challenged. They assess the tolerance, engage the strengths, and compensate to achieve meaningful communication. They know the verbal and nonverbal rules.

I have been privileged in my professional career to witness therapy dogs in action and to work with them to promote patient success in the face of significant communication challenges. When the "voice box" (larynx) is removed surgically, the patient is left without the ability to generate a tone which underlies speech. It takes a while to learn how to produce a vocal sound (esophageal speech) or use an artificial tone generator (electrolarynx) so that verbal communication is possible. The patient is isolated. Not all speech sounds are produced with the same level of effort, so exercises focus on groups of sounds. One therapy dog's vocabulary of commands was made available so I could select those items most likely to be successful. Practice for the patient included communicating to the therapy dog, who recognized the commands and then responded. Although the intelligibility of the patient's speech was not very good by human standards, the "therapist" listened attentively so as not to miss the point. Communication was achieved, the patient's effort was reinforced, and he was validated. It was glorious! Genuine relating and sharing succeeded. There was true communication.

Linda Rosen, PhD, Speech Pathologist (retired)

The most common life forms at the VA Hospital in Livermore—now called a Community Living Center—are long- and short-term residents and patients, doctors, nurses, psychologists, social workers, physical therapists, occupational therapists, recreational therapists, environmental management service people, dietary workers, administrative people, volunteers, chaplains, and the like. And of course, the multitudes of microscopic vermin we all focus so intensively on eradicating—the hosts that carry and spread disease.

A less common life form is a domesticated form of the gray wolf, known in scientific circles as *canis lupis familiaris*, known to the rest of us as the dog. The dog. Man's best friend. I can say that with genuine appreciation, based on a childhood experience where my dog actually saved my life. But that's a story you'll have to ask me about if you want to know the specifics.

The dog—man's (and woman's) best friend. In the environment where I work, the affectionate term is well deserved. Let me share just one story about our faithful canine volunteers at the Livermore VA. On this particular occasion, Old Jim (not his real name) sat in his wheelchair in the hallway, staring blankly at some unseen object out in space. Verbal greetings usually went unacknowledged and rarely altered the blank stare. But then Sparky (not his real name either), one of our canine volunteers, appeared on leash with his handler. Sparky wagged his tail gently, and I'd swear I saw a smile on Sparky's face as he nuzzled Old Jim on the arm.

Almost instantly, a long-forgotten smile was re-born on the face of our long-term resident, and a hand and arm I hadn't seen move in recent memory moved out to touch the head of Sparky. Old Jim's eyes widened and I'm almost certain I saw a faint mist forming in those eyes as one hand invited the other to join in holding Sparky's face. You could see a definite, palpable awakening in the whole body of Old Jim, as the tentative touch became a stroking, petting act, and Old Jim leaned over, putting his cheek on Sparky's head. I wish you could have seen what I saw that day. It's probably fortuitous that Sparky couldn't speak with a human voice and language, for not once had I ever before observed such life in Old Jim—no matter what any of us on staff had tried.

I don't know whose idea it was originally to bring animal/pet therapy to the Livermore VA. Maybe it was somebody who had an early childhood experience like mine. Whoever it was, many thanks!

Rev. Harold L. Rucker, BCC, Protestant Chaplain

I see the therapy dogs in the CLC in the hallways as they interact with the patients. What a blessing they are because just the sight of the dogs brings joy to the patients. And to EMS staff too because of the shedding of fur that occurs when the dogs are being petted is only looked upon as job security for us.

Michael Sewell, Leader, Environmental Management Services;
U.S. Marine Corps, 1974-80

I run a weekly relapse prevention group for patients with alcohol and drug problems here at the Livermore VA. One of the members, a combat veteran, is the handler for the therapy dog, Lawrence, and had been bringing Lawrence to the group for several months. I'd never had a therapy dog in one of my therapy groups, and I was curious to see what this would be like. I noticed during sessions how Lawrence would wander around the group, approaching members who would pet him briefly, before he became interested in someone or something else and would wander on to the next thing. At times, he would move from one member to another for more petting. At other times, he would spread himself out on the floor, blow out a deep breath and lay on his side, relaxing. The effect seemed to have a calming, soothing effect on the group.

Earlier this year, we had a new member come to group, a Vietnam Veteran diagnosed with PTSD and struggling with an alcohol problem. Now, it is difficult for someone to come to group for the first time. Admitting you have a problem and opening up about it in a group of strangers takes courage. Opening up is even more difficult for patients with PTSD, in which physical and emotional withdrawal is common. As a therapist, one of the skills you have to develop is the ability to engage patients so they return after the initial treatment session. If the initial experience is negative, it is a sure bet the patient will not return.

So at one point in the session, the new member started telling his story. As he was speaking, I could see that he was extremely tense. His face was tight and his voice was somewhat hoarse and pinched. He was telling us of the negative effects alcohol and PTSD were having on his life—his personal failings, problems his alcohol use was creating with his relationship with his wife, and the possibility that he could lose his marriage if he did not get a handle on these problems. At one point, I considered thanking him and moving on, as I felt he was experiencing a bit too much anxiety speaking in front of the group, and that giving him a break would help.

But as he continued, a funny thing happened. Lawrence went up to him and perched his nose on his knee. The group member almost reflexively reached down and started stroking Lawrence under the chin as he continued to tell his story. There seemed to be a noticeable change in the patient at that point. His face seemed to soften and his body seemed to relax as he continued telling his story. I decided not to interrupt. The group member got to the end of his story, after which other members gave him feedback and encouragement for coming to the group. In general, I thought this had been a positive experience for him and that the interaction with Lawrence had helped. But I wasn't completely sure if he would return to the next week's session.

The following week the patient did return. And I remember thinking at that time that Lawrence had played a part in this. I remember marveling that a dog had actually been instrumental in engaging this patient in such a way that he decided to come back for that all important second session.

I'd been aware that therapy dogs are good for patients dealing with severe depression and PTSD, and that simply petting an animal can result in changes in brain chemistry that can help someone feel better. But I've come to realize that there may be deeper and more complex levels of therapeutic benefits in using these animals, such as in this case of Lawrence helping a patient to engage in group therapy. So I'm going to keep an eye on Lawrence and the other therapy dogs to see if there are other "tricks" they are capable of to help me and my staff in the delivery of psychotherapy.

I look forward to our ongoing professional relationship.

Darryl Silva, LCSW, Licensed Clinical Social Worker and Clinical Coordinator, Mental Health, Social Work Service

I believe the therapy dogs are great for our hospitalized veterans. It always seems to bring a smile to their faces when they see the dogs approaching. Even if they are not talkative people, they seem to open up when spending a few moments with the dog.

Steve Trigonis, Painter, Engineering

As a spiritual person and a believer in God, I think God gave animals an innate connection to human beings. Being a dog lover myself, and having grown up with dogs in my early childhood and young adult years, I feel certain dogs have the ability to sense humans' emotions and feelings.

The therapy dog program at the Department of Veterans Affairs Community Living Center (CLC) in Livermore has a special group of dogs who are keenly aware of the veterans' emotions, and perhaps spiritual wellbeing. As a chaplain at the Livermore CLC, I often ask the patient, "How is your spirit?" The therapy dogs appear to have a sense of how the patient's spirit is without asking this question. If the dog approaches a patient and the patient is not receptive, the dog quickly senses that its presence is not welcomed, and moves on to the next veteran where it is well received. As chaplains, some of us can probably take a few tips from the therapy dogs!

The dogs bring a glimpse of life outside the VA CLC to resident veterans who once owned pets. Whenever I see the dogs on the units, my spirit is immediately lifted, and a smile takes over my heart and my face. I have seen many of the veterans have a similar experience! I was at the Therapy Dog Awards Ceremony in January 2010 and heard first-hand from several veterans how special these dogs are to them as they presented pins to the dogs.

Thank God for dogs and for the therapy dogs at the VAPAHCS in Livermore.

Chaplain Fleeta Turrentine, MDiv, BCC, Chaplain

I've worked off and on since 1990 at the VA in Livermore. We have a great volunteer program. Our patients are very pleased with all the warm smiles and attention they get. I am not really sure how long we have been using the therapy dogs. But this program has been a smash hit from the beginning. When Albert and Lawrence first started coming here with Pat, the patients actually looked forward to the days the dogs came. I see many patients, who are withdrawn from staff, talk and actively pet the dogs when they are here. After the dogs leave, staff members now have a topic to get patients to engage in conversation when they are questioned about what kind of dog they had. Patients who are normally withdrawn seem to respond well with the pets.

Many of our vets get so involved with pet therapy that they actually buy dog treats with their own money just so they can give a treat to the dogs when they show up. In my opinion, this is a wonderful program for the patients and should be used at all rest homes and nursing facilities. My favorite dog is called Thunder, and I love it when he shows up. It just makes my day better.

David Van Almelo, CAN, Certified Nursing Assistant, Short Stay Unit

The legacy of Animal-Assisted Activities (AAA) at the VA Nursing Home Care Unit is so astonishing that it is hard to imagine what recreation therapy would be without the impact of AAA and the therapy dogs. Kathy Kelley, my colleague and the other Recreation Therapist, and I would always discuss how we could make our program well rounded and add other activities that would reach the total patient populations.

When we added AAA to our program offerings, we were very excited. It gave us an opportunity to reach other patients. We were looking for an activity for patients who love dogs and patients who lost contact with their dogs when they moved into the VA nursing home. Also we needed activities for patients who responded minimally to the other activities, who were bedridden, and/or who had little to no family support. Through AAA, the therapy dogs became a big part of the treatment plan for these patients.

This is my memory of the effect of AAA on a patient in the dementia unit. He loved dogs and had his own dog when he lived at home. When he started to lose his memory, his daughter had him admitted to the nursing home dementia unit to be cared for. He would stay in his room all the time until the therapy dog visits were added to his treatment plan. It gave the patient the opportunity to walk a dog around the grounds a few times weekly. He was so happy and had a gigantic smile on this face during those experiences. The comfort and enjoyment he received during those visits with the dogs were incredible.

The therapy dogs provided so much comfort and emotional support towards improving the quality of life for our patients.

Robert Walker, Recreation Therapist (retired)

—Testimonials from Others—

My father has been at the VA Hospital in Livermore for an extended period following a hip replacement surgery. We always had pets when I was growing up including one or more dogs at any given time. Later in life, when my father lived in an assisted living apartment and now at the VA facility, having his own pet has not been an option.

I have seen him, as well as other patients, absolutely brighten up when one or more dogs make their visits. I had the privilege of attending the ceremony where the dogs were given their pins for the various years of service. The patients spoke about the particular dogs they had formed bonds with, and it was readily apparent the impact these dogs and their owners had made on their lives. The dedication on the part of these volunteers to serve our veterans in this way is very admirable. I want to thank them and salute their efforts! God bless you, and God bless America

David Alvis, Son of a CLC resident; U.S. Army, 1972-75, Medical Corps

I was in Stanford Hospital four years ago with a rare and potentially fatal liver disease. I was miserable. This was the first time I have ever been in a hospital with any type of disease, and it was depressing and horrible. One day, a man came into my room with a black and white Border Collie. He asked me if I would like a visit. I said, "Sure!" The Border Collie jumped up on my bed and immediately laid down in my lap, looking for some pets and scratches. I was on so much medication that I don't remember much of the visit, but I do remember how happy I was to be connecting with such a sweet dog! In my 18 days in Stanford Hospital, the man and his dog came by to see me several times, and each time I remember how calming and happy the dog made me by lying in my lap and allowing me to stroke its soft fur. I came to truly look forward to their visits.

My dad is now in the Community Living Center at the VA in Livermore, and during a few of our visits that my mom and I have had with him, Sandi brought out one of her gorgeous Cockapoos and Pat brought in Albert, a beautiful Lab mix. At the first visit with the Cockapoo, the dog walked into the room and came around for pets and scratches from my mom and me. Then he jumped up on the bed with my dad and laid his head on my dad's lap. My dad had a smile from ear to ear as he was stroking the dog. My dad had rarely smiled before the dog came to visit him.

As I was walking into the Community Living Center on another day, I said to my mom, "I hope a dog comes around while we are visiting today." Sure enough, Albert came walking in during our visit and proceeded to come to my mom and me for pets and scratches. When we weren't petting him, he would lay at my feet, but when I touched him, he would stand up to make it easier for me to reach him. My dad was in a wheelchair this time and couldn't reach down to pet Albert, but really enjoyed my interactions with him and again had a wonderful smile! My mom commented that Albert's bushy tail wagging near her was better than an electric fan.

All the dogs that I have seen here are very well groomed, calm, extremely well mannered, and more than willing to share their wonderful positive energy with those who can feel and enjoy their presence. The owners of the therapy dogs are so very thoughtful and generous with their time to help bring some happiness into someone's life that is not feeling very well at the moment. My spirits were always lifted when the Border Collie visited me in Stanford Hospital, and I can see how my dad lights up when the different therapy dogs enter his room. I personally think the therapy dogs are just as important as the medical care people receive in hospitals, and they should have a recommended daily allowance rating!

To all the volunteers and dogs that do this incredible work, THANK YOU!

Yvonne Buff, Daughter of a CLC resident

I love coming to the VA Hospital to see my husband and Lassie, Albert, and Lawrence. I like talking to the ladies that bring the dogs. My husband and I both love the dogs.

Patricia Burch, Wife of a former CLC resident

I see people who are not communicating with anybody else. And then I see the dogs come in. It doesn't matter which dog—they are all so wonderful! After a veteran sees the dogs two or three times, I see him reaching out to other people. I don't know how that works, but I guess communicating with a dog while they are around other people opens them up. It spreads out and they start talking to the other people there. I have seen it happen so many times. They reach out to other people somehow through the dogs.

Some patients are bedridden and in their own world. But when a therapy dog comes into their rooms, they kick back into our world. They all know the dogs.

I've been volunteering at the VA in Livermore since 1984, and I can certainly see a difference now that the dogs are here so often.

Louise Cobb, Volunteer, Livermore VA

The reaction of the veterans to the therapy dogs is very special because of the unconditional love and friendship these dogs provide to every veteran. Many of the veterans never get to leave their rooms for any amount of time, and the only time they see someone other than the nurses and doctors is when the dog handlers and dogs come in on a daily schedule.

This is a great program for the veterans, and it is very special to see the smiles on their faces when they touch the dogs. It makes their day, and so many of them just wait for another dog to appear. The dogs come in all sizes. This is a program that gives every veteran the opportunity to meet with the handlers and receive love from the dogs.

Each Monday, I teach art to the veterans. Sometimes it takes me three months to get veterans to do their first painting. This is a great program, but when I bring Albert or Lawrence into their rooms, it only takes an instant to get positive responses from the veterans. The therapy dogs give us a wonderful program that brings back great memories to the veterans and provides them an opportunity to stay focused on the moment and not their illnesses.

Charles (Bud) Donaldson, Volunteer, Livermore VA;
U.S. Air Force, 1956-78; Vietnam Veteran

I have often seen my neighbor, Pat Wheeler, taking her dogs to visit our veterans. She invited me to come along and shadow her and Lawrence one day. I wrote the following after the visit.

As morning's light fights for a break in the new day's cloud cover, one strong golden beam slices through and spotlights the bright white edifice, the landmark across the valley—the VA Hospital in the hills south of town. A silent prayer of gratitude, for those who have served, drifts from my lips to the hearing of the Spirit.

As morning warms into noon, we wind up the driveway, past flocks of full-feathered turkeys, with Lawrence, the Livermore Lab, whining from the back of Pat's wagon. Lawrence is dressed in his work uniform, a purple vest, his name embroidered across the back in bright white lettering. A silver and gold pin identifies his rank, "Master Chief Petting Officer."

Today is the day he has promised me for some time. Today, Lawrence is giving me a tour of his workplace, introducing me to all of his friends. As Pat opens the back door of the wagon, Lawrence joyously jumps from the tailgate. I think, "Maybe the small herd of deer resting under a sprawling oak has caught his attention." But no, Lawrence is all business now having spotted two veterans in wheelchairs on the patio across the driveway. These are his people, and they need him now. Well mannered and in work mode, the whining has stopped. There's no tugging on the leash. He moves easily from one man to the other, accepting pats on the head and luxurious back scratches. "That's a good dog," comments one of the men who might not utter another word all day.

Lawrence leads us inside Building 90 to greet his loving fans. At the nurses' station, we sign in and put on our badges. Now it's time to leave his admirers—the chaplain, doctors, the nursing staff—and move on to the men and women who make Building 90 their home.

We enter Earl's room. He is stretched out on his bed, an open laptop on his tray table. Judging from his condition, he has a sad story to tell, but his sparkling eyes and contagious smile give nothing away. When he spots Lawrence entering the room, the laptop is closed faster than a blink, to be opened another time. He greets Lawrence with a scratch behind the ears and the gentle Black Lab responds with a wag of his tail, which makes a thwapping sound against the metal hospital bed.

Down the hall we look for another friend, but discover his bed is empty. His roommate says he's joined the guys in the rec room where a card game is in full swing. I am sorry we miss him. His side of the room is decorated with his handiwork. "It's his therapy," Pat says.

Lawrence moves along as we admire patients' artwork that brightens the hallway. One artist's work strikes my eye. "Is that artist the same man I just met, the one with such challenging tremors?" I ask. "Yes," Pat answers, "He's quite an artist. And, you know, sometimes when the therapy dogs visit him, he stops shaking altogether."

Lawrence and his crew of "Petting Officers" bring an element of normal life to these veterans, broken by war or another of life's battles. A nurse told the story about the lingering effects of the dogs' visits. She said that when she entered the room of two veterans an hour or so after the dogs had left the hospital, they were still swapping stories of dogs they had when they were kids.

Our last stop was a resident room where a volunteer was visiting, talking about the field trip the next day. Specially-outfitted vehicles transport the veterans for an occasional change of scenery. Although they wanted to go, the two veterans needed to be assured they would be back in time for tomorrow's visit by Lawrence or one of his pals.

This was an afternoon I will never forget.

Marilyn Dumesnil, Visitor

As a veteran and a volunteer at the Livermore VA facilities, I have first-hand knowledge and see the effect that the therapy dog program gives to each and every veteran domiciled at this nursing facility. With open arms, each and every dog (and its owner) are greeted by the various veterans domiciled at Livermore. Whether the veteran is ambulatory or confined to bed, each makes time to interact with the dog and its owner. Many of the veterans are without families and rely on these visitations as their form of visits "from family."

The program should also be looked at as a way of healing and helping each one of the veterans while they spend their time awaiting discharge or their final calling. The overall effect this program has had on the facility and the veterans can only be measured by the smiles and the upbeat behavior that one will witness when the dogs approach!

I do hope that this program is replicated throughout the VA system, as it will only help our veterans in the recovery process with its overall calming effect on each one of the veterans it serves.

Conrad Esposito, Volunteer, Livermore VA;
Disabled American Veterans (DAV); U.S. Army, 1969-72

Thank you, Gracias, Merci, Danke to Pat Wheeler and the other loyal volunteers who share their well-trained dogs with hospital veterans. This takes personal devotion that adds joy to a veteran's day. He or she looks forward to these animal visits with anticipation. Petting that furry friend releases tension and offers moments of relaxation. This is a chance to give back to a veteran, who has been in harm's way, a caring friend so that we can live our lives of freedom in the good old USA!

Pat and Clarence Hoenig, Visitors and community volunteers

I would like to tell you how much my late husband enjoyed the therapy dog program at the VA. The dogs are loving and offer much joy to those hospitalized.

I have gone to a nursing home with a friend of mine. It has therapy dogs, and I could see the people's reactions. I never guessed that a similar program would mean so much to my husband. His favorite dog was Lawrence, the Labrador Retriever, though he loved all of them. The dogs made a difference in the last stages of his life.

Ada Hulbert, Widow of a CLC resident

When you asked me to explain how I see those wonderful therapy dogs in action, my first thought was, "Why would anyone not like to pet a dog?" How grand. I feel better when I pet Teddy, my Cocker Spaniel, as he lies on my lap or next to the easy chair. Steve Dale in USA WEEKEND (July 23-25, 2010) included a more sophisticated answer taken from *For the Love of a Dog* by Patricia McConnell, a certified applied animal behaviorist. She writes that levels of oxytocin, a mood-affecting neurotransmitter and "feel-good" hormone in the brain, increases by merely petting a dog. I can see the joy in the faces of the patients when our dogs come through the door and give that special feeling to everyone. Even I have a smile on my face, even though I have Teddy at home every day. Thank you so much for asking me to be part of you and your wonderful dogs.

William Lindke, Volunteer, Livermore VA; U.S. Navy, 1965-92

Lawrence, the Livermore "Lab"rador Retriever, and his charming sidekick, Patricia Wheeler, were among the many participants on New Year's Eve who attended the party at the VA in Livermore.

The party, put on by the Knights of Columbus, featured a six-piece orchestra, headed by me on accordion. Lawrence helped to welcome the musicians and added his special presence to the affair by wandering about to say his "HELLO" to the veterans and guests.

Ken Logsdon, Volunteer, Livermore VA

It is a very important thing that you do, bringing the therapy dogs into the lives of people that don't see much love or hope. The joy that they bring is absolutely amazing. Thank you for doing this. I admire and applaud you.

Leslie Mansfield, Daughter of a CLC resident

Such well-behaved dogs are amazing and the patients love the attention these dogs give them. The reason is simple. We should always remember that DOG spelled backwards is . . . .

Ken Mitchell, Volunteer, Livermore VA; U.S. Air Force, 1951-55

My mom, Josephine Moffat, was a patient at the Veterans Hospital in Livermore, which is part of the Palo Alto Health Care System. While a patient at the hospital, she had a great opportunity to become acquainted with the therapy dogs. She knew them all by name, and they all knew her. My mom was blind and confined to a wheelchair or a bed, but was able to touch and pet the animals. The joy of the touch and the affection that the dogs displayed made my mom's day. It was a break from some of the darkness and loneliness patients feel due to age, limited mobility and, in my mom's case, blindness.

The dogs provided an unbridled love and affection, and I am sure they felt the same from my mom. Her days were brighter because of the therapy dogs, and her quality of life was improved. I know, if she could have, she would have spoiled them like she did all of our pets. These dogs are special and will always have a place in our heart for the love and affection they showed my mom.

John Moffat, Son of a former CLC resident

I have had the pleasure of seeing the well-trained therapy dogs in action at the Livermore Veterans facility over several years. The instant delight on patients' faces when one of the dogs enters their room is heart-warming. I remember one fellow who seemed unaware of his surroundings as we entered the room and unaware of the humans coming into his space. As soon as he realized that a familiar dog had come to visit him, he sat up and carried on a lively conversation with the dog and eventually included both the handler and me.

The dogs open communication again and again just by connecting people with people. It's as if the leash is a communication line between the patient and the handler, and, incidentally, with anyone else who is nearby—possibly even a healthcare professional who has been trying unsuccessfully to get a response from the patient. The therapy dog program is an important addition to the more traditional services available for veterans at this facility.

Joy Montgomery, Representative to the Veterans Affairs Voluntary Service Advisory Committee for the National Society Daughters of the American Revolution (NSDAR)

I have had the opportunity to enjoy the therapy dogs both as an inpatient and as a VA volunteer.

Over a period of several months as a patient stuck up on the second floor I came to look forward to the visiting dogs and handlers with great anticipation. The dogs always seemed to be smiling and were very friendly, as were the handlers. It was always a pleasure to have them come around.

And as a volunteer over a period of several years now, I have seen numerous occasions where a quiet and rather withdrawn patient would be smiling and happy when the dogs came to visit. It is amazing to watch the transformation and very clear that the dogs were having a positive effect on the patients.

Don Odle, Volunteer, Livermore VA; U.S. Navy Veteran

While serving as National Society Daughters of the American Revolution VA Voluntary Service Representative for the Palo Alto/ Livermore Medical Veterans Facility, I observed the therapy dog handlers and their animals' interactions with the veteran patients.

It was an awe-inspiring afternoon that I spent with handler Pat Wheeler and her dog, Lawrence. Lawrence knew exactly how to interact with each patient he approached. One patient I observed was reluctant to touch Lawrence, so Lawrence slowly laid his nose on the patient's knee and waited. Slowly, the patient reached out to pet Lawrence. One patient in particular began talking all about dogs he had back home and kept petting Lawrence and telling him what a good dog he was. This patient was obviously in pain, but it was forgotten for the moment.

It amazed me how Lawrence knew instantly if the person was well and not in need of his attention. I held out my hand, but he just looked at me and went to a veteran lying in bed and waited until the patient acknowledged him. Lawrence knew which rooms to enter and which patients were too ill to visit. He did not bark or jump about, but was a calming influence on all he greeted. The smiles from the patients were a beautiful sight to witness.

It is amazing how much these animals can bring to the veteran patients that we, with the ability to speak, cannot give them. The handlers and their gifted therapy dogs deserve much praise for all the hours they spend each week at the Livermore Veterans Affairs Medical Facility.

Sue Overturf, National Society Daughters of the American Revolution (NSDAR), Josefa Higuera Chapter

It is amazing to see the look on the veterans' faces when one of the dogs walks into their room. What might have started as a rough morning suddenly becomes a little easier. Therapy dogs make the patients happy by their genuine happiness of just being there. That good energy from the animal rubs off on the people in its presence.

Monica Solek, Volunteer, Livermore VA

On January 15, 2011, my husband and I attended a ceremony that honored the therapy dogs that had worked at the Veterans Hospital in Livermore. One of the handlers had told me about this event, so we wanted to attend.

We were greatly moved by the veterans as they entered the room (most in wheelchairs) and were seated around the room. As the therapy dogs and their handlers came in, the veterans acknowledged them with a welcoming smile. The dogs sat down quietly by their handlers to wait until they were called up for recognition of their hours of volunteering. As the program progressed, it was incredibly heart-warming to hear the veterans express their feelings about their four-footed friends. They talked about what it meant to them to see their furry friends arrive each week. It was obvious how much these visits meant to them and how much they looked forward to their visits. Many of the veterans were moved to tears while talking about the therapy dogs.

It was a wonderful experience, and we were encouraged to see that so many people were willing to bring their dogs to see these deserving veterans! Our veterans all over the country should receive this kind of TLC. We hope others will see the value in such a program and start one for the veterans in their area.

Sueva Terry, Visitor

Just as the beautiful grounds provide tranquility and serenity to the veterans, so too do the therapy dogs. Being petted, the wagging of their tails, the therapy dogs bring immense joy and companionship to those who are otherwise consumed with anger, sadness, loneliness, or a lack of company. These dogs put a smile on their souls and what a treasured gift that is!

Barbara Torrison, Volunteer, Livermore VA

My son has really enjoyed the animal therapy visits. Seeing the dogs soothes him. It helps with him missing his dog at home.

Janet Wilcox, Mother of a CLC resident

Thank you for everything you did for my mother. We always had dogs and my mother thrived on your wonderful pets. Please accept my donation to your wonderful book project. This is what my mom would have wanted.

David Wilson, Son of a former CLC resident

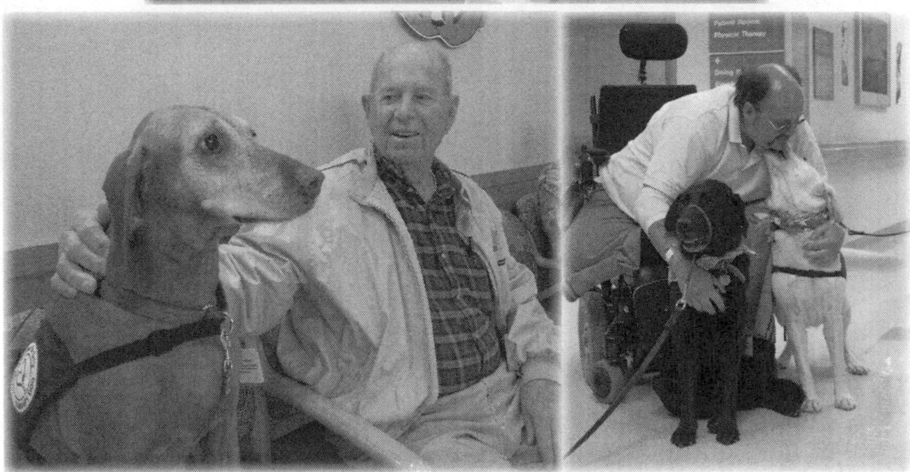

Used with permission of Doug Jorgensen, Photographer for The Independent

—Stories—

Many therapy dogs have gone to the VA. Below are stories for these dogs—Albert, a Border Collie/Black Lab mix; Alfie, a Cockapoo; Belle, an English Cocker Spaniel; Brooks, a Pointer/Lab mix; Buddy G, a Maltese mix; Buddy K, a French Bulldog; Dazzle, a Vizsla; Dori, a Shih Tzu; Elsa, a Black Labrador Retriever; Gunther, a Norwegian Elkhound; Jiffy, a Yellow Labrador Retriever; Klaus, a German Shepherd/Airedale mix; Lady, a Border Collie/Aussie mix; Lassie, a Collie; Lawrence, a Black Labrador Retriever; Maggie, a Golden Retriever mix; Miles, a Golden Retriever; Mitsy, a Havanese/Poodle mix; Patch, a Golden Retriever; Poli, a Yellow Labrador Retriever; Rio, a Bernese Mountain Dog; Rivers, a Queensland Heeler mix; Sailor, a Portuguese Water Dog; Schnoz, a Standard Schnauzer; Shazam, a Sheltie/Longhaired Dachshund mix; Simon, a Shih Tzu; Thunder, a Boxer/Great Dane mix; and Zito, a Cockapoo.

Following the Doctor's Orders—

Lawrence strolled down the hallway and turned into Mark's room. Lawrence hadn't visited Mark for some time. When he went by Mark's room earlier in the month, Mark was on the phone, sleeping, or being treated by medical staff. This time Mark was at his sink, leaning over at a 90-degree angle, bent from the hips. Mark looked at Lawrence, standing in the doorway, and exclaimed, "It's so good to see you. I've missed you. Haven't felt good."

Lawrence snuggled up to Mark as he bent over to rub Lawrence's back. Mark said his doctor has told him that he needed to walk to the nurses' station each day, pushing his wheelchair. As soon as Lawrence heard the word WALK, he was ready to take Mark for a walk and let him know that by rapidly wagging his tail. Apparently Mark sensed Lawrence's excitement about walking and decided to give it a try. Mark unloaded the clothing and books piled on his wheelchair. The chair got little use as Mark stayed in his room most of the time, and the chair had become a storage device. Mark said his doctor told him he would die soon if he didn't start walking each day.

When the wheelchair was unloaded, Mark turned it around and started toward the doorway of his room, with Lawrence right next to him. Mark looked down at Lawrence as he walked down the hallway.

He said, "Lawrence, you look like you have put weight on." I said, "I hope not. He was 65 pounds last fall and that is a good weight for him according to his veterinarian." Mark was still concerned. As they walked slowly down the hallway toward the nurses' station, they passed the scales. Mark stepped onto the scales to check his weight. Then he instructed Lawrence to get on the scales. Lawrence promptly did so and the scales read 64.4. Mark was so pleased that Lawrence's weight was at a healthy level.

They continued down the hallway, with Mark taking a couple stops to rest and get a sip of water. As he approached the nurses' station, staff eyes were wide open and jaws dropped. They were obviously surprised to see Mark there, but Lawrence wasn't. Mark said, "Lawrence is my speed, nice and easy." Mark talked with staff about his cash account and mail, and he reported his weight to the nurse. He stayed there a few minutes, talking with people and watching the activities in the hallway. As he started back to his room, he said, "A journey of a 1,000 miles starts with a few steps."

Mark went straight back to his room without stopping for a break. When he got back, he said to Lawrence, "Thanks a million! I couldn't have done this without you. Now I know I can do it. I have to do it every day or I'll die."

Lawrence and I stayed in Mark's room until he got the books and clothing moved from his bed back onto the wheelchair. Mark was smiling from ear to ear, very pleased with what he had just accomplished.

Special Connection—

Pamela couldn't sit up in her bed and couldn't see well. So I would bring Patch to the side of her bed where Pamela could reach him with her left hand. We had many conversations about her family, of whom she was very proud. She had a grandchild who was in law school, and it was clear that her family meant a lot to her.

One day, Patch and I saw Pamela in the cafeteria in her wheelchair. Patch approached her, and she immediately began to pet him and talk to him. Patch was so attentive and just looked at her. He let Pamela pet him for as long as she wanted. I am convinced that Patch knew that Pamela couldn't see him because of the way she moved to be close to him. It was a different connection than I had observed with other residents.

Giving a Veteran Hope—

While visiting the subacute unit, Lawrence walked into the room of a new young patient. John saw Lawrence and reached out to touch him. Then John looked at me and said, "This dog gives me hope." I asked him why he said that.

John said, "I can't feel my blanket. I can't feel my table. I can't even feel that cup. I can feel the dog!" Tears came to my eyes as I saw what magic the therapy dogs can perform for our veterans.

Therapy Dog Responds to His Name—

Tom was in his room, trying to learn to talk again after having a tracheotomy. The speech pathologist was working with Tom when Albert pranced down the hallway on his way to see the next patient. Tom saw Albert, and, struggling to get it out, tried to say "Albert." Albert heard Tom, made a sharp left turn into his room, and went right up to him. Tom repeated the name, "Albert," more clearly.

The joy on Tom's face was unmistakable, and tears of joy came to the eyes of the speech pathologist. This brief interruption in treatment by the speech pathologist was welcomed by all involved.

Time for Snacks and Time for Love—

Jiffy started her working day at the VA visiting outpatients and staff in the main building. As is the case with all Labs, Jiffy knew where the treats were. She always started near the coffee room where apple slices were waiting for her. Then it was to the cashier's office for more apple slices or maybe jerky sticks. After visiting staff in a few more offices, she went to the fourth floor reception area where the women had carrots for her. Jiffy knew where the snacks were, but she also knew that after the snacks, it was time to visit the nursing home and show her love for her veteran friends.

Bringing Back Memories—

One of the recreation therapists, Lawrence, and I went to visit a new patient to introduce ourselves and find out his interests. As we stood in the doorway, we asked Gene if he would like to meet Lawrence. He said, "No," as he was lying in his bed, looking out the window. Then he looked toward the doorway, saw the dog, and said, "Well, okay." He sat up on the edge of his bed. Gene was a very large man and had to struggle some to sit up.

We went around to that side of the bed so he could meet Lawrence and learn about some of the activities offered. We talked about a variety of other topics—weather, wild turkeys on the VA grounds, etc. At some point, Gene moved from the side of his bed into his wider-than-normal wheelchair. And Lawrence disappeared under the wheelchair, into what he saw as a nice, cozy little den.

Suddenly, Gene started bawling his head off, tears pouring down his face. We asked him if we should get a nurse. He said, "No, no." We asked, "What's wrong?" Gene replied, "My dog was euthanized 29 years ago. Until today, I didn't realize how much I missed her." Lawrence came out from under the wheelchair and comforted Gene.

Precious Last Moments—

Albert was busy going up and down the hallway, in and out of rooms at the nursing home. As he came to Bill's room, he saw a young couple in there sitting next to Bill's bed. Bill was sleeping, close to death. I asked the young couple if they would like to meet Albert. They readily accepted the offer and played with him, giving them a comforting break from the strain of trying to communicate with Bill.

As we got ready to leave the room, Albert tugged me around to the other side of the bed. He put his paws up on the bed rail and licked Bill's hand. Bill woke up and started talking to Albert. The young couple was so excited and also started talking to Bill. Albert and I quietly left the room so they could share some moments with Bill.

Albert continued visiting people in the nursing home. About 45 minutes later, the young couple came running down the hallway towards us, past the nurses' station. They said, "We need the dog. We can't wake Bill up." Albert made a sharp U-turn, walked quickly back to the room, and, with the love only a dog can deliver by licking Bill's hand, woke Bill up again. Bill died a day or so later. But Albert provided some precious final moments for Bill and his young loved ones.

Number One Christmas—

We once had a reporter at the VA writing a story on the Animal-Assisted Activities (AAA) program for a local news magazine. He had been busy interviewing both veterans and staff. After three hours, both of his notebooks were brimming with stories and quotes.

The reporter was getting on the elevator when Mike came up to him and said, "I have to tell you this story." The reporter said he could listen, but he had no more room for notes. Lawrence and I were in the area by the elevators. Mike said, "This dog gave me the best Christmas ever," as he pointed toward Lawrence.

Mike added that he was admitted to the subacute unit a year ago, two days before Christmas. He told us that Lawrence was there and greeted him with unconditional love and lots of licks. Mike said, "That was the best Christmas present I ever got, including all the ones from when I was a child."

Knowing What a Veteran Can Do—

One day, Don was learning to use a walker. He was to go down the hallway to the end and turn around. Albert walked next to or just ahead of Don. When they got to the end of the hallway, instead of turning around, as instructed by the physical therapist, Albert turned right and started down another hallway. Don followed Albert and went to the end of that hallway before turning around. Don, with Albert at his side, walked all the way back to the room where he had started his walk, twice as far as he was expected to go, based on prior walks, and without stopping. Albert seemed to know Don's limits and provided Don the encouragement to keep going. Both Don and the physical therapist seemed quite pleased.

Comparing Dogs—

Carmen loved to read, but also couldn't forget the Pomeranian she used to have at home. Her son had given him a furry dog-shaped pillow that looked like a Pomeranian. Carmen said that Patch's fur reminded her of her dog. She insisted that we wake her up when we came to visit so she could sit up and hug and kiss Patch. She would talk to Patch and pet him while also carrying on a conversation with me. On one of her birthday celebrations at the VA, she wanted a photo taken of herself with Patch next to her wheelchair.

New Assignment for Therapy Dogs—

Every six months, there is a memorial service at the VA to remember those veterans who have recently passed away. One social worker thought it might be nice to have a therapy dog there. Lawrence and I agreed to try this and see if it helped.

During the service, Lawrence and I sat quietly toward the back of the room, near some of the veterans in wheelchairs. Glenn, a veteran who had been discharged from the NHCU several months ago, came back to pay his respects to Arnold, his former roommate. When Arnold's name was called, Glenn started to cry. Lawrence immediately knew he was needed and went over to Glenn, put his head on Glenn's lap, and comforted him. Glenn shared his memories of Arnold, stroking Lawrence while doing so.

The next week, the social worker told me she wants to have at least one therapy dog at every memorial service from now on. And we have been doing that.

Dog Licks Help So Much—

Willard's hands were very sensitive to touch. They tingled, and even being touched by another person or rubbing his hands on his blanket was painful. In walks Jiffy. She started licking Willard's hands passionately. A big smile came across Willard's face. He said, "Jiffy's licking feels great. This is the best hand massage for me."

Later that day, Albert went into Willard's room. He reached out and started petting Albert. "Oh, he feels so very soft, so very gentle." Willard told me that he welcomes the dogs to help him cope with the pain in his hands.

Even When the Dogs Are Not There—

One day someone changed the screen saver on the computer in the veterans' lunchroom in the subacute unit. It was now a Black Lab that looked like three of the therapy dogs. Three veterans told me about this change before Albert and I even got into the building. No one seemed to know who did it. But they said they liked having a dog to look at when the therapy dogs were not on site.

Banana Treat—

Isaac was an avid reader, but really enjoyed seeing Patch and would always put his book down when Patch arrived in his doorway. Isaac's wife visited him regularly and enjoyed giving Patch a banana. Patch remembered that and would always go to the dresser which had the banana on top of it. Isaac got such a kick out the fact that Patch could eat a whole banana, and seemed to really enjoy it.

A Stop to Foot Dragging—

Bob was continuing to practice using a walker. He tended to drag one foot as he walked. The physical therapist told Bob he wanted him to lift that foot and stop dragging it. But Bob always dragged it until one day when Jiffy was there. Walking beside Bob, Jiffy provided a pleasant distraction, and Bob seemed to forget about his foot. For his entire walk that day, with Jiffy by his side, Bob never dragged his foot. Now Bob knew he could walk without dragging his foot. Hopefully, that practice would continue when Jiffy wasn't there.

Concerned About the Therapy Dog—

Lawrence and I went to the memorial service to honor 26 veterans who had passed away during the last six months. After the service, Lawrence was being petted by one of the veterans. I saw another one about 25 feet away sobbing. Lawrence and I went over to try and comfort him. I asked if he was okay, and he said, "I'm worried that the person over there is hurting Lawrence." He was concerned that the gentle petting was more like hard pats, and he didn't want Lawrence to be hurt. I assured him that Lawrence was not getting hurt and the best way to tell was to look at Lawrence's tail, which was wagging rapidly from side to side. He smiled and started stroking Lawrence.

Greeted on Arrival—

Elsa's first day at the VA was amazing. Pat and Lawrence were there to see how Elsa and I would do as a team. It was a beautiful warm summer day. Pat had told me to have Elsa all ready to go with her vest on, and I had goop (i.e., hand sanitizer) at the ready. As we walked up to the front doors, about ten patients in their chairs were taking in the beautiful day and waiting for us. We were so warmly greeted. It took us about 30 minutes to actually get into the building because many veterans wanted to pet the dogs.

Quiet Times—

Neil was bedridden, but his family visited him regularly and would take him outside to certain areas of the VA grounds so he could enjoy the sunshine and fresh air and see the wildlife. I had chatted with the family members many times, and they enjoyed petting Patch. I noticed that Neil rarely spoke. He would nod slightly and smile when I spoke to him. He was not able to reach out and pet Patch. But he would thank us for coming to see him.

One day, Patch and I visited when it was Neil's birthday. We were invited to his party on the patio. His grandchildren were there. They really enjoyed petting Patch and asked me many questions about Patch. I knew that he and the family enjoyed their time with Patch.

Training a New Dog—

Lawrence was showing Elsa, a new therapy dog, how to get attention from the veterans. Lawrence has a way of backing up to a wheelchair and making it known that he wants his lower back, near his tail, to get scratched. Elsa and Lawrence were visiting with two veterans in the hallway. One veteran, Danny, was happily scratching Lawrence's lower back when the other veteran, Dick, said, "I wish you would scratch me that way." Danny said, "I'm not going to scratch your rump like this. But I will do it for any of the dogs." Elsa gingerly moved in, following Lawrence's example, and got her lower back scratched too. There were two happy dogs with rapidly moving tails.

Encouraging Exercise—

One of Lawrence's favorite tasks is getting kicked, almost. While David was sitting, he was instructed by the physical therapist to swing his leg out straight. Lawrence would position himself right past the farthest point that David could extend his leg. With Lawrence there as a "target," David tried harder to kick his leg out farther than on other days. If David almost "kicked" Lawrence, he would back away a couple inches and encourage David to try harder.

Time for Magic—

I was at the VA with Albert on the day before the Fourth of July. I asked Celia, one of the residents, if she knew what was planned for tomorrow. She said there would be games starting at 10:00 AM, then a barbecue, and, after that, a magic show. I knew that Lady was scheduled to come out the next day. I said, "I hope the magician doesn't make Lady disappear." Celia responded, "That would be terrible! I hope he can make lots more Lady's. She is so sweet and adorable."

A Show of Patience—

I had brought one of Lawrence's favorite toys one day, a ring made out of material like a tennis ball. Lawrence, being a Lab and liking to sleep with this ring as a pillow, had hair all over the ring, despite my meager efforts to get the hair off of it.

We were outside on the patio area. Veterans were tossing the ring, and Lawrence was bringing it back to them, a game I call "Bring Ring." When Victor got the ring, the tossing stopped. He started picking off the hairs, one by one. Lawrence just sat there watching him. This went on for quite a while. One of the other veterans on the patio that day said, "Lawrence has more patience than 500 people combined!"

Day Getting Better in an Instant—

We stopped to visit Chuck in his room. He was at the end of the hallway in a large single room. Chuck spent many hours each day doing puzzles—crosswords, word search, and sudoku—which I am guilty of also. I asked him how the puzzling work was going that morning. He replied, "Terrible! There's a fly in this room and I can't think." Suddenly, there was a chomp sound. Albert had caught the fly. Chuck joyfully exclaimed, "My day just got better!"

Getting Feelings Out—

Lawrence entered the room of a patient he hadn't met before. Lawrence went to the far side of Eddie's bed. Eddie never looked at me, but started talking to Lawrence about all his life experiences and challenges. Lawrence sat there, looking at Eddie's eyes and listening to every word. Lawrence made no judgments. He just attentively listened, showing Eddie he was concerned and interested. This went on for half an hour. Eddie spilled out lots of feelings from his childhood to his military service to recent years.

Finally Eddie looked up at me. He exclaimed, "This was worth more than ten years of psychiatrists." Lawrence provided a listener for Eddie, and a chance for Eddie to get lots of things off his chest. Often people will open up to a dog, but are reluctant to share their feelings and concerns with other people. Lawrence was the non-judgmental and attentive listener that Eddie needed so badly at that moment.

A Special Relationship—

Dori had a very special relationship with Nancy at the VA. Whenever we visited Nancy, it was a beautiful experience for all of us. Nancy would hold, and hold, and hold Dori! It seemed like an eternity to me, but not for Dori or Nancy. One time, as Dori and I were about to go visit other veterans, Nancy said, "It's okay if you want to leave since Dori and I are just fine."

Getting Over the Fear of Dogs—

Rachel was visiting her brother, Derek, one Sunday afternoon. Derek's bed was the one near the window, and Rachel was sitting in a chair, her back to the door and facing Derek's bed and the window. Lawrence strolled into the room knowing this was a great place to get gentle strokes on his back. As soon as Rachel saw Lawrence, she said, "Get him out of here! I don't like dogs!" Derek said, "It's okay. He'll be here just a minute and he won't hurt you."

Lawrence went to the window side of Derek's bed to receive the gentle strokes. Rachel sat there, obviously uncomfortable. As Lawrence and I started out of the room, he came to a dead stop, right next to the chair that Rachel was in. He stood there, not twitching a hair. Rachel was shaking, but Derek encouraged her to touch Lawrence's back. After a couple minutes of encouragement from Derek, Rachel touched Lawrence's back ever so lightly. Instantly, the tail wagged rapidly. Derek exclaimed, "See, Rachel. You made Lawrence happy. He won't hurt you." Shortly after that, we moved on to the next room.

A couple months later, Derek told me that his sister, Rachel, had passed away. He added that, "The best thing that happened to her before she died is she got to like dogs."

Missing the Stamp Collector—

When Patch and I stopped in to visit Alfred, he was usually working on a puzzle or his stamp collection. He loved seeing Patch and would talk to him and pet him while I stood in the background. He often said that Patch reminded him of his dogs at home and that he missed them a great deal.

He had a large collection of stamps. One day he gave me a stamp of the state of Colorado, my home state. When Alfred moved home,

Patch and I missed him, but I still have the stamp with Colorado on it to remember him by.

A Tough Moving Job—

Tony was a new patient in the Alzheimer's unit. He was outside, on the enclosed patio area, tightly grasping the fence. Lawrence was visiting the five patients in the multi-purpose room of the Alzheimer's unit. A nursing staff member went outside to get Tony to come back inside and take his medication. Tony was standing there, rigid, grabbing onto the bars enclosing the patio, and wouldn't move. Tony was a large man, well over six feet tall, and we didn't want anyone hurt.

Next thing I knew, Lawrence became aware of the situation, went outside to the patio, nudged Tony in the leg, and gently steered him back inside and towards a chair. He stood in front of Tony and made him back up and sit down. As soon as Tony sat down, Lawrence plopped down on his feet. Tony was going nowhere. And Tony took his medication with no further problem.

Knowing When She Is Needed—

One day, Lassie and I were walking down the hallway. There was a family visiting their loved one, who was close to passing. Lassie knew she was needed there and pulled me into the room. She quietly brought relief to those family members during a hard time.

The Therapy Dog There Even in Death—

The door to the ward where Ivan had been was closed. Jiffy had visited Ivan the day before, and she had provided some fun playtime for him. But Lawrence couldn't see Ivan today. Ivan had passed away that morning.

A gentleman came that afternoon to pick up Ivan's body. Ivan was on a gurney, covered with a brown sheet. The gentleman wheeled the gurney down the hallway toward a back doorway through which he was to take the body. Lawrence and I were visiting people in the hallway when the gentleman said he had to go get the key to unlock the door. He left the gurney at the end of the hallway and quickly walked back to the nurses' station.

Lawrence pulled me gently, but firmly, down to the end of the hallway, past several patients' rooms and veterans in the hallway. Lawrence stood at the foot of the gurney. Then he went to the side of the gurney, made a 180-degree turn, and stood by Ivan's head. Lawrence looked straight ahead, down the hallway, tail straight out. He didn't flinch. Lawrence was there to be with Ivan in death as he had been in life. He was Ivan's bodyguard. The nurse coming down the hallway saw Lawrence by Ivan's body, and said, "That is so charming. He is still protecting him." When the gentleman came to take Ivan's body to the waiting vehicle, Lawrence watched them leave and then returned to his regular therapy dog duties. Lawrence had said farewell to Ivan in his own special way.

Making a Thunderous Impression—

Lawrence was at the VA to train a new therapy dog, Thunder, on his first visit. When they arrived, they visited several veterans on the patio area outside the main entrance. Thunder needed little training as he gently visited each veteran, pouring out his unconditional love. Then we all went inside and started visiting veterans in the hallways. About 20 minutes later, we started down the hallway for the subacute unit. We passed Cliff's room where he was lying on his bed. I said, "We saw Cliff outside, so we don't need to visit him now." We were two doors down the hall when Cliff yells out, "Thunder!" Of course, Thunder had to respond and provide more love to his new fan. And Cliff was very pleased to see him twice that day.

Therapy Dog Sent on a Search and Rescue Mission—

We arrived one afternoon with Dazzle and Albert. We were visiting patients in the patio area outside the main entrance, when a nursing aide came running out saying one of the veterans, Ronald, had left the building with his cane and was last seen swinging it at a groundskeeper. She asked us to watch out for Ronald.

Next thing I knew, the nurse manager appeared. He owned a German Shepherd who was a trained search and rescue (SAR) dog, but his dog was not there on site. His dog was at home. He looked at Albert and gave him a search and rescue command. Next thing I knew, I was flying behind Albert, trying to hold onto the leash. Dazzle stood by, continuing to visit the veterans in the patio area and keep staff calm.

Albert headed off in a totally different direction from where Ronald was last seen. Albert headed up into the woods behind the building, and there was Ronald. We walked Ronald down to an open grassy area. I told Ronald that Albert wanted to hold his cane. Ronald said,

"Okay, if Albert wants it, he can have it." Ronald dropped his cane onto the grass. Albert put his paw on the cane and looked up at me. I said to Ronald, "Albert just asked me if I could hold your cane for him so he can play with you." Ronald said, "Fine, if that's what Albert wants."

Next thing I knew, Ronald was sitting on the grass playing with Albert. The nurse manager was coming with a wheelchair. And we could see a police officer heading our way. As soon as the police officer saw Albert on the ground by Ronald, he waved goodbye to us. He knew Albert could take care of the situation, and the Police Department's services were not needed in this case.

We managed to get Ronald into the wheelchair so we could take him back to his room. Twice on the way back, Ronald slipped out of the wheelchair onto the ground to play with Albert some more. Once back in his room, Dazzle and Albert spent 45 minutes with Ronald, trying to calm him down and make him realize that this was his home right now.

Eventually a staff member came in and said, "You can go now," meaning Dazzle, Albert, and the two of us. But Ronald took it to mean him, stood up, and started walking down the hallway. Dazzle stayed with Ronald, while Albert and I went ahead to ask a staff member to lock up a fenced-off patio area, which he did promptly. Dazzle and Albert walked Ronald out to the fenced-in patio area. We walked back and forth for a while, some times with Dazzle and other times with Albert. Eventually we managed to get the two dogs back into the building. Ronald continued walking for a while until he was ready to go back to his room for a long nap.

What amazed us is that Albert had never met Ronald before, and I have no idea where he learned to follow search and rescue commands, but he sure knew what to do and did it very successfully.

Love Goes Beyond the Veterans to Their Families—

One couple that comes out regularly to visit their father, Harvey, has a son Jimmy, who is autistic and afraid of dogs. At first, Jimmy backed away from the therapy dogs. But when he saw his parents, grandfather, and others enjoying the company of the dogs, he started to reach out and gently touch them. He is still a little startled when the dog moves suddenly (e.g., sits down, turns to look at another person), but his mother said now he keeps asking, "When we gonna see grandpa and the doggies?" Sounds like the dogs have won over another fan.

Love Affair—

Jiffy first met Gregory at the nursing home during one of her weekly visits to the VA. After a few visits, they became very close friends. Jiffy discovered that Gregory would come over to the main building on the VA campus in the morning. As she would visit with other patients and staff, she always kept an eye towards the hallway, waiting for Gregory to come around the corner in his wheelchair. When she saw Gregory, there was only one thing on her mind—go see her friend! This was a love affair that lasted until Jiffy's passing.

Special to Feel—

A new patient who is blind and deaf had his first interaction with a therapy dog when Lawrence came by to nuzzle up against him and encourage him to rub his back. Later, I heard one of the staff members say that he told her, "I may be blind and deaf, but I did something really great today. I got to feel Lawrence."

Moving Closer—

Larry was lying on the gurney in his room, his hand shaking and having a challenging time reaching out. Schnoz moved gently toward the gurney and then backed underneath the gurney just enough so Larry could reach him. Schnoz stood there, thoroughly enjoying getting his head petted. And Larry was obviously enjoying his visit from Schnoz.

Finding a Cell Phone—

Albert was making his rounds one afternoon when he pranced into Vince's room. A nurse was in the room trying to find Vince's cell phone. They were both glad to see Albert, who immediately put his paws up on the rail of the bed. Then we found out why they were so happy to see Albert. Vince held a cord for his cell phone to Albert's nose, and said, "Albert, find my cell phone."

Albert immediately had his nose to the floor (even though he had never been trained, as far as I knew, for the command "find"). He spent a good minute sniffing around and under Vince's electric scooter on the other side of the bed. He checked under his chest of drawers and sniffed into one open drawer. Then he turned around and stuck his nose under the bed. He went under the bed, next to some equipment there. Albert came out and looked up at me. Then he put his nose back under the bed. So I bent over and looked carefully. Albert reached under the equipment with his paw and pushed the cell phone out a little. It was hard to see, but I saw the cell phone and pulled it out. Vince was so happy and exclaimed, "Now I can call my wife!" The nurse was pleased too.

The next day, I saw the nurse at the VA when I went out there to deliver some documents. She told me she was so glad Albert found the cell phone. She added, "I spent 30 minutes looking for it and Albert found it so quickly!" Other staff overheard her, so Albert might be called on again to "Find . . . ." He certainly seemed to understand that command. Over a week later, when Vince saw Albert, he exclaimed, "Four people couldn't find my phone after looking for half an hour each, but you found it right away, Albert. You're awesome!"

Special Label for the Therapy Dog—

Christopher was learning to use a walker. Christopher went down the hallway, the physical therapist at his side and following Albert. As he walked down the hallway, Christopher started to laugh. The physical therapist asked, "Why are you laughing?" Christopher replied, "Albert keeps stopping and looking back at me." I said, "Albert wants to make sure you are coming with him and that he is not walking too quickly." Christopher replied, "I'm following Albert. He's my pacemaker."

Remembering a Very Special Dog—

Twice a year, the social workers hold a memorial service for all residents who have passed away during the last six months. This helps bring closure to the veterans' family members and friends at the VA. Dazzle was so special to the veterans that the social workers included her in the memorial service in the fall of 2007. Remembering Dazzle brought tears to the eyes of many in attendance that afternoon.

Dazzle was the first therapy dog to be remembered at one of these services, but not the last. Jiffy and Patch were both remembered at the memorial service in the fall of 2009. The therapy dogs have become such a part of the family at the VA.

Fan of the Big Dog—

Thunder and I walked into a two-bed room. The person in the first bed was sitting in a wheelchair with his back to us. I asked both veterans if they wanted to see my dog. The man in the wheelchair said, "Which dog is it?" As soon as I said Thunder, he got all excited and said, "Yes!" Then he said, "Let me get my wheelchair backed up." I got the biggest kick out of that. I guess Thunder already has a good reputation with the veterans on his third visit.

Rainy Day Doesn't Stop Dogs—

It was a rainy day, so I waited until the rain let up to bring my dog in. I told Peter that I was sorry we were late, but that we know what wet dogs smell like. Peter said, "This dog when he's wet? He smells beautiful!" We can't let rain stop the therapy dogs from visiting our veterans.

Irresistible Loving Eyes—

Two family members were visiting Joe. Maggie came by to greet all of them. Joe was particularly taken by Maggie, who was only on her second visit to the VA. While gently stroking Maggie's head, Joe looked at his wife and said, "Hey, I want you to get me a dog like this." Maggie looked at Joe with her loving eyes. It must have been love at first sight.

Pain Drainers—

Matt's arm was hurting, and, when Albert came to the doorway of his room, Matt said he didn't want to see the dog today because he was in pain. I pointed out that Albert is a "pain drainer." Matt agreed to have Albert come in. He petted Albert with his left arm. As we got ready to move to the next room, Matt said, "My left arm feels better now. Thanks for coming."

During the next few visits by Albert and other therapy dogs, Matt was very excited to see the dogs. He told one handler a week after Albert's visit that he was "feeling fine now, thanks to the dogs."

Choosing Whether to See the Dog—

Lassie was entering Jerry's room. It looked like Jerry was in the middle of a telephone call. So I asked if he was on the phone, and Jerry replied, "Yes." Then I asked him if he wanted us to come back later, but he loudly proclaimed, "NO!" So Lassie and I turned around, telling Jerry, "Have a nice day," as we started to leave. Jerry exclaimed, "Wait! Where are you going?" I replied, "Oh, I thought you didn't want to see

Lassie today." Jerry said, "I don't want to see her later. I want to see her NOW, even if I am on the phone!"

Support to the Family When Needed—

Louise was close to death, surrounded by six loving family members, some of whom had seen several of the therapy dogs at the VA before. Although we had been advised by staff to leave people alone in such situations, the family requested that Albert come into the room. They wanted Albert on the bed, snuggled next to Louise who had been non-responsive for a few hours.

Albert rested next to Louise. Louise raised her left arm. She wrapped her finger around Albert's front right leg, and her lips started moving as if she was talking to Albert. The family was so pleased at this precious moment of Albert bringing end-of-life joy to Louise.

Opens Patient Up—

We were asked to visit one patient who rarely leaves his room and won't participate in activities. But once he sees Lady, he brightens up and can't stop talking about the dogs. He even comes out into the hallway now and looks at the bulletin board with the dogs' photos on it, including one of Lady catching a disc in midair.

Sharing Special Time—

Jacob often sat outside in his wheelchair. He was always so happy to see Gunther. Gunther would sit right next to his chair, and they would silently share some quality time together, as Jacob petted Gunther and talked to him.

Not the Usual Room—

Betty and Norma, both avid therapy dog lovers, had shared a room for many months. Betty had passed away, and Norma was moved to another room. One day, when I took Lawrence to the VA, he made his usual "pull" down the hallway to the room that Betty and Norma had been in. I was skipping past that room, knowing it was empty now. But Lawrence wanted to check it out. He entered the room and spent about two minutes looking and sniffing, searching for his good friends. He later found Norma in a nearby room. I hope Lawrence knows that Betty went to Heaven.

Veterans Want the Same Service—

A group of four veterans were sitting in the hallway. They saw one of the nurses scratching the therapy dog's head and rubbing its back. One of the veterans said, "Why don't you do that to me? I'm a better looking dog than he is!"

Denomination of Therapy Dogs—

We were waiting for the elevator when Louis came around the corner in a wheelchair and asked if we could push him to the religious ceremony. I said, "Sure. That's where we're going now." I pushed him into the elevator, and Lawrence stood at the left side of his wheelchair. I leaned over and said, "This is Saint Lawrence [a name one of the Protestant chaplains called Lawrence once]. The veteran said, "I'm Protestant, not Catholic!"

Telling His Neighbors About the Dogs—

A couple from the neighborhood where Fred used to live comes out to the VA once or twice a month. They would visit with Fred and update him on the neighborhood news. One day the couple asked Fred, "What do you like most about the VA?" Fred instantly replied, "I love it when the dogs come in!"

Can't Resist the Dogs—

Charlie, a small Terrier mix, and Lawrence were strolling around the Community Living Center. They entered one room with two patients. The one near the window rolled over, saw the dogs, and pulled the blankets over his head. The other man, Joel, said, "I don't want to see any dogs!" Lawrence immediately sat down near the foot of his bed, and, with those irresistible Lab eyes, made Joel change his mind quickly. Joel reached out for Lawrence, who came up next to his bed for some welcomed petting. Charlie came closer to the bed. Suddenly, Joel invited Charlie up to his bed and started playing with Charlie while Lawrence stood by waiting for his turn for more petting. It seems like Joel really did want to see the dogs and the dogs knew that.

A Howling Good Time—

Klaus can be very vocal at times and often makes weird grumbling roars which can sound very intimidating to people who do not know him, but he only makes his unique happy sounds after he feels comfortable with someone. We need to discourage the therapy dogs from making noise at the VA. We don't want any loud barking without a really good reason. But Klaus found a way around this. When he has something to say, which is most of the time, he lets out soft howls. These make the veterans howl with laughter, even thought they aren't sure what Klaus is trying to tell them. A few veterans who have heard Klaus "talk," love it, and some tell him do it again and again. They ask me to "make him do it again," hoping they will understand him if he repeats himself. I think all Klaus wants to do is to be sure the veterans have a howling good time when he's there.

Need Some Rest—

Thunder had come back from a busy weekend camping in the mountains and romping in the woods. He was very tired when he arrived for work Monday morning. Thunder entered Rich's room, and Rich noticed immediately how tired Thunder looked. Rich took the pillow off his bed and put it on the floor. With no coaxing, Thunder, a very large dog, settled comfortably on the pillow and closed his eyes. Rich and I were talking for a while about the camping trip. Rich looked down at Thunder and asked him how he was doing. Thunder opened one eye and gave Rich a look as if so say, "Leave me alone! I'm sleeping now."

Controlling the Shaking—

Maggie gently came up to Wayne's outstretched hand. Wayne's hand was shaking uncontrollably. Wayne rested his hand on Maggie's head. Suddenly the shaking stopped, as Wayne gently petted Maggie's head while Maggie looked at Wayne with her adoring eyes.

Crowded Elevator—

Staff members were encouraging Bart to go downstairs and hear the music. He told them he would if they could find someone to wheel him downstairs. Two of us were there with Albert and Lawrence that afternoon, and we offered to wheel Bart downstairs. Bart said, "Okay. If they have the dogs, I trust them." All of us, three people (one in a wheelchair) and two dogs, entered the elevator. When the door started to close, Lawrence's tail wasn't completely in. Bart pointed out that the door was closing on Lawrence's tail and added, "That would be disrespectful!"

Visit So Special—

I went into Vernon's room on a Sunday afternoon. His ex-wife was there visiting because Vernon had not been doing well, and it seemed like the end could be near. He appeared very weak and uncomfortable. I lifted Zito up to see Vernon. He smiled at Zito and tried to pet him. I talked to Vernon and told him that when he gets to Heaven not to forget that he is supposed to look up my husband. Vernon said he would tell my husband that he knew me. Vernon smiled and then closed his eyes in discomfort.

Vernon's ex-wife followed me out of the room, gave me a hug, and told me that I had really made his day and that Vernon had valued my visit. She said that Vernon knew the end was near, but that he was so happy that we had come to see him. Vernon had always liked Alfie and Zito very much and called them "Baby" and "Sweetie."

Art Stroll—

In 2009, Elsa and I attended the Art Stroll in Downtown Livermore. Our friend and VA volunteer, Bud Donaldson, was setting up an area to display and showcase artwork from the art classes at the VA. I was so touched to see the artwork, with paintings of some of our dogs proudly displayed. It was so interesting to see another side of the men and women we meet in our therapy dog rounds. There were some really nice pieces. I bought two postcards that just "spoke" to me. When I see the painter on our visits, I always remember those post cards, and I am amazed at his creative output, despite his physical challenges.

Family Invites Therapy Dog to Funeral—

Schnoz had visited Phil often, and they had become good buddies. But it wasn't until Phil passed away and a member of his family called me that I learned how special Schnoz was for Phil. They said that Phil had often told them about Schnoz and how special he was to him and how much he enjoyed visits from Schnoz. They wanted Schnoz to be at his funeral. Of course we went. And the family members got to visit the therapy dog that had provided so many special moments for Phil in the last weeks of his life.

Therapy Dog Awards Ceremony Means So Much—

It was a week before Christmas, and we were working on plans for the annual therapy dog awards ceremony. Roy was talking about his upcoming schedule and seeing family members. I said that it is so nice to see family at the holidays. Roy said, "I'm talking about the show, the awards day for the dogs. Christmas is nothing!"

Irresistible—

Buddy K, a friendly French Bulldog, was a big hit on his first day at the VA. As he walked past Doug in the hallway, Doug said, "Hey. You want to sell him?"

Playing Hard To Get—

Albert arrived on a sunny Sunday afternoon to visit some of his best friends. Three veterans were outside on the walkway area enjoying the fresh air and sunshine. Albert went up to them and stood in the area between all of them. As Keith reached out to pet him, Albert stepped back a little. I said, "Albert is playing hard to get." Keith replied, "That's okay. He should play hard to get. He is so beautiful."

Where Are You Going?—

Lawrence was sitting in front of Ken, enjoying the scratching of his head and shoulders. Ken was talking with me about the upcoming therapy dog ceremony at which Lawrence would receive his 750-hour pin and be promoted to "Captain." Lawrence was getting tired, as he had already worked over two hours that afternoon. He gradually slid down, under Ken's bed. Ken said, "Hey. Where are you going? Can't we talk this over?" Lawrence slowly came back out to accept Ken's thanks for all Lawrence had done for him and others at the VA.

The Entry of the Giant—

One Saturday, I was with Pat Wheeler as she was breaking in a new dog team. She told me the new dog was going to be big. Little did I know how big she really meant. Pat and I gathered out front to greet the new handler team. Up walks Dan Schack with his large Bernese Mountain Dog named Rio, now nicknamed "Rio Grande!" Elsa and I started our rounds, being followed by Rio. Rio was a big hit. Residents started coming out of their rooms to make sure they caught a glimpse of the huge dog. Up until Rio arrived, Thunder was the largest dog in our team. The men were all smiling and laughing that Rio was taller than they were in their wheelchairs. The entire floor was abuzz talking about how much he weighed, how much he might eat, and how much poop a dog like that makes. I knew this was going to be a very popular dog!

Supporting Dogs—

One veteran who had been at the VA for about a year said he was so taken with the therapy dogs, he wanted to do something to help dogs. Now he makes monthly donations to the ASPCA.

Special Aroma—

Buddy K and Lawrence walked up to Jeff, a new patient. They sniffed him. I said, "Don't worry about that. They are getting to know you and you have a special smell." Jeff replies, "Guess I'd better take a shower." Then he began meeting the two dogs. They really didn't care how Jeff smelled. They just wanted to have a way to remember him next time.

Reminder of Another Dog—

Shane loves it when Alfie and Zito come into his room. He especially enjoys seeing Zito because Zito reminds him of a Cocker Spaniel he had when he was a child. Shane was sitting in his wheelchair next to his bed. I placed Zito on this bed to he could reach him easily. He rubbed Zito's soft ears with his weaker hand. He said, "This is a nice workout for my fingers."

I showed him the photos of Alfie and Zito on the bookmark. Shane said, "I love these pictures. Please put them up there [on the bulletin board in his room] for me."

Steady Improvement—

Darryl was being visited by his daughter and her dog. A nurse came to me and said that Darryl had requested to see Lady because she is his favorite dog. We visit Darryl regularly, and he has been improving every week, probably in part due to Lady's loving.

Mutual Pleasure—

Albert pranced from the parking lot to the outdoor patio area where Gordon was waiting for him. Gordon started scratching Albert on his lower back near his tail. Albert had made it very clear to Gordon in the past that he loved being scratched there. With Albert's tail going a mile a minute, Gordon said, "That feels good." I asked Gordon, "To you or to the dog?" Gordon replied, "Oh, it makes me feel good that the dog feels good."

Big Foot—

Rio's second visit to the VA was for the Therapy Dog Awards Ceremony where he would be introduced to people and receive his "Petting Officer" pin. After the ceremony, Frank came over to meet Rio. Frank stood up from his wheelchair and Rio stood next to him. Frank looked down, and then up to say, "Looks like Rio and I take the same size shoe."

More than a Couple Words—

Earl was asked to present the award rank and hour pins to Belle, one of the dogs receiving awards at the Therapy Dog Awards Ceremony. Beforehand, Earl had been told he could take up to a minute or two to say what Belle meant to him and why Belle was such a special therapy dog. Earl said, "Only one or two minutes? I need half an hour!"

The day of the ceremony came, and Earl was downstairs early, ready to do his part. When it came time for Belle's awards, Earl told the audience, "I have a couple words to say about Belle. I am going to read them to you." Earl unrolls about four feet of paper and holds it up in front of the audience. He provided a good laugh for all of us, followed by his special words about Belle, a very special dog.

Loves Food—

Adam usually had a bag of Cheetos in the sack on the back of his wheelchair. And Thunder knew that. Adam got a kick out of seeing Thunder start to drool as soon as he saw him down the hallway.

Want to Meet the Big Dog—

Rio and Lawrence headed down the hallway of the second floor of the Community Living Center. It was Rio's third time at the VA, and he was still learning the tricks from Lawrence. There were about six veterans in their wheelchairs in the hallway. Eric bent over slightly, looked at Rio, and said, "Now you're a BIG dog! I want to meet you!" Lawrence didn't like being ignored by Eric, and finally Eric turned to Lawrence and said, "I didn't mean to ignore you, but I'm already acquainted with you."

Taking a Walk—

The nursing staff was working with Jim, trying to get him out of his wheelchair and to encourage him to walk. After walking to one end of the hallway from Jim's room, Jim sat down in his wheelchair for a break. Albert came down the hallway, ready for some back rubbing from Jim, which he promptly received. Then it was time for Jim to get up and walk some more. Albert walked just ahead of Jim, looking back periodically to make sure Jim was still coming.

When they arrived at the other end of the hallway, Jim sat down again to rest and petted Albert some more. Then it was time for Jim to turn around and go back to his room. Albert led the way back. We stopped in the hallway outside Jim's room. Jim thanked Albert profusely. He said, "Usually I have to sit at least three or four times during my walks to rest. Today I sat only twice. Thank you, Albert. You are fabulous! I hope you do this again with me."

Quick Change of Mind—

Although Patrick wasn't really ready to have a dog visit, when we stood in the doorway and Patrick saw what a little dog Simon was, his mind quickly changed. I put Simon in his lap. Patrick couldn't resist him. He petted him gently and then glanced up at me. Patrick said, "What are you looking at? He's my dog now!"

All Are Navy Dogs, But . . .—

All the therapy dogs are Navy dogs since they are all "Petting Officers." They received their various levels of "Petting Officer" pins based on their hours of service at the VA. But sometimes this upsets veterans from other branches of the service. One day, while looking at Lawrence's "Master Chief Petting Officer" pin, Sam said, "I want him to get a Marine Corps pin!"

Later, when Lawrence got a "Captain" pin, veterans in other branches started to claim him since the Navy Captain pin is the same as the Colonel pin in the Army, Air Force, and Marine Corps. When Lawrence became a "Rear Admiral," they wanted to call him a "Major General."

There at a Difficult Time—

Belle had a special connection with veterans' families. It is always a difficult time when one is waiting for a loved one to pass. Interacting with Belle seemed to give them a moment or two of pleasure. They would want to pet Belle, ask questions about her, and always add, "Thank you for bringing Belle here."

Mutual Snorting—

Buddy K, being a French Bulldog, is prone to heavy breathing and snorting. When he entered Ralph's room, I put him on a guest chair so he could be close to Ralph's bed and at the right level. Buddy K started "talking" to Ralph with his usual snorting. Ralph sat up, leaned over, and the two of them were snorting back and forth at each other. I'm not sure what the "conversation" was about, but both Buddy K and Ralph were having a memorable time together.

Tail-Wagging Contest—

One afternoon, Miles and Lawrence went out together with us to the VA. Both thoroughly enjoyed seeing their good buddies at the VA. This was clearly shown by the rapid wagging of their tails. José came by and asked, "Which one is the winner at wagging their tail?"

Helping with the Arm—

Vivian was in a unique special bed that could be lowered to just a few inches from the ground. She had limited use of her hands and arms. When lowered, the bed was just the right height to be eye-level with Klaus. When Klaus entered her room, their eyes locked on each other as he walked closer to her. She would reach out for him with her impaired hands the best she could and start to giggle.

When Klaus reached Vivian's bedside, sometimes her arm was tired. So Klaus would nuzzle his nose under her hand as to help her to put her hand on his head. She could not open her hand all the way and would always say she was worried about poking him in the eye as she petted his head. Klaus never complained about being poked in the eye, and they certainly enjoyed each other's company.

Bringing Back Long-Term Memories—

Albert pranced into George's room, ready to meet and greet him for the first time. George smiled from ear to ear as he saw Albert. We talked for a few minutes. Then George recalled an experience in World War II about a special dog. He said he was in the Army Air Corps, stationed in southern Europe and making flights over North Africa. One of the men in this squadron had a dog, which became like a mascot for all of them.

One day, the dog's owner was sent on a flight mission over North Africa. The dog became somewhat agitated at not having his owner around, despite all the attention he was getting from the rest of us. Then one day, the dog went berserk. He was chasing his tail, not eating, not sleeping, not wanting to interact with us. We couldn't figure out the reason until we learned that his owner's plane had crashed, over one-thousand miles away, just about the same time that the dog went berserk.

George concluded, "How did the dog know what had happened to his owner? Dogs are so special and so smart. I really love seeing dogs like Albert. He reminds me how wonderful dogs are."

Back When I Was a Mailman—

Arthur used to work for the post office, delivering mail. When Alfie comes to visit him, Arthur likes to share his experiences with dogs. Arthur said that dogs used to follow him like a pied piper down the street to the next house. He added, "Some dogs would wait for me to come with the mail."

Visiting with Alfie brings back joyous memories for this former mail carrier. Arthur enjoyed my bringing Alfie so much that he wanted us to spend more time in his room and requested that a guest chair be brought in so we could sit down and stay longer.

Providing Badly Needed Doses of Love—

Floyd was a new patient at the VA, and Lawrence was seeing him for the first time one day. Lawrence came up to Floyd's bed where Floyd could reach him and feel his fur. Of course Lawrence's tail wagged with joy. Floyd was very happy being able to stroke Lawrence's back and rub his ears. It was a wonderful time for both of them.

A couple of months later, we were at the six-month memorial service at the VA where they remember all of the veterans who had passed away in the last six months. Floyd was among them. Lawrence and I were there, as the social workers always want at least one therapy dog at every memorial service to provide badly needed comforting.

At the end of the ceremony, a woman came up to me since I had a dog with me. She described her brother to me and his telling her about a dog who visited him when he first came to this VA facility. I told her that the dog was Lawrence. She was so pleased that Lawrence was there. She said, "I wanted to meet the dog that made my brother so happy in the last days of his life. And now I have."

Always Have Treats for the Dogs—

Marvin always welcomes the therapy dogs into his room with a dog treat in hand. Lady likes to sit, stand up, or do some kind of performance to earn her treat, and, at the same time, make him smile.

Please Wake Me Up When the Dog Arrives—

Often Scott is sleeping during the day and can miss the opportunity to see the therapy dogs. Yesterday, he saw Thunder for the first time, although he had already met some of the other therapy dogs since arriving a week or so ago. He said to me that he told the nurses that, even if he is sleeping, he wants the people with the dogs to stop in and see him.

Miles of Smiles—

Miles always enjoys visiting his friends at the VA. One day, Perry said, "Miles, you'll walk a mile for me. And I like Miles' smiles." Of course, Miles just sat there looking at Perry and grinning from floppy ear to floppy ear.

Meeting the BIG Dog—

Rio was meeting Lee in the hallway for the first time. Rio, a Bernese Mountain Dog, was very large, soft, and fluffy. Lee was petting Rio, extending his arm to reach the full length of Rio's back. One of the nurses came by and said to Lee, "He doesn't want you to pet him. He wants to you ride him!" That gave Lee a good chuckle and he continued stroking Rio's back, and Rio gently let him know how nice it felt.

A Special Opportunity—

The therapy dogs move through the "Petting Officer" ranks (unique to the Navy and Coast Guard), as they "work" more hours at the VA. Once they become "Master Chief Petting Officers," at 500 hours, the next rank is "Captain" for 750 hours and "Rear Admiral" for 1,000 hours. The pins for Navy Captain and Rear Admiral are the same as those for Colonel and Major General in the Air Force, Army, and Marines. So, now that Albert has his Captain pin, Aaron, a U.S. Marine veteran, calls him "Colonel." Aaron exclaims, "The only time I get to pet a Colonel is when Albert is here!!"

Special Talk—

Lassie and I walked up to a man in the hallway who could not talk. Lassie pushed her way up to Myron and snuggled against his leg. Myron looked up at me, with tears in his eyes. He didn't need to be able to speak to talk with Lassie.

Dog Gets Through—

One of the veterans that Klaus and I would visit regularly was Norman, a gray-haired gentleman in his sixties who could walk a little, but used a wheelchair most of the time. After about five visits, Norman and Klaus took a special liking to each other. Norman smoked cigarettes, and, often, when Klaus and I arrived, he was on his way to the patio to smoke a cigarette or on his way back to his room after smoking. I would hand him Klaus's leash, and Klaus would slowly walk in front of him as he moved himself in his wheelchair. It became the routine every time we saw each other in the hallway or in his room or in the smoking area.

Later, the nurses told me that Norman was cognitively disabled and not capable of following simple instructions or completing such tasks. Then it occurred to me that all the staff were so intrigued and impressed with Norman's ability to walk a dog and interface with me as the handler when he could not remember the names of the nursing staff or carry out other simple tasks.

Dog Hair Is Special—

Lawrence, being a Lab, always had a ready supply of dog hair to share with others, no matter how much we brushed him. One morning, he visited Owen who was still in his yellow pajamas. Lawrence affectionately rubbed against Owen's legs, covering his pajamas with dog hair. Owen looked down at his pajamas and exclaimed, "I wear his hair with pride!"

Off on Maternity Leave—

Elsa is not only a visitor to the men and women at the VA, but she is also a working mother. When she returned from being on maternity leave for Guide Dogs, we went out to our first visit with a few photos of her pups. Of course, I am biased and think Elsa's six pups are beautiful, just like their mom. Laura looked at the photos over and over again, petting each photo as a fun gesture. I only wish I could have placed one of those pups on her lap.

We continued on our rounds and went into the TV room. Two gentlemen, who usually don't communicate with other people, were in the TV room watching a movie. I don't think I've ever heard these two men speak. I took the stack of photos over to show off Elsa's beautiful babies. I had silly voices for each pup and a cute story about each personality. One puppy, with a particularly dirty nose from digging, actually got one of the men to laugh out loud! It was the first time I'd ever heard him make a sound. Here he was laughing at my silly dog voices and funny stories.

Need the Dog—

Howard would often be in his bed, sometimes sleeping. He requested that he be awakened whenever Gunther came around, as he was such a "loving dog." There were many occasions when Howard was not feeling well and asked that Gunther be put onto his bed with him. Gunther would snuggle up to him, put his head on Howard's leg, and stay there for as long as Howard would pet him and hug him.

A Special Question—

Shazam and I had been visiting Dennis at the VA each time we went for many, many months. Never once was there ever a word spoken in his room, just the mutual love and admiration for Shazam. One Sunday visit started like all the others, but it ended dramatically different.

Shazam and I had spent time, like we always did, letting Dennis pet and gaze into Shazam's beautiful brown eyes. We made our way to the door, saying our goodbyes. But this time the silence was pierced with a question that came out of nowhere. "What's her name?" I said, "Her name is Shazam." He gave us a gracious smile, and we were out the door to visit the next waiting resident.

That was the first, and only time, I ever heard Dennis say a word to us. I will always remember those words, and I now know just how near and dear Shazam was to this wonderful hero of ours. To this day, in a very special way, Shazam and I were given one of the greatest gifts we have ever received by anyone visiting the VA.

Where's the Dog?—

I arrived one afternoon for a meeting, without my dog. Andy saw me in the lobby and said, "You forgot something." I was loaded up with papers for the meeting, and said, "I hope not. What did I forget?" "Your dog!" Andy replied quickly. They next day I was there with Lawrence. Andy was so glad to see I remembered him this time.

Time to Visit Others—

Luke was lying is his bed, eyes closed, when Miles and I arrived. I knocked on the door and said, "The dog's here." Luke's eyes slowly opened, fixated on Miles who was looking back at Luke. Luke reached out for Miles and petted him. After a few minutes, I said, "Well, we need to go see other people now. Okay?" Luke said, "No, I want you to stay right here." We stayed a little longer before heading out into the hallway and going to the next room.

Climate Control—

Raymond was sitting in his wheelchair when Lawrence and Albert entered his room. Albert turned around and backed up to Raymond, rapidly wagging his tail back and forth. Lawrence put his head between Raymond's knees. Raymond said, "This is great. I am getting cooled off and warmed up at the same time."

Talking Dog—

Thunder likes to introduce himself when he sees someone with a soft, gentle sound. One day, he went into Brent's room. Brent said, "I love to see Thunder. He always talks to me when he's here. In fact, he has told me his life story."

Can't Let You Go Home—

Irene was sitting in her wheelchair in the hallway near the nurses' station as Brooks and I walked by. She reached out to pet Brooks, asking what the dog's name was. I told her "Brooks," and she immediately took to petting and crooning over her. Irene told me she had a dog at home and wanted to keep Brooks. I told her Brooks would love to stay with her, but then no one else would be able to visit with her. After quite a few loving moments, she reluctantly allowed us to continue our visits with other VA residents.

Almost six months later, we were at the annual American Legion Riders (ALR) barbecue when Irene came up to us again. She remembered seeing Brooks and how she wanted Brooks to stay with her and not go home with me. Brooks was much obliged to sit and let Irene once again pet her and give all the love she could give. Apparently Brooks is very special to Irene.

Spoiling the Dog—

Lady was getting her back scratched and ears rubbed. She was obviously thoroughly enjoying this. I asked Walter if he was spoiling my dog? Walter replied, "Yes! And it's my pleasure to spoil her!"

From Pictures to Reality—

Marsha was looking at the bulletin board by the nurses' station that had photos of many of the therapy dogs on it. As we walked around the corner from the elevator, Marsha exclaimed, "There's a real dog! Get over here, Lawrence. I want to touch you." Marsha gave Lawrence lots of nice pets and backstrokes. Lawrence's tail was wagging wildly, as Marsha tried to grab the tail and slow it down, saying, "I don't want his tail to get too tired." As we started to leave and visit other patients, Marsha said, "Lawrence, you and the other dogs make our life worth living."

A Memorable Thanksgiving—

We were the only therapy dog team going to visit on Thanksgiving Day. As I approached the Community Living Center, a few vans were taking veterans to a special dinner provided for them downtown. A few with local families were being picked up for the day or the weekend. I thought, "Wow, there won't be too many folks here to visit with

Miss Elsa." We stayed almost three hours and only talked to about 30 patients that day. I came home learning a lot about fishing, NASCAR, and retirement property in Mexico!

Reflections on the Past—

Miles strolled into Calvin's room. Calvin looked at Miles and then started reminiscing about a dog he used to have. He said, "When I went into the Marines at age 18, I gave my dog to my father who lived on a farm. But just after I left for the Marine Corps, my dog laid down and died." I said, "He really missed you." Calvin replied, "I would have taken him with me if I had known that would happen."

Shoe Polishing—

Lawrence loves to lick shoes. When he does it, I tell the veterans that they are getting a "spit and polish" shine. One morning, while Lawrence was licking Ed's shoe, I said that to Ed. He said, "Have Lawrence send his bill to me. He's doing a great job."

Just Had to Pet the Dog—

One of the most memorable visits we made with our veterans came about when I asked Reggie, "Would you like to pet the dog?" I did not know that he could not speak and that he had limited range of motion with his arms. It became very evident from his eyes that he wanted to pet the dog. As I maneuvered Sailor into position so that Reggie's hand could touch Sailor, he extended his arm and began petting the dog. Just at that moment, a nurse passed by and said, "Wow, that is the first time in two weeks he has moved his arm." I was completely overwhelmed as Sailor and I stood there at his bedside for about five minutes while Reggie grinned and continued to pet the dog, an extremely rewarding moment for all of us.

Taking His Medications—

Two nurses were in Bert's room trying to get him to take his medication. I almost wasn't going to go in right then, but the nurses wanted us to come in to help them get Bert to take his medications. I knew Bert liked Thunder and I wanted to be sure that he took his medications. I took Thunder right up to the side of Bert's bed. The nurses encouraged Bert to take his medications with Thunder being there, which Bert did. We stayed for a few minutes and then left.

I returned to see Bert again before I left the VA that day. When I left his room the first time, the nurse said she thought they were going to lose Bert last Friday night because he had been talking about "going home," but more importantly, about "seeing his mother," who passed away 20 years ago.

Treats for Simon—

Whenever a dog enters Martin's room, he has a treat ready for him. He fetches it from the dog treat bag, always there on his table, places it in his open hand, and hangs his hand over the side of the bed after making sure the dog is sitting quietly. But the treats were somewhat large for Simon. So Martin carefully broke one treat into four pieces. I said, "Simon doesn't usually take treats." But this time there was no hesitation. Simon apparently realized that Martin's hand was a well-known place for yummy treats for good therapy dogs. He quickly ate the first piece, his tail wagging like a fan. Simon finished all four pieces of the treat from Martin. I am sure they are both looking forward to the next time they are together.

Outside or Inside—

Albert came into Wally's room and immediately was looking out the window. His tail was wagging, his back wiggling back and forth, his ears up, and his eyes focused on something. Wally asked Albert, "Want to go outside today?" Wally wasn't sure what Albert was seeing, but he sure knew that Albert saw something. A couple of moments later, Albert's attention turned to Wally for some mutual admiration. Albert would much rather be with Wally than looking at a squirrel or whatever he saw.

Love the Dogs—

Zachary was bedridden and usually quite sad. But Zachary was always so happy to see Gunther, and Gunther was happy to see him. Whenever Zachary saw him, he would say, "I love dogs. I love this dog!"

Tired on a Hot Day—

With his thick, black coat and the 100-degree-plus temperatures outside, Lawrence was getting tired during his visits to veterans at the Community Living Center. Oliver saw Lawrence lying down on the floor in the hallway near the nurses' station. Lawrence often plopped down on the floor to rest and to cool off. Oliver said to Lawrence, "When you got no place to sleep, come see me. I'll let you sleep in my room. I miss my dog and would like to have you with me." Lawrence seemed to appreciate the invitation.

Those Blue Eyes—

Something Klaus has, that none of the other dogs at the VA has, are beautiful crystal blue eyes. They are always sparkling, and we have found that Klaus' eyes are a great way to brighten up anyone's day. When he enters a veteran's room, it is almost as though a light is turned on. And he comes with so much loving and comforting for the veterans, which really pours out when they start to pet him.

Losing a Special Friend—

At a recent visit, we learned that one of Belle's special friends had passed away. It was a comfort to us to know that his suffering was over and a comfort to the family that their loved one was not alone. He always waited for us on our Friday visits. We were touched by this veteran. He once told us, "You can never do enough for a veteran." We agree. We will never forget his unique personality, which was a mix of humor and sarcasm.

As it became clear that his health was failing rapidly, we were preparing for an extended vacation and would not see him for a couple of months. He always reminded us that he waited for Fridays so that he could see his beloved Belle. Upon our return, he was very weak and in decline. We had several good visits with him in the two weeks prior to his passing. We were honored to be with his family and friends on that special Friday before he passed away. He will always be remembered as a great person and a great American.

Special Time Together—

I was walking through the hallway with Simon when Kurt asked if Simon could sit in his lap. As Kurt sat in his wheelchair with Simon on his lap, Klaus came around the corner with his handler, Tom. Klaus saw Simon and walked right up, putting his head on Kurt's knees. Kurt has only minimal mobility in one hand, due to a stroke. But he found just enough strength to pet Klaus on the snout when holding his other hand around Simon.

Kurt smiled from ear to ear and bent down toward Klaus' nose, trying not to squish Simon. He whispered to Klaus, "You're a good boy." Klaus kept his head perfectly still on Kurt's lap as his tail whipped back and forth. We just stood back and let the three of them have their special time together.

Wants Dog to Stay—

One of the hardest parts of being a therapy dog handler is leaving a patient when he doesn't want the dog to go. But we need to share our dogs with all the patients at the VA who want to see them, and that is almost all of them.

One afternoon, Linda was more alert than usual. I took Lassie in to see her. She had owned Shelties and Collies, and loved Lassie. After about 15 minutes, I told Linda we had to go now and see some other patients. We quietly left the room, but all the way down the hallway, I heard Linda calling, "Lassie, come home." We did stop by after seeing all the other patients on that floor, but Linda was peacefully napping now, maybe dreaming about Lassie.

Both Husband and Wife Love Seeing the Dog—

Chester had suffered from a stroke, and Mitsy and I often spent time with him. His wife was always there with him, and she is delightful. They loved seeing Mitsy come to visit and wanted her on the bed with Chester so he could pet her. He loved to hug and pet her. His wife says he enjoyed it when Mitsy came to visit because it reminded him of the small dogs his daughter has at home, and, since she cannot bring her dog in, he wanted to pet Mitsy. They both were so thankful for the visits and blessed Mitsy and me for coming.

Can't Miss the Dog's Birthday—

As we entered Hugh's room, he was lying down on his bed. He said he didn't want to see Lawrence that day because he was too tired. I said, "But it's Lawrence's birthday and he is here for back scratches." Hugh quickly sat up and started rubbing Lawrence's back. Then he talked about dogs he had when he was younger. It was a special day for both of them.

Love the Bookmarks—

Charles had been at the VA for three weeks, but had not yet received a set of the bookmarks yet with the dogs' photos on them. When I offered the set to him, he was ecstatic. He said, "I love to read and my books are getting all messed up by the rubber bands I use. These are much better!"

He immediately replaced the rubber band on the book he was reading with these bookmarks. And he enjoyed looking at the photos of the dogs and trying to recall which ones he had met so far.

Bringing Out a Smile—

James' son came to me and asked if we would visit his dad. Lady sat in a chair next to James' bed and brought a faint smile to his face. Those are the visits I like, the special requests. Lady enjoys lighting up many rooms when a patient has family members present.

Maggie in Song—

Ben is one of the residents that Maggie and I like a lot and spend time talking to. He had his wife there that day. It was the first time we met her. She asked what my dog's name was, and I told her, "Maggie." She said, "Oh, that is a lovely Irish song." I told her I knew that, and, in fact, Maggie was named after that song. I added that, when I was on my way to Mexico, I was listening to an Irish CD that I had and when that song came on (it is so beautiful), I decided to call my new dog "Maggie." We left and went on to visit other veterans.

A couple of hours later, Maggie and I were getting ready to leave and decided to stop in and say goodbye to Ben. His wife was still there and said, "Oh, I am so glad you came back." She reached over to a CD player, hit a button, and the song "Maggie" started playing. Ben smiled and I started singing. Maggie stared at the CD player like she knew that was her song. Ben's wife said she ran down to her car and found the CD when we left the first time. She said she was so glad we came back to hear the song, "Maggie."

A Christmas Remembrance—

I am a teacher and my students know that I go to the VA with my dogs to visit our veterans. So, at Christmas time, two of my fourth graders made a Christmas tree wall decoration for Henry. I had told them how interested he was in my class of students. That tree stayed on his wall in plain view for him through December and January. He said that he received many compliments on the tree. I brought him pictures of the boy and girl who made the tree for him. He put the pictures on the wall beside the tree. He sent a thank-you note to my students. He really valued that tree and the connection that he had made with the real world. Of course it is because I visit with my dogs that Henry got to know me and became connected with my students. Henry is a real dog lover and always misses his own dog, so he really appreciates the therapy dogs' visits with him.

Nurses Love the Dog—

Staff particularly favor Buddy G because he is so small and can be easily passed from nurse to nurse. They smile and say what a beautiful and nice dog he is. Many nurses want to take him home.

Mr. Handsome—

All of the men and women at the VA are special. After the Therapy Dog Awards Ceremony in January 2010, one of the men had pictures taken by a family member. When we went in for a visit, he pulled out his stack of photographs. He said, "Look at that handsome dude," pointing to a photo of himself at the ceremony. The name stuck, and after that Elsa and I always referred to him as Mr. Handsome.

A Big Smile Moment—

While visiting the VA, Maggie and I saw, Claude, a new patient. We asked if he wanted to see Maggie, but he seemed lost in his thoughts. I put Maggie's paw on the edge of his bed, and he reluctantly petted her. Maggie suddenly looked into his face and got right next to his bed. She nuzzled next to him, putting her head next to his chest. An enormous smile appeared on Claude's face, and Maggie closed her eyes, relaxing at her success in getting him to respond to her. Claude wanted us to stay for a while more, and we did, for about 15 minutes.

A Challenging Day—

Roger was having a challenging day and was hard for the staff to manage. Lady entered Roger's room, and he immediately calmed down. There were visitors in his room at the time. One of them showed me a picture on her iPhone of a dog they had at home with facial features similar to Lady's.

Inviting the Dog into His Room—

Justin was lying in his bed, looking toward the door to the hallway, when he saw Rivers walk by. I saw him stretch his hand out, as if to be calling Rivers into his room. Although Justin could talk, he could not talk loudly enough to call Rivers into his room and he didn't know Rivers' name yet, as this was their first meeting. But we got the message and Rivers walked right up to the side of his bed. Justin really enjoyed petting Rivers and asked to have his picture taken with her so he could see her when she wasn't at the VA.

Baseball Game Versus Dog—

Daniel was busy watching a baseball game when we peeked around the corner and knocked on his door. Simon was peering at Daniel through the hair dangling from his forehead. Simon won out quickly over baseball. He curled up in Daniel's lap like a cat, and Daniel started "purring" like a cat, so pleased at his newly-found lap buddy. Daniel commented to me on the few gray hairs on Simon. I said, "Well, he is 12-years old, and, when his hair grows out, it is much grayer." Daniel promptly suggested we try "Just for Men" on Simon. He continued stroking Simon for a few more minutes before returning to the baseball game.

Last Moments—

Lady and I were asked to visit a room in hospice. Warren was unresponsive and was surrounded by family members. One of his family members, Ruth, asked if I could bring Lady over to him. She then put Warren's hand on Lady's head, and Warren woke up. He petted her, smiled, and went back to sleep. I ran into Ruth later. She said he woke up and asked what the dog's name was, and then he went back to sleep. I believe he passed away a short time later.

Loves to Cuddle—

Herb loves to cuddle Alfie and has had several wonderful times snuggling with him. Herb's roommate had a situation that required immediate cleanup by staff. I looked out the door of his room for a nurse in the hallway so I could report it. Herb wanted Alfie to stay with him while staff cleaned up the other part of the room. Herb cuddled Alfie, hugged him close, and talked all the time about how much he liked Alfie, and how Alfie liked him too. He did not want to let Alfie go. It was very apparent that Alfie was fulfilling a need for Herb. Alfie was the object of Herb's sentiment at the time, and his spirit seemed to improve from our visit. The look on Alfie's face indicated that he was bonding with Herb and enjoying the love that he was receiving.

Need to Keep a Memory of This—

As an outpatient, Noah was waiting at the counter to make an appointment. He saw Lawrence interacting with a staff member and wanted to meet Lawrence. He played with Lawrence, a big smile on his face. Noah was having a joyful time. He then turned to his wife and asked her to take a photo of him and Lawrence with her cell phone. "I don't want to forget today," said Noah. Hopefully, neither Noah nor his wife will forget their meeting with Lawrence.

Quick Wake-Up—

I came to the doorway of Grant's room. Although he appeared to be asleep, I knocked on the door and said, "Zito is here to see you." Grant woke up quickly and asked me to set Zito next to him on the bed. I did that and Grant put his head right next to Zito. Grant said, "Are you a good pup today, Zito?" They enjoyed a few moments of special time together.

There for Family Too—

Some days it's not about the patients. Some days, it's all about the family and friends of the patients. As the VA was getting ready for an upcoming holiday weekend, you could feel the excitement in the air. A barbecue with all the fixings was underway. It was a few days before the Fourth of July. Most of the patients were downstairs listening to the wonderful guitar music and singers that come to play on Friday afternoons. But up in the rooms, there were family members, sitting while their loved ones slept. That day, I spent more time with the family members who wanted a dog visit so they could take a short break, or have something different to talk about for a few minutes. I asked one daughter if her dad wanted to see the dog and she said, "No, he is too ill. But I sure would." She put her arms around Elsa's neck for a few seconds and then said, "Thank you," and went back into her father's room.

Which Branch of the Service—

Buddy K is a Navy dog, since he is a "Petting Officer" with our therapy dog crew. However, since he is a French Bulldog, the Marine Corps veterans want to claim him as a fellow Marine Corps member. Buddy K was standing on a chair in the recreation room next to Brian, a Marine Corps veteran, who was sitting in his wheelchair. Brian told a Navy veteran in the room that the Marine Corps laid claims to Buddy K since Bulldogs are the toughest. They started arguing over which branch of the service Buddy K was in. As they were arguing, a VA police officer entered the room and said, "Hey, Buddy looks like both of you." They laughed and settled down right away, both petting Buddy K on his head and stroking his back.

There to Snuggle When Needed—

Edgar had just woken up and was very sad and crying. Alfie snuggled up to Edgar. This helped him to feel better, and he stopped crying. I told him that Alfie loved him and that he should think about Alfie instead of the other sad thoughts. We spent a longer time in his room than we usually do because the need was apparent. A loving snuggle from a warm little dog brought some distraction from Edgar's plight and some measure of comfort. I was glad Alfie was there when Edgar needed him so badly.

Job Benefits of a Therapy Dog—

Sometimes staff members give treats to the therapy dogs at the end of one of the hallways. Rio was anxious to get to that location. After getting a treat, he wanted more. He is a large dog, but one treat was all he should get. Ward was nearby in that hallway. He saw that Rio needed to be distracted from the "place of treats." Ward called Rio over to him, and Rio went right to him. Rio forgot all about the treats (or at least seemed to) as soon as Ward started petting his head and stroking his back.

Tight Quarters—

Lawrence and Albert came by to visit Russ. He was in his room on his motorized scooter with his back to the door. But when we knocked and told him Lawrence and Albert were here to see him, he immediately said he wanted to see the dogs. He started to spin his scooter around, finding it a challenge with the table and the walker in the way. We said, "Good thing you don't have a leash." Russ looked around, envisioning the tangle he would be in if he did have a leash. But soon Russ had spun around and was getting love on both sides from Lawrence and Albert, who found space in Russ' cozy quarters that afternoon.

Is This a Therapy Dog?—

"Is this a dog therapy dog?" asked Elaine, who was visiting her father. I said, "Yes, this is Lawrence." "Can you help with my father? He is outside sitting on the patio and they need to bring him inside and they are having trouble. He liked Alfie, the little dog. Lawrence might be able to help," Elaine said. I looked to Pat Wheeler for advice. She said to me, "Take Lawrence outside. See what you can do. Tell him that Lawrence wants him to come inside with him. Ask him if he'll come in with Lawrence." I said, "Okay," and started walking outside with Lawrence to the patio. Elaine said, "Thank you."

I walked outside to Mel, who was sitting in a wheelchair wearing a Navy baseball-style cap turned backwards. A nurse wearing a medium-blue scrub suit was sitting on the bench next to Mel. I said, "Hi, this is Lawrence." "Hi," the nurse said, but she was obviously focused on Mel. I observed for a few minutes. Mel was taking off his wheelchair seatbelt and trying to hand it to the nurse saying, "Put this over there," while looking and motioning across the patio. "I don't want it!" Mel exclaimed. The nurse, after a couple of attempts, buckled the seatbelt, only for Mel to unbuckle the seatbelt, and the process began again.

Mel started leaning forward in his wheelchair and looked on the ground to his right. He said, "I am looking for a brass nut." The nurse pulled out a bag of shelled sunflower seeds and proceeded to offer some to Mel. "That's not a nut!" Mel growled. "The kind of nut that attaches to a bolt?" I asked. "Ohhhh," the nurse said, as she put her bag of sunflower seeds away. Mel said, "Yes, and you can attach it to a flange . . . and if I were to put my mark on it, I will have won the argument." I thought to myself, "What argument?" and asked Mel, "Do you like Lawrence, the dog? Lawrence likes to be petted." I began to pet Lawrence. "Joey, the dog?" Mel asked. I said, "Lawrence, the dog," as I attempted to correct Mel. "Bobby, the dog?" Mel asked.

Taking a different approach, I said, "Do you like the dog? He came out here to see you." Mel reached to pet Lawrence on his head and said, "Yes, he's okay." "Would you like to come inside with Lawrence?" I asked Mel. He grunted, "No." I said, "Lawrence told me he wants you to come inside with him. Will you follow Lawrence inside?" "Okay," Mel said.

By this time, the nurse was standing up from the bench. I said to the nurse, referring to Mel, "How do you want to do this? Do you want to back him in?" The nurse replied, "That's probably the only way we can do this." The nurse began to back the wheelchair towards the door to the building, and I started walking Lawrence as close in front Mel's wheelchair as Lawrence could get so Mel could keep seeing Lawrence while the nurse backed him into the building. As the nurse took Mel through the doorway, Mel tried to take Lawrence's leash from me and commanded, "Give him to me!" "I can't let you take him. I'm sorry," I told Mel. "Oh, okay," Mel said begrudgingly.

The nurse backed Mel all the way down the hall to the other end of the building and into his room. Lawrence and I followed closely behind. Mel was focused on Lawrence and was quiet the rest of the way to his room. When we arrived at Mel's room, Mel growled, "I need to use the men's room." I think he realized that he had been tricked into coming in and he was making a scene about using the men's room as his way of expressing his frustration. The nurse said, "Ok, are you ready to use the restroom?" "Yes," Mel said. "Thank you," the nurse said to Lawrence and me. We left Mel and the nurse in his room and went to other end of the building to visit more veterans.

Checking on Moustaches—

Alan and Schnoz both have gray moustaches. Each time Schnoz visits Alan, he compares their moustaches—length, color, and texture. This activity makes Alan look forward to each of Schnoz's visits. Alan told another handler that he had seen Schnoz and that their beards were the same length, but that Schnoz's was grayer now.

Wagging the Tongue Instead of the Tail—

When dogs are happy, most are known for wagging their tails. But Zito wags his tongue. He loves throwing kisses to people. He wants me to hold him as close as possible to their faces. I guess that is because he wants to be sure the kisses arrive quickly so they know how much he loves them.

Getting a Patient Out to the Barbecue—

It was a beautiful and pleasant summer day, perfect for a barbecue picnic at the Community Living Center. Lady was asked to attend so she could do her disc-catching demonstration. While others were eating, Lady and I went through the hallways trying to encourage reluctant residents to come to the barbecue. Lady actually convinced a patient, who has never wanted to participate in anything, to come outside and join in the picnic. I pushed the wheelchair while Kathleen held the end of Lady's leash. Lady literally pulled Kathleen down the hall and outside.

We had many good visits with patients and their families. We then put on the disc-catching demonstration for the residents and their family and friends who were there. Kathleen had a great time and was smiling the rest of the day, as were we.

Charming the Staff Too—

Belle, it seemed, could charm almost anyone at the VA, and even the doctors and nursing staff were not immune. One of the staff members would always stop what she was doing so she could pet Belle. She would say that visiting with Belle always lowered her blood pressure. Some of the nursing staff would also spend a minute or two visiting with Belle. They would all say that they looked forward to Fridays because they knew that they would see Belle.

Rescuing Dogs—

Lester loved to spend time with Mitsy. When he found out I had adopted her, he said he rescued his dog too and that she was the best friend he had. She was always happy to see him and to greet him with her wagging tail. Lester said he would rescue all the dogs if he could.

Time with Family Too—

Clyde was not responding. However, Lady had a good visit with the family, including three small children. We then went into the hallway where she entertained the children and their parents, including one little boy who was afraid of dogs, but ended up bonding with Lady. Hopefully, he is no longer afraid of dogs.

Thanks from the Sister—

I was walking down the stairs with Lawrence after our group session when a woman was on her way up the stairs. As we approached each other, she recognized Lawrence by his therapy dog vest with his name on it. She seemed very happy and said, "So this is Lawrence? I know Lawrence. My brother goes to your group and talks about Lawrence. He is doing much better now because of Lawrence." I replied, "This is Lawrence. We all enjoy having Lawrence in our group."

I proceeded down the stairs with Lawrence and toward the Community Living Center so Lawrence and I could visit with some of the residents. I know Lawrence means a lot to them too.

What Is It?—

Wade was coming out of his room and looking down the hallway. He saw something large and hairy approaching, and thought it was a bear. He knew about all the wildlife around the VA—deer, wild turkeys, etc. But Wade didn't expect to see a bear. Yet this animal kept approaching him. He was very relieved when he realized it was Rio, a large and gentle Bernese Mountain Dog, on his way to deliver love.

Bringing Good Luck—

Upon our arrival on Tuesday afternoons, Alfie and Zito walk into the main dining room where residents are playing card games. The two dogs walk around the table, encouraging the veterans to scratch their backs. This gives the veterans a momentary stretch for their arms before they return to the card game. Hopefully, the dogs bring them good luck.

Too Late—

A group of nursing students were heading out to the parking lot after their day at the CLC just as I was arriving with my dog. One exclaimed, "Oh no! We're leaving too early. The dog is just coming."

Love at First Sight—

Lady was meeting a new patient one afternoon. It was love at first sight. Lady has no tail, but she was wagging her ears in delight. A short while later, we were in the hallway on our way to see other veterans when Lady's new friend signaled her to come back into his room. So we returned to his room. He wanted to know if Lady had a boyfriend. He said he was hoping she would say no, because he loved Lady so much.

Knowing What to Do—

Belle has a special talent for knowing how to respond to the individuals that she visits. Jules loved to have Belle on his bed, and Belle would promptly relax and go to sleep next to him. When Belle would arrive for a visit, Jules would smile and say, "Here's my special pain medicine." Even when Jules was not feeling well, he always wanted to have Belle next to him. When it was time to leave, Jules always said, "Come back soon!"

Missed Rio—

Rio and I walked into Trevor's room. Trevor was so happy that Rio was actually there that day. He pulled out the "baseball-like" card, which I had given him a few weeks ago, from his top drawer. It had Rio's picture on the front and information about Rio on the back. Trevor said, "I look at that card every day and wonder when the real Rio will be here again." That certainly made me aware of how important Rio was to the veterans.

Got Fleas?—

As Albert and I were walking down the hallway, Wendell stopped us. Sitting in his wheelchair, he told me, "I got fleas from Albert last time you were here. Don't you use flea powder on him?" I explained that I use another product for flea prevention on Albert and that he has no fleas. Wendell said, "Well, my hair was full of fleas last week just after Albert left." Wendell took his hat off and rubbed his bald head, with not a hair on it. "See, it is still full of fleas." Wendell then let out a hardy laugh and gave us a good chuckle.

Just What Is Needed—

Stanley was working out on the treadmill one morning with Lawrence watching him. The staff member commented, "Your endurance is a lot better today." Stanley said, "Yeh. Lawrence is an inspiration to me." The staff member added, "And your cheerleader." Wagging his tail happily, Lawrence stood there attentively watching Stanley's feet moving on the treadmill.

At the Barbecue—

VA staff requested that Lady attend the family barbecue in August to do her Frisbee ® catching. Although she wasn't up to doing it at this picnic, she visited family members, many of whom remarked that they had already heard about Lady. She visited people and shook "paws" with them. And she helped two young twin boys overcome their fear of dogs. What a busy day for her.

Dogs Have Good Noses—

Zito walked up to Rob and sniffed his leg. Rob said, "Zito probably recognizes my smell. But I haven't taken a shower today. Hope that's okay." Rob continued talking about what a wonderful sense of smell dogs have and how he has read about their use in tracking and searching.

A Lab's Face—

It was a beautiful October Sunday when I accompanied Pat and Lawrence, the Livermore Lab, to the Livermore VA. The sun was shining, there was a gentle, pleasant breeze, and the VA grounds were populated with humans, deer, and wild turkeys. And then there was Lawrence; he was here to work. After visiting in numerous rooms, Lawrence and Pat spied some veterans sitting outside in the sun, and so they went outside to visit.

We were sitting with Shawn, who greeted Lawrence with a term of endearment. "Hey, buddy—hey, my buddy—how's my guy doing today?" Shawn sat idly, patting Lawrence and telling us stories of other dogs he has known, including his daughter's dog and dogs from his youth. As we sat there chatting, Nick approached and joined us. Nick was interested in discussing Lawrence's pedigree, and he made observations about Lawrence's graying muzzle and calm, sweet manner.

At this point, Lawrence had his head tucked under my chair and his body out for a good back scratching, his tail wagging happily. Nick noted that, to him, Lawrence didn't look like a Lab. When I asked why, he said, "Well, his face doesn't look like a Lab's face." Shawn pointed to Lawrence's wagging tail and quipped, "Well, that's not his face you're looking at there!" A good laugh was had by all, and Lawrence just continued to wag his tail, happy to be bringing joy to all of us.

First Meeting—

Thunder and I were walking in the hallway on the first floor, and met Barney for the first time. I told him, "This is Thunder." His immediate response was, "I have a dog named Thunder also." At first, I thought he was just repeating what I said. So I asked him, "You said you also have a dog named Thunder?" His response was, "Yes." I then asked him how he came to name his dog, Thunder. He said that he got him on a day when there was a lot of thunder. My mouth dropped open, and I said, "That is why I named my dog Thunder, because we found him the day after a huge thunder and lightening storm here in the valley." Barney said his dog was a six-year-old German Shepherd. His story sure made my day.

Camouflaged Dog—

One of Alfie's favorite things to do at the VA is snuggling, whether next to someone in bed or on a lap. Steve was sitting in the hall outside his room. He was wearing all tan-colored clothing. And Alfie is a cream-colored Cockapoo. Alfie was curled up on Steve's lap and blended right in.

We chatted with Steve about upcoming football games, holiday activities, and other topics. When we looked down at Steve's lap, Alfie was totally zonked out. I lifted one of his front legs and it was limp. Alfie was not responding to our saying his name or moving his leg. Steve kept petting him. Alfie was sound asleep.

One of the staff members walked by and looked at Alfie, so comfortable on Steve's lap, though he admitted that he didn't notice Alfie at first because he blended in with Steve's clothing. Alfie was snuggled so tightly up against Steve that the staff member said, "We are going to have to surgically remove Alfie from your lap, Steve." I finally managed to lift Alfie off Steve's lap, but it was like dead weight. Alfie was so sound asleep, but needed to wake up and visit others at the VA.

Thankful for the Touch—

After my Tuesday group afternoon session at the VA, I was riding the elevator with Lawrence down to the first floor with Kevin, a new member of the group. Kevin said to me, "I like this dog. He made me feel better every time I touched him." I replied, "This is Lawrence. He's a therapy dog here at the VA. That's what he does." Kevin replied, "Yes, he does. Thanks."

Christmas Time with Lady—

Lady and I make sure the veterans are not forgotten at Christmas time. She joined the Rotary Club and students from Granada High School in Livermore at the VA. They sang Christmas carols for the veterans. Lady went to the VA on Christmas Day too. This was very rewarding for her and me, as well as being a great gift for the veterans.

Victory at Sea—

Each January, the Pleasanton Community Concert Band presents a concert at the VA Community Living Center in Livermore. One year, all pieces were associated with a branch of the military. One of the veterans in attendance kept a record of how many minutes of music were played for each branch. He later complained to the band that the Navy had way too many minutes, compared to the other branches, primarily because of "Victory at Sea."

A few years later, the band was presenting its January concert and had "Victory at Sea" on the program. I suggested to the conductor that he tell the audience that the band is playing this at the request of "Rear Admiral" Lawrence, who was in attendance. As soon as the music started, Lawrence stood up. He remained standing or sitting in front of the band for the entire six plus minutes of "Victory at Sea." Once it was done, he returned to the audience area and plopped down. No complaints about the Navy having too much time for this concert!

Good Job at the Car Shows—

As a member of the P-Town Push Rods, I go to the VA regularly for car shows. Of course Poli accompanies me. She likes walking around and showing the veterans the variety of cars we bring.

Helping a New Arrival—

One Friday when we arrived at the VA, one of the social workers met us in the hallway and said, "Oh good, you're here! Can you come with me to visit a newly arrived young veteran?" She wanted to see how Burt would react to Belle.

Burt was quite agitated when we got to his room but, once he saw Belle and started to pet her, he seem to calm down right away and was even able to engage in conversation with us. It turned out that Burt loved dogs and used to have dogs. So he responded very favorably to Belle.

Memories of the Therapy Dogs—

I was waiting in line with Lawrence at a clinic on the third floor of the VA when Drew noticed Lawrence and started talking to him. I asked Drew, "Do you know Lawrence?" He said, "Yes. When I was staying at the Veterans Home over on the hill [the Community Living Center], all the dogs used to come visit. They always brought up peoples' spirits." I said, "Yes, they are very good at that." And Drew agreed.

Dog Goes for a Ride—

Buddy G has several special friends that look forward to his visits. One resident liked to have Buddy G sit in his lap. Then he would take Buddy G for a ride around the hallways in his wheelchair. He said that visiting with Buddy G always made him feel better!

This Is Tough Work—

I often wonder why Sailor, after almost two hours of visiting veterans, gets anxious and wants to leave. He truly enjoys his time with the veterans, but looks up and says it is time to go. While I was visiting a relative in a Santa Monica hospital, a therapy dog came to visit. His handler and I struck up a conversation about the value and character of our respective canines. I mentioned how Sailor, after two hours, was ready to leave.

This handler, who had thousands of hours of therapy dog service, knew right away what I was talking about. He explained that the dog actually gives positive energy to the patient and takes negative energy from the patient. So after about two hours, the dog becomes very tired and wants to rest. His visit was the last for that day for him and his dog, and, as he was telling me this, his dog was lying on my feet taking a nap. So I have come to learn that, for the dog, it is rewarding work and I do mean work! It is work that Sailor loves to do. But it is a tough job. No wonder he is tired.

Headache Treatment—

Tracy was napping when Albert and I arrived at his door. We knew from prior visits that Tracy loves seeing the dogs. So I quietly said,

"Albert is here and would like to visit with you." Slowly, Tracy rolled to the side and sat up. He said, "Seeing Albert will help my headache more than anything else in the world." Tracy continued petting Albert while we chatted about recent TV programs we had seen. Before we left to see the next veteran, Tracy said, "My headache is better already. Thank you, Albert."

Making Veterans Day More Special—

Poli made sure we recognized the service of our veterans by attending the Veterans Day Ceremony at the VA. She greeted all arriving veterans. And I don't know how she knew to do so, but she stood at attention during both the "National Anthem" and the playing of "Taps."

Break from Belt-Making—

Nolan was in leather class, making a belt for his son. Zito looked up at him. Nolan said, "I want to see my friend." Nolan invited Zito to come up on his lap, so I placed him on Nolan's lap. Nolan said to Zito, "Where have you been today? You're such a good dog. I love seeing you." Nolan put a piece of leather from the belt in front of Zito's nose so he could smell it. Then I put Zito back on the floor so Nolan could get back to his project.

Not My Wheelchair—

One afternoon, Lawrence and I were visiting the veterans in the Community Living Center. We heard someone yelling and banging on the wall. I asked the nurse, "Is he ok?" She replied, "Herman thinks we took his wheelchair, but the one he has *is* his." I said, "Oh, okay." Lawrence and I decided to enter the room to see if we could help this situation.

I asked Herman, "Are you okay? What's wrong?" Herman shouted, "This is not my chair; they took my chair!" as he hit the wall with his fist. I said, "Lawrence is here. Can he help?" Herman put his hand on Lawrence and began petting him and talking to him. "You're a good dog. You always know." Herman continued to pet Lawrence, and, for a few minutes, he had peace.

The Dog Is So Trusting—

Troy was in the hallway, petting Albert. Both were having a fun time, as evidenced by the smile on Troy's face and Albert's tail wagging. A staff member was coming down the hall and there wasn't room for him to get past us with his large cart. So Troy had to move over. Albert moved to the side just a couple inches. Troy moved his motorized wheelchair over, commenting on how Albert wasn't moving over very much. He said, Albert is so trusting of us. He knows I won't hit him." Troy moved right up against Albert and the petting continued.

Never an End to Snuggling—

Alfie loves to lie on the bed and snuggle. One day, André was in his bed, watching a movie when we arrived. Pat placed Alfie on the bed, next to André's right leg, while I went to the other side with Zito. André petted Alfie and then rolled over onto to his left side to pet Zito. As soon as André was lying on his left side, Alfie snuggled against the back of his left leg. André decided to sit up so he could reach Zito more easily. As soon as he sat up, Alfie snuggled against André's lower back. André decided to stand up, as he couldn't move anywhere else with Alfie against his back. Alfie looked up at André as if to say, "Where did you go? How can I snuggle now?"

—Quotes from Veterans—

- I smile every time I see one of the therapy dogs.
- I always feel better when people bring out the therapy dogs. I cry, but I feel better.
- Dogs are great stress relievers. All you have to do is hug them.
- Can you start a pet rental program like they are doing back East? I want to rent a pet for a long time!
- That dog is a big lover baby!
- These are special dogs for special people.
- Everyone should have a dog at least once in their lifetime.
- If these dogs didn't come here, I wouldn't have any friends visit me.
- These dogs are fabulous! I love every one of them.
- You know you take second fiddle to these dogs. [said to a nurse]
- You have two dogs? Can I have one of them?

- These dogs always cheer me up. They are so friendly, so nice.
- It's really magnanimous of you to come here with your dogs and visit us old goats.
- This is the most unusual ministry, but it is wonderful because the dogs are so friendly.
- They're beautiful dogs. Are you ready to get rid of them? I'll take them!
- I think it's terrific what you do! It gives us an uplift.
- All of them are so good and so well trained.
- I wake up every morning wondering which dog is coming today and what time it will get here.
- We are so grateful you bring the therapy dogs here. At home we either have dogs or see our neighbors' dogs. But when you are in the hospital, there are usually no dogs. These dogs make this feel like home for us. We appreciate them coming here.
- You're always welcomed here, dogs. You wag your tail and don't bite with your teeth.
- What cuties! Thanks for coming, big guys.
- Look at him wagging that tail. I wonder if he realizes how happy that makes us. I love these dogs.
- When I was in the hospital, these dogs sure made my day. When I was dozing off, I felt something. It was a dog's nose. Sure made me happy.
- I love that little dog. I want to steal him.
- These animals are so nice. They'll give you everything you want and ask for nothing.
- These dogs remind me of home—kinda makes me homesick.
- I love it when the dogs come in.
- The best friend you can ever have is a dog. They're so loyal. They'll die for you.
- Lawrence wants you [his handler] to go and leave him here. I have no problem with that!
- I really appreciate having the dogs come out here.
- One day, I was sitting at the entrance when the dog came in and put his head on my lap and looked at me. That was so nice.
- The dogs make everybody's day—the employees, the patients.
- They like me. That's the important thing. They lick me to death. They make me feel better.

- I wonder if they know how much good they do and what they think.
- I like having the dogs here. I love to pet them.
- That's a job I could get—walking a dog around.
- I'll be with my dog soon. When I go to Heaven, my dog will be there.
- Is there anyone who doesn't like dogs?
- There's nothing like a good dog.
- I really appreciate the chance for a little dog talk. They let me chatter.
- These dogs are sweethearts. That's what we need more of out here.
- This is the best therapy there is for people. There is something special about a dog.
- Lawrence, the Livermore Lab—he's an Atomic Technician, not SLAC!
- He comes to see me. That's important. He cares. He likes to get his ears rubbed.
- Wow, he's husky. I wish I were half as big as him.
- I love dogs. They're so cool. How can you not feel something when they look at you?
- These dogs are really special. So gentle and mellow.
- The dogs—that's a nice way to wake a guy up.
- There are so many dogs here, and I love every one of them.
- You're late! I missed them so much.
- Thank you for bringing her because we need them. Many of us have nobody else. The dogs light up our lives.
- That's an amazing animal that God gave us—the dog.
- It's remarkable how you can talk natural to an animal.
- Thank you for bringing the dogs here. They make my day!
- The nice thing about this program with the dogs coming so often is that they become your friends.
- These dogs are too smart for words.
- All dogs should be spoiled.
- Thank you for bringing the dogs here. They're so nice, so very friendly.
- What I like about you guys is you enjoy doing this and so do the dogs.
- Thanks for bringing them in. It always breaks up the monotony.

- I always know it's Friday when I see Belle.
- I relax when I know you're here with the dog.
- There is nothing like a dog for a friend.
- I thoroughly enjoy the dog visits.
- Thank you for coming. It makes me feel better already.
- I'm so glad to see the dogs here. They spark up the day for me.
- You're welcome to come here any time.
- I wish I could relax the way that dog does.
- God bless you people and dogs for coming. Thank you, God.
- Thank you for bringing the dogs here because we need them. Many of us have nobody else. The dogs light up our day.
- The people that run this place need to know how much good these dogs do.
- I look forward to visits from the dogs because I don't get any visits from my family.
- The dog visits make me feel needed.
- The dogs are like friends.
- I always look forward to the dog visits for comfort and love.
- You dogs are sweethearts! You bring a lot of joy to a lot of people's lives.
- These dogs make a world of difference when you are hurting and not feeling well.
- Miles keeps secrets so well. We can tell him anything and he won't tell anybody.
- You're a gentle pup to put up with all this!
- These little angels love to visit us and they make us so happy.
- Everybody loves Thunder because Thunder loves everybody.
- You're not an animal, Albert. You're a people. And a better man than most people.
- Lawrence is a colorful guy. He always has something to say.
- I love dogs more than people because dogs understand me.
- Seeing Albert for Mother's Day was more than enough for me to make this day special.
- Everyday I go down to the counter to see if a dog is signed in. The bookmark helps me to know which dog to look for. I don't want to miss them.

—Quotes from Others—

- The more dog hair around here, the better, because then the residents and staff are happier. *(EMS staff)*
- These dogs deserve all the love that they can get. *(nursing staff)*
- It's surprising how much they do for patients—even with a short visit. *(long-time volunteer)*
- This is such a good idea. People really respond. *(family member)*
- Are you putting smiles on everyone's face? I know you're putting a smile on mine. *(nursing staff member talking to a therapy dog)*
- My grandpa's here and he really loves to see the dogs. We really appreciate it. *(granddaughter who visits regularly)*
- Belle is good for my blood pressure. *(staff doctor)*
- Thank you for volunteering. Our loved one misses his dogs so much. The dogs remind him of home. *(family member)*
- These dogs make you feel like you are the center of attention. *(staff member)*
- Are you giving him away? I'd like to take him home. *(visitor to dog handler)*

—Poems by Veterans and Staff—

Albert

Albert wags his tail every time he sees me.
When he comes to visit me, I feel better. It
improves my day tremendously. He doesn't fib to me, and
he always seems so pleased with me. We have an extremely
good relationship. I call it a very good friendship. He is a fine
dog and stays calm, until he sees a squirrel, at which time,
he alerts me about looking at something,
something exciting too.

Robert Alvis
U.S. Air Force, 1941-66

Poli

This is a corny poem about a hot dog
Who comes over the hills from Tracy to see us.

She didn't pass mustard for Guide Dogs,
But she relishes being a therapy dog.

I want to ketchup on getting to know her
'cause Poli is a really hot dog!

Tortillas Bailey
U.S. Air Force, 1986-96
U.S. Air Force Reserves, 1996-99

Lawrence

Lawrence has only been here at the VA since '04.
Lawrence started after I came here.
I like Lawrence because he is always there
and always good to me.
He has liked me as long as I have known him.
He always remembers me.
He knows who I am
and that means something to me.

Michael Brown
U.S. Navy, 1964-65

Zito

Zito has curly black hair
And he doesn't shed.
He is cute and cuddly.
He's always a lot of fun.

He likes to be in my lap.
He likes me and I like him.
All the dogs like me,
And I like all the dogs.

Michael Brown
U.S. Navy, 1964-65

Shazam

Shazam is the most beautiful dog
I have ever seen. I love dogs, especially
Shazam. She is very special to me. Shazam
is sixteen years old—that's 112 in people years!
In my opinion, she is the Queen of the therapy dogs.
Shazam makes me feel good on her visits,
and I love her more just thinking about
her daily, until she visits me again.

Thomas Bruton, Jr.
U.S. Marine Corps, 1957

Lady

Lady is not a big dog.
She is pretty and full of fun and energy.
She loves running after the Frisbee.
When she visits the veterans,
she is as
friendly as can be.
The vets love her and feel
good when they pet her.
I enjoy her very much and wait
for her visits each week.

Looking at her and
touching her lovely coat
is so much fun.
I believe
she enjoys it all too, because her
expression is so happy.
She makes me happy too.

Joe Clay
U.S. Army, 1955-59

Lawrence

Lawrence is the name of a dog.
He's a special therapy dog,
who comes to visit the patients at the
VA Hospital. We pet his back and head,
and he sits up to be friendly with lots of us.
His fur is black and he is gorgeous. He has
a beautiful way about him, standing strong
and sitting near our beds.
He likes contact with patients, and
we always find time to be with him.
I look forward to his visits on
the ward. He brings a 'togetherness'
between veterans, giving us a closeness
with him, that feels good. I look
forward to seeing him again, and again.
Just talking about him and his kind
of beauty gives me pleasure.
I love his visits.

Sam Marrazo
U.S. Air Force, 1949-53

Miles

This dog would walk a mile to
see me. He's a beautiful dog with a beautiful
coat. It's a good winter-weather coat,
and he needs it for these
cold, cold days.

Tony Miranda
U.S. Marine Corps, 1942-78

Miles a Year Later

Miles likes to put his nose under my jacket.
It's warm under there,
But there are no cookies for him.

Miles doesn't look a day older
Than he did last year,
Just a rank higher.

Tony Miranda
U.S. Marine Corps, 1942-78

Therapy Dog Visitors

When therapy dogs come to visit
It makes the vets all smile
'cause petting a dog seems to wash away cares
And makes us happy for a while.

Mark Mosegaard
U.S. Navy, 1973-77

Mr. Alfie

I love Mr. Alfie because he has a lot of nice
hair and has never bitten me.
One time he chased a fly out of my room,
and guess what! He didn't even use
a broom. He wags his tail at me when
he says good-bye. Even though
I miss him, I do not cry. I'll
just look forward to
his next
visit.

Ed Proffit
U.S. Marine Corps, 1942-45

Alfie

I did not like dogs when I worked in
The Post Office, but I do now.
Alfie is a dog I like.
He's such a wonderful dog.

When I see him, my blood pressure
Goes down—great medicine for me.
And he loves to lie on the floor, roll over
On his back, and let me rub his tummy too.

James Ricks
U.S. Army, 1950-53

Sailor

Sailor is a special dog because he loves Marines.
He loves me, yes he loves me, even though
he loves his owner too. Sailor recently welcomed home
a Marine Staff Sergeant, who had completed four
tours of duty in Iraq and one in Afghanistan.
He truly is a great dog.

John Schultheis
U.S. Marine Corps, 1941-45

Lady

When Graham Scott talks to Lady, he says
"Are you ready to go to work?"
Lady is always up to the challenge
To come here and see us.

It's great when she puts her paws on my bed.
She is even-tempered and willing to entertain us,
Especially outside catching Frisbees.
I don't know anyone who doesn't like to watch her do that.

James Sellers
U.S. Navy, 1960-69
(Corpsman with the Marine Corps)

Maggie

Maggie is a raving beauty, a striking blonde.
She's very tied up with her owner
And she'll do whatever Dusty wants her to do.
She is very obedient.

Any time such a good-looking blonde walks in the room,
Things stop. All our worries stop.
Maggie brings in bright light
And makes you think of nothing but good things.

Michael Sturdivan
U.S. Air Force, 1965-70

Zito

Zito is very friendly,
kind, and not rambunctious.
He loves to crawl up on my bed
and go to sleep. Zito is very calm, and he has a
calming effect on me. He doesn't meow, because Zito is
a handsome Cock-A-Poo!

Michael Sturdivan
U.S. Air Force, 1965-70

Pet Angels

The dogs are such a wonderful gift.
It brightens the days of those they lift.
To put them on the laps and pet.
Brings tears to the eyes of the vets.

To see their eyes come alive and respond
Makes all the nurses shout with joy.
Pets are great therapists who are put to the test
Making vets happy and full of zest.

A dog has so much healing power from their souls.
It makes them companions of young and old.
Carefree and full of grace
Therapy dogs are put to their pace.

Happily they wag their tails
Making memories for all the vets.
With one wrinkle of the nose
They look up to the sky and pose.

They are family and friend
For those who are in need,
Making them angels indeed.

Rose Wilkins
Licensed Vocational Nurse, NHCU

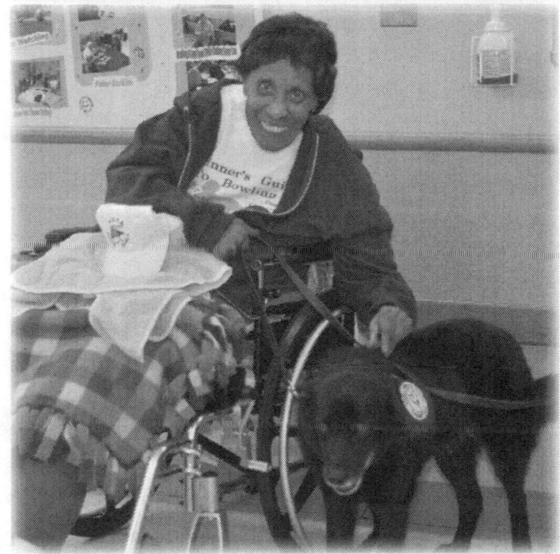

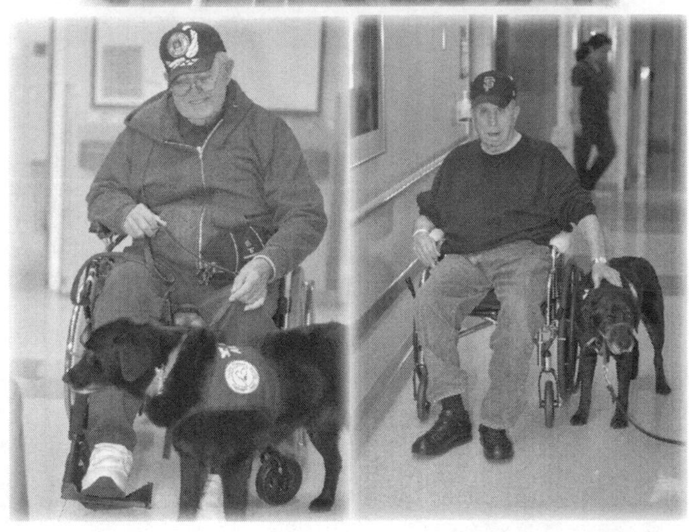

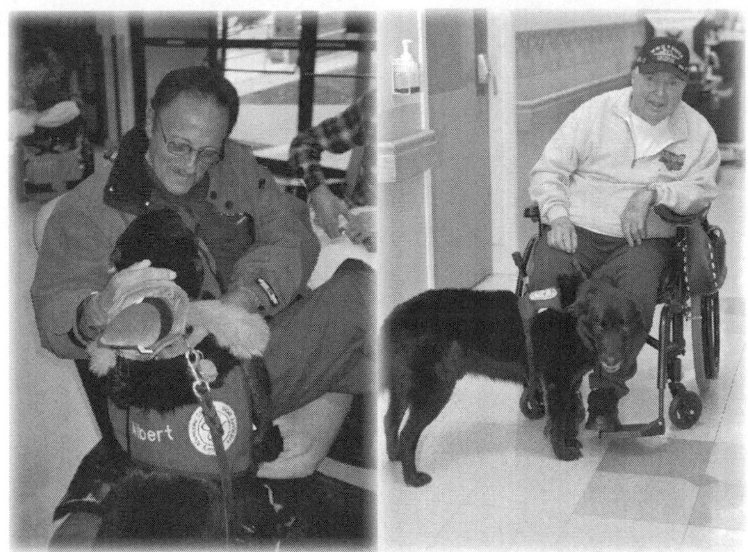

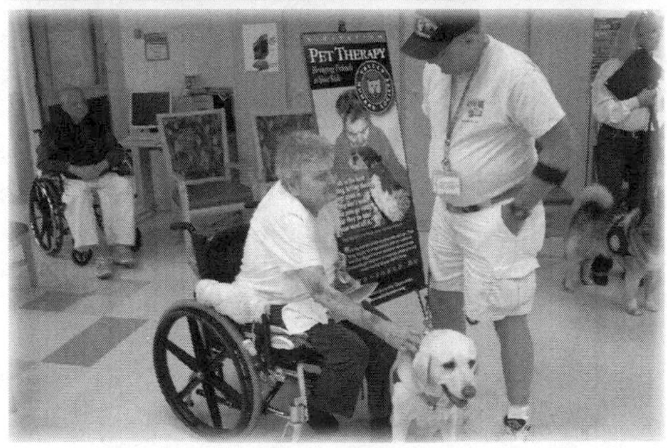
PET THERAPY

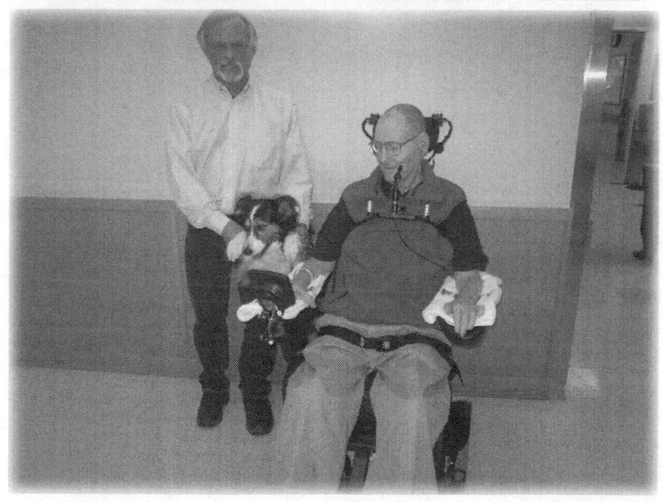

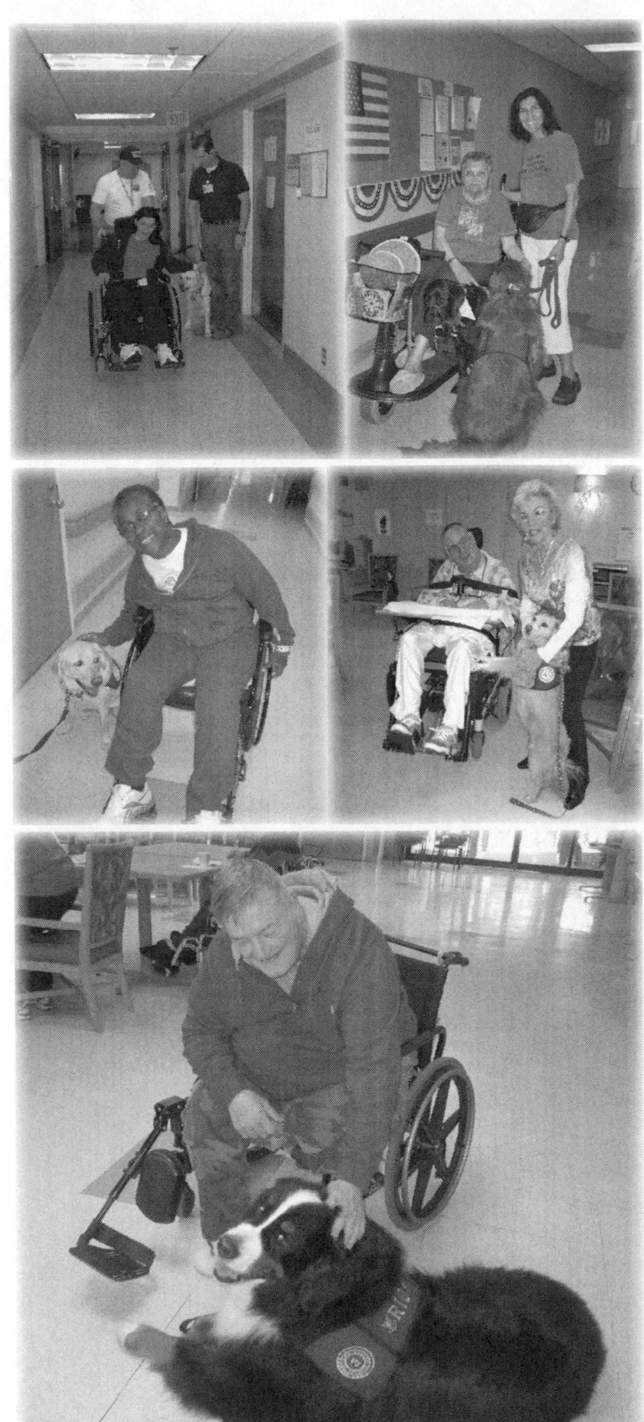

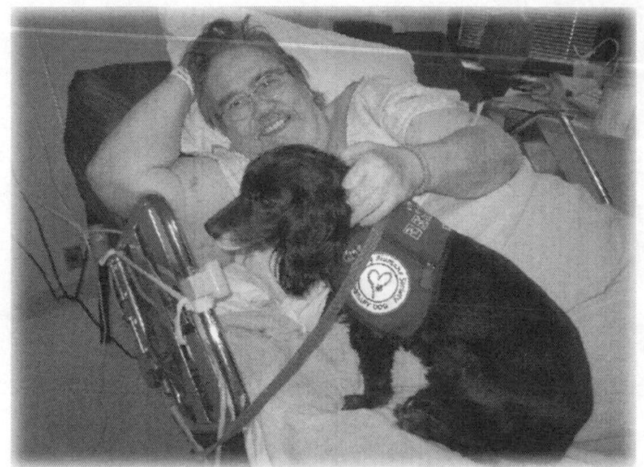

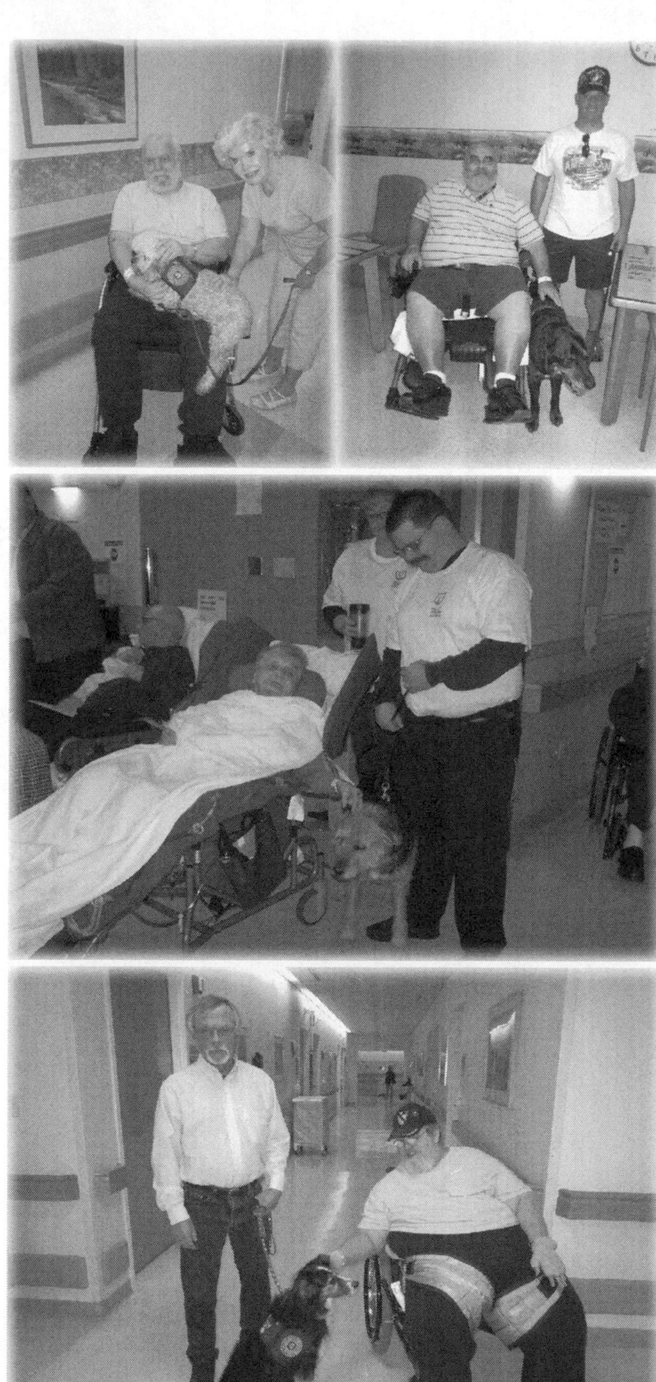

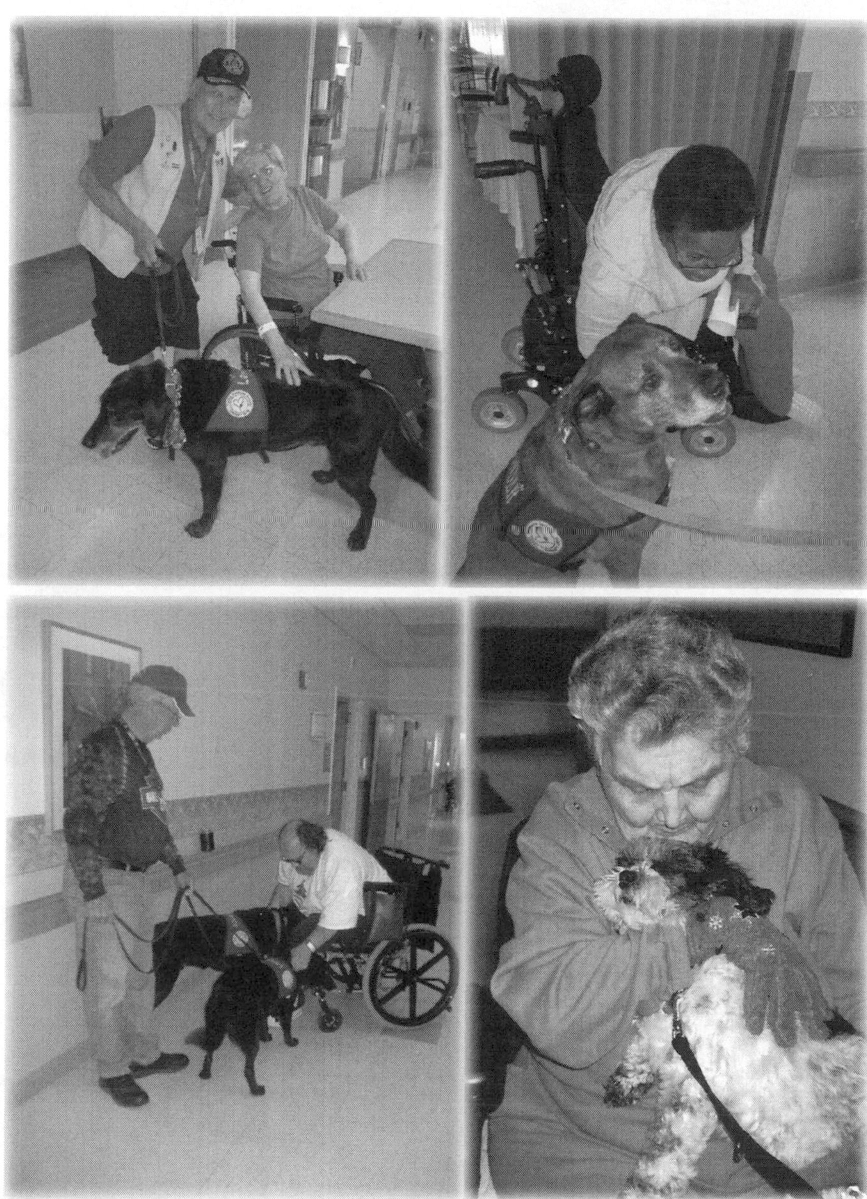

~CHAPTER 14~

other sites, programs, and events

Many of these dogs have gone to places and participated in programs and events in addition to the ones featured in this book. These testimonials, stories, quotes, photos, and the poem are as special as the ones earlier in the book. Rather than omit them from the book, I have included them in this chapter.

—Testimonials—

Shirley, a Castro Valley resident, had been struggling with her biggest question, "What will happen to my dog when I die?" Her dog was the most important thing in her life, having no other family members. Hope Hospice discovered that her goal was to die with her beloved dog at her side. Partnering together with Valley Humane Society, Hope Hospice was able to help Mary reach her goal. Valley Humane Society sent caring volunteers to walk and feed Shirley's dog, twice a day, for many months. During those months, Mary was able to meet a loving volunteer and selected her to take her precious dog after her death. Through Hope Hospice's and Valley Humane Society's support, she was able to die very peacefully with her loving dog and her long-term volunteers at her side.

Hope Hospice has sent Valley Humane Society's therapy dogs and their handlers to visit with end-of-life patients who are agitated and often non-verbal. The comfort of petting a dog is soothing, and it allows our patients to relax, bringing them peace. Many of our patients live at homelike care facilities and miss the pets they once had. Often a therapy dog's visit will trigger memories of beloved pets that the patient once had and bring them comfort at the end of life.

The role of pets is important in the lives of our patients. Since 2007, together Hope Hospice and Valley Humane Society have supported the patients' needs regarding the care of their pets and allowed them the comfort of holding onto memories of their loving animal companions throughout life.

Wendy Celeste, Coordinator of Volunteers, Hope Hospice, Inc.

Throughout my years as Mayor of Pleasanton, I have seen therapy dogs at numerous places. I first met Lawrence at the open house for a new business, Workday. Although not a typical therapy dog work assignment, Lawrence made all of us feel comfortable and probably helped encourage people to network with each other as several people would pet him at a time and then start talking to each other.

I have seen the therapy dogs at various community events. They have "marched" in our local Veterans Day parades. They have attended several Welcome Home Celebrations for our troops in Pleasanton. At one ceremony, the emcee mentioned my daughter's fight with cancer and that she was now cancer free. This brought tears to my eyes, and those tears brought Lawrence to my lap, where he rested his head, and I rubbed his head and ears. He was so comforting to me. For much of the rest of the Welcome Home, he rested on my feet. This was his way, I guess, of letting me know he was concerned about me and wanted me to relax, just as he was doing.

I have also seen the therapy dogs at the Pleasanton Public Library in the Paws to Read program. Those dogs work wonders, encouraging the children to read, to love books, and to want to come to our library.

All the therapy dogs are lovely dogs, and I so much enjoy meeting them and petting them. And I appreciate the handlers sharing their beautiful dogs with us at various events and places in Pleasanton. They help make our city a better place to live.

Jennifer Hosterman, Mayor, City of Pleasanton, 2004-2012

The healing capability of animals has been documented many times. In fact, some patients actually spoke, moved, or smiled as a result of an animal being there. I always felt I was a better person when I was able to share my own dog, watching him perform his "magic" to someone with a kiss or snuggle. Seeing that person smile for just a few moments made my day.

Gay Maestas, VHS Pet Therapy Program Coordinator/Volunteer, 1994-2000; Therapy Dog Handler, 1993-2000

Animal Services Officer Roy Ficken came into my office one morning. Roy had a six-pound puppy in tow. It was wide eyed and eagerly exploring his surroundings. I assumed it to be a stray, but Roy proudly introduced him as his new dog. Roy, mirroring the excitement of his little friend, told me that this was Gandalf. Roy had long taught school children how to safely approach and handle a dog. He asked if he could bring Gandalf to work with him each day as an "assistant." The work half of their partnership was cemented that day.

There was not a day, thereafter, where Roy would come to work without his little partner. Gandalf joyfully walked through the Police Department in such contrast to the 80-pound-plus German Shepherds who often roamed the hallways with their handlers. Soon Gandalf had a badge and uniform. The Shepherds' egos were slightly dented, but little Gandalf became as well known in the community as Roy. He was a hit! From public relations to putting people (big and small) at ease, this little fella did what his big brother police dogs just could not quite do. He connected with the hearts of everyone he met. He became a part of virtually all programs geared toward connecting with children, a part of our Citizen's Police Academy, and an ambassador for our Animal Services Program.

Timothy P. Neal, Pleasanton Chief of Police, 1999-2007

Although my service time in the U.S. Navy did not involve any major conflicts, I was involved in the 1979 Iran Rescue Operation and then in the 1979 Jonestown suicide. In 1983, I went to Beirut for the Marine Barracks bombing. These three events had a major impact on me.

In 1986, I was admitted to the Menlo Park VA hospital for severe PTSD and severe alcohol and drug addiction. My stay in the program at Menlo Park was Long Term, for two years. This was my first encounter with having a therapy animal (in this case, a dog) in the program with us. I have always been an animal lover and have owned German Shepherds all my life. I knew already that animals bring immeasurable comfort to a human. They give unconditional love that cannot be described. They know when you are hurting, when you are sad, and when you need them. I cannot tell you how many times this dog came to me without even calling. She knew I needed her.

Now, many years later, clean and sober, I see on a daily basis how the therapy dog program has grown to what it is today, especially in the case of our "Petting Officers" that attend the Welcome Homes for our returning troops and visit patients at the VA in Livermore. They bring smiles to the patients, no matter how much they're hurting. The spirit within these therapy animals is HUGE! I was not only taken aback by what they do for adults. It's even more so at a children's hospital.

What a difference it makes when this four-legged, furry creature walks in, wagging its tail. To see a child with cancer, having their worst day, in pain, sad, scared, and, in just one moment, when the therapy dog arrives, all of it's gone is amazing. You would have to see it to believe it! The therapy animals program cannot be replaced by anything!!

Fred "Spike" Schau, U.S. Navy Veteran, 1977-91; U.S. Navy Reserves, 2002-05, 2009 to present; Northern California State Coordinator, Warriors' Watch Riders

—Stories—

Stories in this chapter are provided for the following therapy dogs—Alfie, a Cockapoo; Bosco, a Black Labrador Retriever; Chex Mix, a Newfoundland; Dori, a Shih Tzu/Poodle mix; Elsa and her friend Arbuckle, both Black Labrador Retrievers; Gandalf II, a Chihuahua/Schipperke mix; Kody, a Samoyed; Lawrence, a Black Labrador Retriever; Mitsy, a Havanese/Poodle mix; Mojo, a Welsh Corgi; P.I.P., a Border Collie/Cattle Dog mix; Tedi Bear, a Newfoundland; and Zito, a Cockapoo.

Laughing at the Dog—

Throughout his career with the Pleasanton Police Department, Gandalf II participated in Safety Meetings. One day, we went to a private home in Pleasanton for a Girl Scout meeting. When we arrived, Florence answered the door and started laughing at my dog.

After the meeting, I asked her, "Why were you laughing at Gandalf when you answered the front door?" She told me to wait a moment, as she ran up the stairs. Florence brought a book back with her, *Officer Buckle and Gloria*, by Peggy Rathman. This became the book that Gandalf II "reads" when asked to read to various groups, and it is a symbol of his job with the Police Department.

Lawrence Can Read!—

Lawrence and I were invited to visit a second/third grade classroom to talk for 30 minutes about what dogs do for us. I started telling them about therapy dogs. But then I talked about guide dogs and service dogs, police dogs, sniffing dogs, search and rescue dogs, and other working dogs. Lawrence had been staying near me during this time. As I closed my presentation, I said dogs can actually read. Of course the students wanted evidence.

I wrote the word "SIT" on the white board with a red marker. I explained that I didn't know if Lawrence could see red letters on a white board since he was used to reading black letters on a light grey background. Lawrence was sitting in the middle aisle at the other end of the leash, about six feet from me. I pointed to the word "SIT" on the whiteboard. Lawrence walked to the front of the room, looked at the whiteboard, and sat down. "Wow," said some of the students. So I erased "SIT" and wrote "DOWN." Lawrence immediately plopped down on the floor. Then I said it was time for us to go. But this upset several students. They said to the teacher, "Lawrence read to us. We want to read to Lawrence!" The teacher said she had to get on with their regular reading program now. I quietly said to the teacher, "Isn't oral reading part of your regular reading program?" She agreed and told the students they could read one book to Lawrence.

Three students rushed to the bookcase and pulled out a book about a police dog. Each student read one page and then passed the book to the next student. Lawrence moved from desk to desk, sitting attentively, listening to each student read his or her page. When the book reached Ryan's desk, Lawrence stood back a couple feet. Lawrence knew Ryan was afraid of dogs. Ryan read the page, and, as he did, Lawrence slowly inched forward. By the time Ryan had reached the bottom of the page, Lawrence had his head in Ryan's lap, and Ryan was petting Lawrence on the head. The teacher had a tear in her eye. She told me that Ryan's mother had told her how afraid Ryan is of dogs, even though they have two dogs at home. The teacher said, "I will have to tell Ryan's mother about this. She'll never believe me." The teacher also commented on how well the children read that day and that none were reluctant to try new words, as they usually are.

Teddy Bear Picnic—

Chex Mix and Tedi Bear participated in the Teddy Bear Picnic one afternoon at a local hospital. Chex Mix's job was to pull children around in a small cart while Tedi Bear walked along side the cart. The children really enjoyed being pulled around in the cart by a dog and getting to pet both dogs.

Dogs Are Unforgettable—

I was a special education teacher, and, before retiring, I would bring my dogs, Alfie and Zito, to school. Todd, a third-grade boy, was particularly affected by my dogs. He had an unstable family background and had been bounced around from family member to family member.

He came to my school from Arizona where he had been placed with one relative and then moved to Livermore with another relative.

Todd had a hard time concentrating and sitting still to do his schoolwork. He loved my dogs, particularly Zito. He could sit with Zito on his lap and pet him with one hand while doing his schoolwork with the other hand. At the end of the school year in Livermore, he was sent to another relative and went to another school. A year later, I saw him at a grocery store. The first words out of his mouth were, "How is Zito?" That shows how much of an impression Zito had made on him.

Change of Mind—

During our visits to a local hospital, I always knocked on the door of a patient's room and asked if they wanted a visit from Kody. Sometimes, I was turned away. Most often, we weren't. On this one occasion, a mother met us at the door and told us she didn't want a visit for her son. However, as we walked down the corridor, she came running after us and asked us if we could come back.

In the bed, lay her son Marty. He couldn't communicate with us because he had a terrible injury. Marty's eyes sparkled when he looked at Kody. The mother asked if Kody could get on the bed. I told her that the therapy dogs aren't allowed on the beds. But she pleaded. So, I told Kody to get on the bed. He wouldn't, no matter how many times I asked. He apparently knew the rules. So, I lifted Kody's paws onto the bed. Marty leaned over and touched him. It brought tears to all of our eyes because, even though Marty couldn't talk, he was communicating with Kody.

Helping the Field Sergeant—

While on night duty, the Field Sergeant called me and Gandalf II to a local neighbor's house to help with a young man named Craig who had run away from his home and gone into a neighbor's home where he went to bed.

When we arrived, I opened the door to the bedroom and asked Gandalf II to jump onto the bed and to befriend Craig. After about ten minutes, with Gandalf II calming him down, Craig walked out of the bedroom and was taken to a local hospital. This saved the police from having to be more assertive with Craig, and hopefully Craig is doing okay now.

A First Time Experience—

In 1998, Bosco had his first visit with seniors. It was at a recreational facility where seniors came for various programs and activities during the day. Bosco, proud canine that he was, walked in as if he owned the place. When he saw Gloria strolling across the room with her walker that had tennis balls on the ends, he couldn't resist checking into the tennis balls further. Gloria started laughing at Bosco's response to seeing the tennis balls. Others also got a good laugh out of watching Bosco. He was bringing joy to all of them who saw him that day.

All the Things Dogs Can Do—

A friend of mine who teaches fifth grade invited Lawrence and me to visit her classroom on a Friday afternoon just before a holiday weekend. She knew students were always restless at times like this, more restless than they usually are on Friday afternoons, and didn't want to be presenting a heavy academic lesson.

I talked for an hour about the wonderful things dogs do for people. I went into much more detail and specific examples than I did when visiting the second/third grade classroom. One area I spoke about was how dogs help in diagnosing medical problems. I talked about how dogs can detect certain types of cancer by sniffing air or urine samples, how dogs can anticipate heart attacks and seizures, and how dogs can tell when a diabetic needs insulin.

At the end of the hour, I opened it up to questions. One boy raised his hand and asked, "Does that mean next time I go to the doctor, I'll be sniffed by a dog? And will the insurance pay for it?" I said, "Not now, but maybe sometime in the future when people realize how valuable dogs are to us and what a good job they can do detecting health problems for us. We need more lab tests and cat scans done by our canine and feline friends."

The students were very well behaved and attentive the entire hour. The next time she saw me, my friend told me that she was really amazed at how calm and well behaved the students were for the remaining hour that day. She said she wished Lawrence could be in her classroom every day.

Special Last Hours—

There was an elderly woman at a residential care facility in Livermore which I had visited occasionally. Eleanor had suffered a stroke and needed assisted living services. Her husband came to visit her every day. My dogs, Alfie and Zito, and I got to know the couple, and Eleanor loved to have one of my dogs sit on her lap. She would smile and pet the dog, obviously enjoying that doggie love. Eleanor never talked, just murmured and smiled.

One day, when I came for my visit, her husband and daughter beckoned me into her room. She had suffered another stroke and had only a limited time to live. When I came into the room, she was lying on her side and either asleep or semi-conscious. I began talking to her and lifted Alfie onto her bed. When she felt Alfie's body beside her, she opened her eyes, turned over a little, and petted Alfie. She also smiled a great big smile. That was the last smile Eleanor ever made because she died a short time later. I am very happy that Alfie's visit made her last hours a little better.

Helping a Confused Lady—

One day, an older woman named Natalie was lost. She thought she was in Pleasant Hill, but instead Natalie was in Pleasanton. She was quite upset and needed to be calmed down. Who better to do this job than Gandalf II? He was called to duty by the Pleasanton Police Department's Field Sergeant. Upon arrival, he went straight to work. He jumped into the car and got on the seat next to Natalie. She started stroking him and then calmed down. By the time her family arrived to take her home, Natalie and Gandalf II were best friends.

A Special Person, A Special Jacket—

Lawrence went to the Church of Latter Day Saints to attend the memorial service for one of his handlers, Harold Swartz. They had been good buddies for over two years. Harold had had a stroke and was recovering when he was asked by a friend of mine in the Livermore Veterans Foundation (LVF) if he could march in the Rodeo Parade with Lawrence. This would be a new experience for Harold, but Lawrence was a parade-pro by now, and was marching in the Rodeo Parade, with his "brother," Albert, to honor the veterans at the VA. Harold wore his Army blue dress uniform, and Lawrence was decked out with a patriotic neckerchief and military hat along with his therapy dog vest.

Harold continued as a handler for Lawrence for the next two plus years. It was wonderful for both of them. Harold recovered from his stroke more quickly as he got out of the house almost every week, walked with Lawrence, and talked with the veterans whom Lawrence was visiting at the VA. Harold said, though, that he would never wear his Army blue jacket in the parade again—too hot!

The last time Harold and Lawrence were together was on a Sunday morning at Camp Arroyo, a camp for developmentally delayed youth. Harold was scheduled for heart surgery and said he would call me when he was ready to go to the VA again. That call never came. Harold passed away four weeks after the day at Camp Arroyo.

Lawrence and I went to Harold's memorial service. Lawrence was very well behaved throughout the service. Afterwards, Lawrence and I went to the reception to greet people and for him to provide the loving care they needed at their time of grief, especially to Harold's wife, Karen. She encouraged us to go to the area where there were photos and mementos of Harold's life. Hanging there were two items, his Contra Costa County Sheriff's Department shirt and his Army blue dress jacket. Lawrence had done no sniffing at the service until he came to that jacket. He sniffed it and rubbed against it. Obviously, he knew it belonged to a very special friend of his. Lawrence will always miss Harold.

Meeting in the Neighborhood—

Tedi Bear and I were taking a walk on our local streets one day and met some neighbors whose granddaughter, Amy, was visiting them. Amy was very comfortable petting and chatting with Tedi Bear while I talked with her grandparents. Suddenly, all was quiet. I turned around and saw Tedi Bear lying down and Amy sitting next to Tedi Bear, leaning against his side with her eyes closed. Apparently, they had quickly become good friends.

To Sit or to Stand?—

Lawrence, with his many years of work as a therapy dog, has attended several memorial services at various churches. He had gotten used to the routine—when to stand, when to pray, how to go up and down the aisle, and where to sit. At Ernest's memorial service, the minister called for the congregation to sing a certain hymn. I don't know what clue(s) Lawrence used, but he immediately stood up. We were sitting on the end of the row on the center aisle. Nobody else was standing, because the tradition at this church was to remain seated when singing. Lawrence looked around, with a confused expression on his face. After a moment, though, he sat back down while the congregation sang. For the next hymn, he remained seated at this church. He had learned his lesson.

Stroller Dog—

Whenever we went to a senior living community in San Ramon, everyone remembered Dori, but not me. Yet to be honest, who wouldn't? She is a-Dori-ble. Though only 12 pounds, she is full of love. Dori enjoys sitting on people's laps.

What residents really enjoyed is when I brought her in the doggy stroller. It turned out to be a great purchase. The stroller put Dori at a good height for those residents in wheelchairs and beds. And the stroller, itself, drew attention, making our visits there an adventure for sure!

Safety Club Honoring the Dog—

The students in the Safety Club at both Amador Valley and Foothill High Schools in Pleasanton were developing a safety newsletter for their school. They contacted me to see if they could use Gandalf's name in it. Now called the *Gandalf II Newsletter*, high school students prepare it and distribute it to elementary schools in Pleasanton. The Gandalf II Safety Club is involved with drug and alcohol use, stranger danger, safety around wild animals, pet safety, Halloween safety, and staying safe when home alone.

How to Stop the Screaming—

One day, we were walking into the skilled nursing facility when we heard a woman screaming. As we approached the visiting area, a nurse waved at me to hurry over. The nurse turned to the patient, and said, "Oh, look who is here to visit you today." When the woman looked at Kody approaching, she clasped her hands together, stopped screaming, and reached down to put her face in Kody's fur. Kody did not mind the attention one bit. The nurse turned to me and told me that the one time when patients are always calm is when Kody comes to visit. Then she gave Kody a big THANK YOU.

Can't Forget the Dog—

Bosco and I visited the patients in a convalescent hospital where he was a big shot, the popular one, the visitor that patients couldn't wait to see. I can't recall the number of times we would see a patient there, and he or she would remember Bosco's name, but not mine.

One day, Gwen called out, "Bosco, Bosco, come say hello. I've been waiting for you!" Of course Bosco went right up to her for a visit. That made my day, Bosco's day, and, most importantly, Gwen's day.

Performing with the Band—

Lawrence was invited to perform with the San Ramon Symphonic Band when it played Arthur Pryor's "The Whistler and His Dog." Lawrence attended three rehearsals so he could practice parading around and sitting during the music at specific times, and, at the end, retrieving the duck and taking it to the conductor. Since he had his therapy dog vest on, he would not bark. So we asked a trumpet player to do that.

On the evening of the concert, Lawrence was prepared for his performance. He was on the program for the last piece before intermission. The band started playing, and Lawrence began parading around through the audience, stopping briefly to visit a young child in a wheelchair. At the end, a band member tossed the stuffed duck out, and Lawrence quickly retrieved it. He went to the conductor and gave it to him. But then Lawrence surprised us. He stepped up on the podium, bowed to the audience, turned to the conductor, and stuck his paw out to shake the conductor's hand, all with no commands or signaling from me. The audience loved it, and youngsters in attendance couldn't wait to give Lawrence a cookie during intermission. What a challenge I had to let him interact with the audience members and keep him from the cookies during intermission. I think only one cookie got through.

Lawrence later performed "The Whistler and His Dog" with the Windjammers Circus Concert Band in Carmichael and at a joint concert with the Golden Gate Park Band and the Las Positas College Band in San Francisco. He was also invited to do it with the San Jose Symphonic Winds, but had to decline because I had just had total knee replacements three weeks earlier.

In 2012, he was invited back for repeat performances with the Golden Gate Park Band on Father's Day and the San Ramon Symphonic Band on the Fourth of July. He knew the routine so well that there was no need for a rehearsal for him, even though it had been almost two years since he last performed it.

Entertaining Dogs—

When I went to a senior residential facility, I would take not only my dog Elsa, but a friend of mine would come with her therapy dog, Arbuckle, also a Black Lab. Between the two of us, we would have our dogs do some simple tricks, and Elsa would do a few of her dance steps. All the residents seemed to enjoy Arbuckle ringing the bell on command and Elsa dancing in place with her front feet. When the dogs got tired, they usually rested on someone's feet.

Fun Playtime—

Bosco and I visited a private home with a small number of residents who needed rehabilitation services or were struggling with the beginning stages of Alzheimer's. This beautiful home had a pool. On warm days, the residents would bundle up, get a seat out front by the pool, and watch Bosco as he put on a water show for them by launching himself into the pool after the infamous tennis ball. The residents participated by tossing the ball into the pool and having Bosco bring it back to them. The looks on their faces when he did this were unforgettable. Who would have thought that tossing a tennis ball into a pool and having a dog retrieve it would bring so much cheer and laughter as well as the desire for Bosco to keep doing it again and again. When the weather didn't allow us to go outside to the pool, Bosco did tricks and played catch inside the house.

Bringing Out Words—

Kody enjoyed going to a rehabilitation center when the speech therapist was there working with patients who had suffered strokes. The patients loved to touch Kody's amazing white coat. Since this was a wonderful tactile experience for the patients, it gave them lots of opportunities to use adjectives to describe him.

Special Olympics Mascot—

When Mitsy was first certified, she was anxious to get started in her new job! I decided that, since we didn't have any regular visits scheduled, we could go and be with the Special Olympics athletes at their track practices in Pleasanton. After checking with the coach and getting the "paws up," we went to cheer on our special athletes while they practiced. Mitsy would get so excited when she saw them coming toward the finish line and would be waiting for each athlete, doing her little dance for them, almost like a "high five." Even the athletes, who were not used to animals and were a little nervous, became so happy with Mitsy cheering them on that they would eventually come over and give her a pat. They considered her part of the team—their mascot!

Misty also attended their softball practices and the Regional Softball Tournament for Pleasanton's Recreational Activities for the Developmentally Disabled (RADD) Special Olympics team held at Heather Farms in Walnut Creek. The players enjoyed seeing Mitsy dancing and cheering for them behind the dugout and Mitsy watching them take the stand at the medal ceremony.

Knows Where His Friends Are—

Over the years, Bosco got to know the residents by their first names. When I said, "Bosco, go visit Ted," he would head right to Ted's room and find Ted there in his wheelchair waiting for the love and joy that Bosco was always ready to deliver. Ted would talk about Bosco's tail and its strong wagging motion. Ted just loved watching Bosco's tail go back and forth, and Bosco seemed to enjoy wagging it for Ted.

Can Remember the Dog—

Last year, I found out that my girlfriend's mother was in an assisted living home near where I live. P.I.P. and I decided to go visit her. We were very warmly received by all residents and staff in the home. My friend's mother was suffering from dementia. Every few minutes, she would ask me what my name was and how she knew me. I would explain how her daughter and I had grown up together and remained friends. Interestingly, she remembered P.I.P and would call him by name. P.I.P. only visited twice before she passed on, but I know she loved seeing him because she told me so.

Increasing Parental Awareness—

For two years in a row, we have attended the Parents Reading Night at an elementary school in Livermore. During this program, about 90 minutes are set aside for parents to come into designated classrooms where they can either read with their children or see the children read in a group to a dog. This is a very popular event, and there are at least 30 students in grades one to three waiting in line to read to only a few dogs.

Several parents say that their dogs at home would never be so calm with the noise and commotion going on. Mojo seems to not mind that at all, as long as he has a lap to cuddle up to while listening to a child read to him. Hopefully some of these parents will encourage their children to read to their dogs at home or take their children to the Paws to Read program at the local libraries.

Final Exam Stress Relief—

Stress Relief is going to the dogs at St. Mary's College in Moraga. ARF Pet Hug Pack members and their dogs were invited to a lunch break Stress Relief program the week before finals. Six dogs, including Elsa, and their handlers were set up in the common area with other programs, such as a massage and a brain food station. The dogs and students got to spend quality petting time together. Most students said the dogs reminded them of their pets at home who were anxiously awaiting their arrival for summer break. Approximately 60 students came by to visit and take a needed break from studying for finals.

Dog of the Queen—

Each summer, the Pleasanton Public Library holds a Summer Reading Game. It runs for eight weeks, during which there are entertainment activities, weekly movies, story times, and craft projects. The theme varies each year. Since 2012 was the year of the Olympics in London, the theme was "Readers Are Good Sports!" And many of the activities reflected the London Olympics theme.

It started this year, on opening day, featuring Mojo, a Welsh Corgi. Why? Because Queen Elizabeth II has Welsh Corgis, her favorite breed of dog. She reportedly has over 30 of them. The 2012 summer program was kicked off with children carrying a copy of the Olympic torch down Main Street to the library where Mojo and I were. I was dressed as Queen Elizabeth II and Mojo was just being himself. We greeted many of the children as they arrived at the library for this exciting program. Some children had their picture taken with us. It was a fun time for all and a great start to the 2012 Summer Reading Game.

—Quotes—

- The Black Lab was a wonder dog! He stole the show!! *(concert audience member)*
- Oh, Lawrence. You're such a sweetie. *(community center staff)*
- I couldn't believe how many kids wanted to meet Lawrence afterwards. *(concert audience member)*

—Poem—

My Four-Legged Friend

I lie in my bed, as lonely as can be.
No one comes to visit, no family.
I'm getting sleepy and my eyelids are sagging,
When all of a sudden, I see a tail wagging.
For years, this four-legged friend
has been coming here to visit me.
He likes to rest his head on my lap
and he's as nice as can be.
He always brightens my day
and he loves me in every way.
Thank you, my friend.
Please, please come again.

Catherine Lynas
Visitor, VA and Easy Living Care Home;
Attendee, Welcome Home Celebrations

HOLIDAYS

APPENDIX A

VALLEY HUMANE SOCIETY

Valley Humane Society (VHS) is an animal welfare organization that advocates for responsible pet ownership. In addition to its animal shelter and adoption program to eliminate unnecessary euthanasia, VHS offers programs to enrich the bond between people and animals through community events, humane education and other educational outreach services, collaborative programs, and its therapy dog program. VHS has been endorsed by the American Kennel Club (AKC) as a Therapy Dog Certified Organization. This allows VHS therapy dogs with at least 50 hours of service to be recognized as AKC therapy dogs.

Founded and incorporated in 1987 by a group of volunteers, in 2003, it became a board-directed organization with paid staff. VHS moved from a former veterinary office in downtown Pleasanton to a modular building on Nevada Street in April 2007. In June 2011, it moved into the new 5,200-square-foot animal shelter and office building.

VHS has always provided animal care and adoption services for dogs and cats. Committed to its no-kill policy, the organization works closely with county shelters to pull animals that are scheduled for euthanasia and brings them into the VHS network. These animals receive medical treatment and behavior modification as needed. Once the animals are deemed adoptable, new loving homes are identified. VHS also works closely with the local community providing an avenue for people who must surrender guardianship of their animals.

By the early 1990s, VHS began its pet therapy program, offering certified therapy dog teams to visit people of all ages in various settings throughout the Tri-Valley. It was started by a volunteer who had a beautiful Golden Retriever that was trained as a Guide Dog, but had a career change and became a therapy dog when it was seen how this dog was interacting with hospitalized people.

The program started with four or five teams visiting a few sites. Initially managed by volunteers, the program grew each year as more and more people learned about the program. With each new manager and more VHS outreach activities, the program was expanded and continues to grow.

Through this program, handlers and dogs are covered with liability insurance by VHS, and participating sites and programs can be assured that the teams are well behaved and suitable for work in various settings, and that the dogs are healthy and current on required shots and tests. The focus of this book is on the value of these therapy dogs in service to others. This book includes only some of the sites and programs where VHS handler/therapy dog teams work.

In addition to the animal care and adoption services and the therapy dog program, VHS runs a pet-food pantry for low-income families with pets (AniMeals), educational programs to help children learn about being responsible pet owners (Humane Education and Critter Camp), and a fund to help provide financial assistance for emergency veterinary care (Just Like New).

VHS relies heavily on individual donations for its operations and programs. It is a 501(c)3 nonprofit organization which receives no government funds, tax dollars, or money from national humane organizations. To make a donation, send a check, payable to Valley Humane Society, to 3670 Nevada Street, Pleasanton, California 94566 or go to the website at www.valleyhumane.org.

APPENDIX B

DOG BIOS

This appendix includes bios about each of the 51 dogs featured in this book. They range in size from under ten pounds to over 130 pounds. They include several purebreds and a variety of mixes. About two-thirds (31 of 51) are males. Sadly, several of these 51 dogs have passed away, but while alive provided loving service to many people.

Since four of the dogs are named Buddy, the initial of the owners' last names have been added so it is clear to which Buddy we are referring.

Albert was found wandering on the streets of Livermore one evening in August 2002. Pat Wheeler had been out doing some errands and was heading home when she saw him in the street about half a mile from her house. At first, she thought it was her Black Lab, Lawrence, and was wondering how on earth he got out of the house. She pulled over and opened the back of her car. Albert dashed over, jumped in, and started licking Pat's face. No one nearby knew to whom he belonged, and he only had a rabies tag. So Pat took him home to call Animal Control and the veterinarian's office where he got his rabies tag. As soon as she walked into the house with him, he and her dog, Lawrence, were best buddies.

Pat left a message for the veterinarian. Animal Control said they had no one available to pick him up now and asked if she would keep him until someone could come by to get him next week. The next morning, she got a call from the veterinarian's office. Albert's temporary owners were out of town and the pet sitter lost track of all their animals (they had, as Pat recalls, four other dogs and four cats). The pet sitter came to pick him up, and she saw how sad both he and Lawrence looked as she put Albert into her car.

The next evening, the owners arrived home. They called Pat and said they had been trying to find a home for Albert. While camping on the north coast of California, they had been given Albert by a homeless family that couldn't afford to keep him. Pat instantly agreed to come and pick him up. Lawrence and he are still the best of buddies, and Albert has brought lots of joy to her household.

Albert started as therapy dog at the VA in May 2005. By 2010, he had given 750 hours of service at the VA and was promoted to "Captain" by Navy veterans for these hours of service and for helping Lawrence oversee the "Petting Officers" and their handlers. In February 2006, he was welcomed as the first therapy dog ever at Shepherd's Gate in Livermore. This is a shelter for battered and homeless women and children. At the end of his first year, Albert earned the "Volunteer of the Year" award at Shepherd's Gate.

Since September 2006, Albert has also gone to Easy Living Care Home sites three or four times a month, participated in parades (e.g., Livermore Rodeo Parade, Veterans Day Parade), and attended Welcome Home Celebrations and other military events. He is an AKC Canine Good Citizen, Canine Partner, and Therapy Dog. His favorite command is WORK. He won't wake from a sound sleep to the words "treat" or "walk," but jumps up instantly at the word "work." We think Albert is a Border Collie/Black Lab mix, born in the spring of 2001. The Border Collie in him sure makes him focus on work.

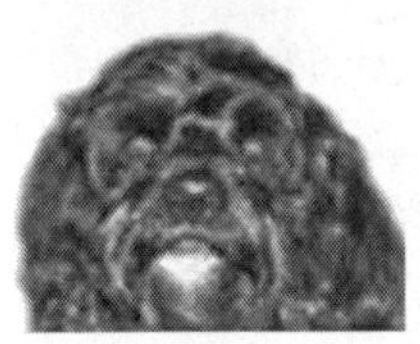

Alfie and **Zito** are the first small dogs that Sandi DeTata has ever owned. Previously, she always had larger dogs like German Shepherds. Her former dog died of cancer, and, being a dog person who has always had a dog in the family from childhood to adulthood, she missed having a dog. Sandi researched dog characteristics on the Internet and decided that a Cockapoo had the characteristics that she wanted. She researched for good breeders and found one in the nearby town of Brentwood that interested her. She visited and chose Alfie from the litter when he was seven weeks old. He was an adorable little cream-colored fluff ball and a very sweet puppy.

After she had Alfie for two weeks and just loved him, she decided to get him a brother. Alfie's littermates were all sold by then, but Cockapoo breeders throughout the United States network with each other. Alfie's breeder found Zito in Tennessee, and he was close in age to Alfie. A picture of Zito was sent to Sandi on the Internet, and she wanted him. Zito flew out here from Tennessee. He is five weeks younger than Alfie. They bonded right away, and Alfie potty trained Zito. They have been true brothers ever since. Even though Alfie is smaller than Zito, Alfie is the alpha dog and kind of looks after Zito. Zito is a little shyer than Alfie and lets Alfie lead the way in many instances.

Sandi loves her two little Cockapoos and would recommend this breed to anyone. Sandi and her dogs have been volunteering weekly at the VA in Livermore since June 2009, and both have reached the rank of "Chief Petting Officer" for 100 hours of service. They also went to Quail Gardens in Livermore, an assisted living facility, from April 2009 to June 2011. Both Alfie and Zito have gone to Welcome Home Celebrations for military troops and marched in a Veterans Day Parade in Pleasanton.

Augie was a Golden Retriever, born on August 31, 1998, in Dublin. Caroline Gary obtained Augie from his breeder and 4-H dog instructor, Laura Finco, in Dublin. From the get-go, Augie was a "people dog" who preferred interacting with people rather than other animals. At the young age of one, Augie started participating in the pet therapy program. He visited The Friendship Center for seven years (2001 to 2008) where he was always greeted warmly by the staff and clients. Augie enjoyed his visits and provided many laughs because of his antics. Augie passed away, surrounded by his family, on Christmas Day in 2010, at the age of twelve. He will forever be remembered as our dear sweet boy with the gentle soul who was placed here on Earth to show us how to love each other.

Bear was born in 1988, and the Rogers family adopted him in 1998 from Norcal Golden Retriever Rescue in Fresno. He was almost ten years old at that time. But he loved people and tennis balls. So he was very happy to visit Merrill Gardens as a therapy dog. Bear loved tennis balls and could carry two balls in his mouth at once, and also enjoyed seeing the tennis balls on walkers. Bear worked at Merrill Gardens weekly from 2001 until he died in 2003. He also went to the Paws to Read program at the Pleasanton Public Library when it first started in 2001. Bear passed away on May 1, 2003, at almost 15 years old, a very dignified and special dog.

Bella is a Shetland Sheepdog, more commonly called a Sheltie. She was born on January 30, 2009, in Fremont. The Beckers obtained her from Susan Garcia of Salina Kennels. When she was just four months old, Bella started going to The Parkview to visit an elderly family member. It soon became evident that she was a natural therapy dog and able to give joy to many.

After Bella officially became a therapy dog, she started going to the Paws to Read program at the Pleasanton Public Library and continued going to The Parkview. She loves working with both young and old, and, as soon as her vest is on, she gets into working mode. When not working, Bella loves running on the beach off leash, taking walks down Main Street in Pleasanton, and walking on the trails in the forest in Pacific Grove.

Belle, an English Cocker Spaniel, was born in August 1999 in Wales, United Kingdom. Joan and Lou Gigliati obtained her from a trainer in North Dakota. Belle has been going to the VA in Livermore since December 2007, where she has attained the rank of "Chief Petting Officer."

Although Belle is a trained and practicing bird-flushing/hunting dog, her enthusiastic and sweet nature led her owners to believe that Belle would be a great therapy dog. Belle's enthusiastic "tail wagging" has won over both patients and staff at the VA. Belle particularly likes to visit with patients in wheelchairs, which are just the right height for her to be petted. Belle just can't seem to get enough petting, which endears her to all who try. When not working, Belle likes to go for walks and lie in the sun.

Benji was born in a trash-filled trailer park in Los Baños, a rough beginning for a dog. With nothing to eat, Benji and the other dogs were forced to eat rocks and scavenge for food. Fortunately, his mother and his siblings were rescued, and all were adopted out through Companion Animal Rescue Effort (CARE). Unfortunately, his mother succumbed to complications of another pregnancy. But Benji's new owners, the Payne family, give his mother a lot of credit for helping these puppies survive and doing a wonderful job of raising such amazing dogs.

Lynley Payne knew, the moment when Benji entered their home, that he was something special. His love and gentleness were so apparent to everyone that met him, and Lynley knew that he had plenty of love to share with others. He is a dog that has never growled or snapped at anyone, and pretty much does whatever his owners tell him to do, whether he wants to or not. People often ask Lynley how Benji was trained, but in truth Benji pretty much trained himself. At an early age, he decided that this was a good home, and he had no need to wander, often sitting on the front lawn and watching the world go by, an activity for which he has became famous in our neighborhood.

Benji is probably a Collie/Labrador Retriever mix. Benji was born in December 2007 and came to the Payne family when he was five months old. He is a real people-pleaser and will do anything to get approval from people. His favorite thing is "Walk," even more so than "Food," and he probably has actually learned how to spell those words. Benji has been visiting The Parkview since May 2009 and also participated in some sessions of Paws to Read at the Pleasanton Public Library in 2009 and 2010.

Friends, neighbors, and even his veterinarian have proclaimed that Benji is "the best dog ever," and, though Lynley could be just a little biased, she tends to agree. Pets are with us for such a short time, and it seems that Benji decided early on he was going to make the most of this time by being the best he can be. We should all take a leaf out of his book, so to speak.

Bizi was born in 1998 in Tracy. Pat Jacobson obtained Bizi from NORCAL Golden Retriever Rescue when he was nine months old. Bizi died of cancer at age six-and-a-half years. Bizi always had that wonderful Golden personality and temperament, but it took a couple of very difficult, out-of-control years for Bizi to finally begin showing good behavior. In his former life, he received no discipline whatsoever, as evidenced by the first day that Pat got him. A neighbor stopped by to meet Bizi, and Pat pulled out a chair for her to sit on. As fast as a lightening flash, Bizi was in the chair! Throughout his life, Bizi was convinced that every empty chair was put there for him. Chairs, and, oh yes, tennis balls, all belonged to Bizi, he was certain.

The day finally came when Bizi was to be tested as a therapy dog. Pat and Bizi entered the rehabilitation facility. Bizi was on Pat's left and on leash. What would you expect Bizi to see, just inside the door on the left? An empty chair, of course! With a firm "NO," Bizi responded properly, and Pat praised him. As they walked down the hallway, they saw an elderly lady coming toward Bizi, using her walker, which just happened to have two tennis balls attached to the legs. Another "NO!" and praise. Bizi passed the rest of the test with flying colors, and he was now truly a therapy dog. He began working at a nursing and rehab center in Danville in 2002 as well as the Paws to Read program in Pleasanton. He also went to Camp Arroyo in the summer of 2004. When not working, Bizi liked to swim and hike, and to be petted by everyone in the world.

Bosco was a Black Labrador Retriever who was born on December 29, 1995, in Bend, Oregon, and passed away on May 26, 2006. Frances Hewitt got Bosco from Three Sisters Labs in Bend, Oregon. He was a natural born bird hunter, but also a gentle giant who made a wonderful therapy dog, working with children and seniors. He was loving, kind, playful, caring, and, most of all, smart!

Bosco began his work as a therapy dog in 1998 at the Pleasanton Senior Center. He then went to a convalescent hospital in Pleasanton and also to Chardonnay Home Sr. Solutions, Inc., in Livermore, a residential care facility for people needing 24-hour care. Bosco was also a regular participant in the Paws to Read program at the Pleasanton Public Library.

In 2005, Frances Hewitt decided to retire Bosco as a therapy dog because he was beginning to slow down. Although he was deaf at this point in his life, Bosco's other passion was pheasant hunting, and he continued doing this until his passing in 2006. Bosco is no longer with the Hewitts, but they know that, with all the visits he made, he brought joy and laughter to many people, young and old.

Brooks was a Pointer/Lab mix born in McCall, Idaho, in April 1998. She started working at the VA in July 2010 with her sister, Rivers, and Cecile and Rich Porter. As old as she was, she still loved her walks to the park and chasing her tennis ball on a rope. She would have you throw it all day long. When she tired of catching it, she'd let you tug with her. She never lost. She loved to tease you by offering one end to you and then jerking it away at the last second.

She had endless love to share with all. Brooks and her sister, Rivers, also would wear the American Legion Riders (ALR) patch. She loved going to Welcome Home Celebrations with the Warriors' Watch Riders (WWR) and the Patriot Guard Riders (PGR). There is nothing like a "mug and hug" from a loveable Lab. Sadly, Brooks had to be put down on August 17, 2012.

Buddy G, a Maltese mix, was born in January 2007. Joan and Lou Gigliati adopted her from the White Cat Rescue Group in Walnut Creek. Buddy G started working as a therapy dog at the Livermore VA in February 2010. He saw her sister Belle going to the VA each week and wanted to go too. Buddy G likes nothing better than snuggling next to a patient. Since he is only 11.5 pounds, Buddy G is well suited to visiting with those patients that are confined to bed. His calm, soothing demeanor is especially suited to this program. He is also liked by the staff and loves to visit with them as well. When not working, Buddy G likes to play with his toys and lie in the sun next to his sister, Belle.

Buddy H is a Queensland Heeler/Golden Retriever mix who was born in Livermore in August 2000. Joanne Hamilton adopted him from a woman at a soccer game when he was six weeks old. He grew up with two girls (who are now in college) and numerous animals (five cats, three chickens, and many visiting dogs).

Buddy H is loving, smart, gentle, sweet, and very friendly. His mission in life has always been to serve and help people the best way that he can. As part of this, he became a therapy dog in 2003, working with the Paws to Read program at the Pleasanton Public Library, visiting assisted living facilities, and going to The Friendship Center in Livermore on special occasions. He retired as a therapy dog in 2005.

Buddy K is an adorable French Bulldog, who was born on October 23, 2007. He started working as a loving and snorting therapy dog at the Livermore VA in September 2009. He also goes to the Paws to Read programs at both libraries in Livermore (Civic Center and Rincon branch). Buddy K visits the students at Marylin Avenue Elementary School too. He likes to be in your face. And how can one resist a cute face like his. When not working, Buddy K likes taking walks in the neighborhood with his owner, Randy Kirchner, and going to the dog park.

Buddy W is a Golden Retriever/Yellow Lab mix that Paul Wankle adopted in March 2008 when his dog Chamois, a Chow mix, died at age 13 of a stroke. Buddy W was a rescue dog, born in 2004 in Sacramento. Paul rescued Buddy W from a foster care facility sponsored by the local Labrador rescue group. Although he had no history on Buddy W, it wasn't long before he exhibited the best qualities of both Golden and Lab breeds. Buddy W is intelligent and gregarious, but extremely gentle, and absolutely in love with everyone he meets. He seems to thrive when exposed to people, especially children, the elderly, and those in need. We noticed that children seem to be his favorite. At 75 pounds, Buddy W is relatively large and is totally unaffected by the unintentional "abuse" that young children can dish out. He also has an excellent stature for visits to care facilities and is anxious to reach out to solicit petting from bedridden patients.

When it became apparent that Buddy W might be a good candidate for the Paws to Read program, his owner Paul Wankle began the process of qualifying for the program by contacting Valley Humane Society and meeting with their staff. Buddy W passed the testing with flying colors, but it would take a bit longer to become totally familiar with the details and logistics of the program. Once Buddy W was certified, Paul met with Reneé Freidus at the Pleasanton Public Library. They spoke about the program, she met with Buddy W, and now they had the necessary authorization to participate in the program, starting the next Tuesday evening. Buddy W has been participating in Paws to Read since January 2009.

Since 2011, Buddy W has gone to Camp Erin, along with occasional visits to senior care facilities. He and Paul also participate in a number of VHS-sponsored events throughout the year. In April 2012, Buddy W was recognized as an AKC Canine Partner and Therapy Dog. When not working as a therapy dog, Buddy W enjoys "working" at Classic Cars Ltd. where he is the Vice President of Human Relations.

Cabo, a large Yellow Labrador Retriever, was born on November 17, 2004, in Bend, Oregon. He is Bosco's great-nephew. Frances Hewitt obtained Cabo from the same place that Bosco came from—Three Sisters Labs in Bend, Oregon. Cabo became a therapy dog in 2006 and knows that when he is wearing his therapy dog vest, he is at work and that means business! He followed Bosco by visiting residents at nursing homes and The Parkview in Pleasanton, where he is well-loved by residents and attends many special events. Since 2009, Cabo has been visiting a third-grade class at Emma C. Smith Elementary School in Livermore. In 2011, he started participating in the reading programs and BELIEVES! at Marylin Avenue Elementary School. In addition, Cabo participates regularly in the Paws to Read program at the Livermore Public Library's Rincon branch.

Cabo has also assisted in community events. While wearing his patriotic bandanna, he proudly marches in local parades including the City of Pleasanton's Veterans Day Parade. He loves to be kept busy. When not working, he enjoys spending time pheasant hunting at his club in Rio Vista with Frances' husband, Don. Cabo has also become Frances' "running partner" and has run up to nine miles with her on a given day.

Caper is a Golden Retriever, born in Dublin on July 5, 2005. Caper joined Nancy Rogers' family on April 3, 2008. Her breeders used to take Caper to shows, but then she was "retired" at age three to be bred so that she could have puppies. However, Mother Nature had other ideas and motherhood was not to be for Caper. Nancy was already involved with the therapy dog program, and so Caper moved into that career.

In 2008, Caper started participating in the Paws to Read programs at the Pleasanton Public Library, and, the next year, at both the Civic Center and Rincon branch libraries in Livermore. She also started visiting The Parkview in 2008, and visits Camp Arroyo in August and sometimes in November. She also goes to Marylin Avenue School. Her favorite job is working in the Memory Care Unit at The Parkview. Caper has been recognized as an AKC Therapy Dog. When not working, Caper enjoys taking long walks, playing, and just spending time with "Daddy."

Chex Mix is a Newfoundland who came to Hazel Jacoby from Newfoundland Health and Rescue, Inc., at age 22 months. He was born on December 25, 2004 (yes, he's a Christmas baby), in Elkland, Missouri. Hazel and Chex Mix went to obedience training, as they both required some! He wanted so much to be a good boy that he passed his AKC Canine Good Citizen (CGC) test on the first try.

He does not have the drive to be in the water like many Newfies, but he can swim and does not object to the water. He has learned to pull a cart. Starting in 2007, Chex Mix participated in the CARH activities. He currently goes about once a month to one of their activities, just to be available for loving. He was named CARH's "Volunteer of the Month" in August 2011. He pulls his cart, decorated appropriately, to bring party favors to attendees on special occasions such as St. Patrick's Day and Halloween. Chex Mix also visited a rehabilitation center, and, in April 2012, started attending Welcome Home Celebrations for our troops. He has participated in the Castro Valley Library's Paws to Read program since it began in 2010.

Chex Mix is known in his local neighborhood for pulling his cart and sometimes giving rides to small children. Once he even gave a ride to a boy and his dog. A picture of that ride was in a magazine article about the neighborhood in Castro Valley where he and Hazel live.

Christy, like her housemate Gunther, was bred in New Jersey at Bjorn Lass Kennels. She was born in July 2000 and became a member of Paula Huettig's household. Unlike Gunther, Christy was not interested in conformation showing at all, but tolerated obedience class. However, she really loved being the "demo dog" at obedience class, and, because she was a quick study, she was the demo dog most of the time! She just loved the praise and attention the instructor gave her (not to mention the extra treats!). Christy, along with Gunther, became a therapy dog in 2006 and participated in various community events.

Christy began working with the Paws to Read program at the Rincon branch library in Livermore in the spring of 2011, and, shortly thereafter, at Marylin Avenue School for students in grades two to five. Christy has also participated in the special sessions held at the Livermore Civic Center Library for children with autism. Christy is very popular with the children.

While more reserved than Gunther, she too loves to be hugged and to snuggle, and really looks forward to visiting the library and listening to the children. For some reason, the little boys are particularly attracted to Christy, sometimes meeting her outside the library, before the program begins, to pet her. And Christy enjoys being with them. It is her time to shine and have attention paid to her, and she is also happy to have some time away from her two much younger canine brothers so she can give and get attention without competition.

Dazzle was the third VHS therapy dog to work in the program at the VA in Livermore. She was a Vizsla who had been a service dog for a paraplegic woman in Florida. Lisa Clowdus rescued Dazzle after her owner passed away. Dazzle was nine years old then. Given her experience as a service dog, Lisa thought Dazzle would be great as a therapy dog. She learned about the therapy dog program at the VA when talking with Pat Wheeler at a meeting of the Daughters of the American Revolution (DAR). Pat invited Lisa to come shadow her and Lawrence at the VA. Lisa felt this was a natural for Dazzle and immediately became involved in the program.

Dazzle worked with the Paws to Read program and at the VA from April 2005 until she passed away of cancer in September 2007. She achieved the rank of "Chief Petting Officer" at the VA. Dazzle was remembered at a memorial service at the VA for all veterans who had passed away in the last six months. This was the first time that a dog had been remembered at such a service, and the memory of Dazzle brought tears to many eyes in the room.

Dazzle brought so much love and joy into Lisa's life as well. She enriched Lisa's life in so many ways by being her therapy dog. But she also brought happiness and hope to hundreds of people that she visited in hospitals and nursing homes and to all the children who read to her in the Paws to Read program. Dazzle's name was the most fitting name of any dog in the universe. She brightened up so many lives and radiated her love to all while working at the VA. She was, quite simply, the most "dazzling" girl in the world. She is missed, but held in our hearts forever.

Dori is an a-Dori-ble Shih Tzu/Poodle mix and the poster dog for the VHS pet therapy program. Sandra Wing started taking Dori to the Livermore VA in December 2005, but they had to transfer to Villa San Ramon when Sandra wasn't able to go to the VA anymore. Dori was so loved by one of the veterans at the VA that the photo of the two of them wrapped up together was selected by Valley Humane Society for publicity about its programs (http://www.valleyhumane.org/index.php?s=program_service). It clearly shows how much love a therapy dog can provide for someone.

Ella, a Cavalier King Charles Spaniel, was born on September 9, 2002, in Sacramento. Her owner, Debbie Lunning, bought her from a breeder when Ella was five months old. Ella began socialization training right away, using her abundant energy to walk around the neighborhood, ride in the car to interesting places, and visit people in many settings.

Ella went to agility classes in 2003, and, while she excelled, she preferred a life as the queen of the house, the neighborhood ambassador, and the best friend to Debbie's grandchildren. Ella passed the AKC test to become a Canine Good Citizen (CGC) and became a therapy dog in July 2007. Her first job was listening to children read at the Pleasanton Public Library's Paws to Read program. She really enjoyed her evenings with the children.

In 2008, she became a weekly visitor at The Parkview, an assisted living and memory care facility, with the goal of putting smiles on as many faces as possible. In 2009, Ella was invited to join the reading class of special needs children at Alisal Elementary School. Being small in stature, she became particularly good at teaching fearful children how to make friends with a dog. This talent of putting fearful children at ease has helped Ella give joy and comfort to special needs campers at Camp Arroyo since 2010. In 2012, Ella was recognized for her work with an AKC Therapy Dog certificate.

Ella enjoys chasing tennis balls and playing "Go Find It." Yet, her favorite thing to do is to seek out a person of any age whom she thinks needs a melting glance, a soft touch, and a smile on their face. She has perfected "The Look" that she gives to charm a visitor and to reap the rewards of making a new friend.

Elsa, a Black Labrador Retriever, was born to help others. She was born on May 12, 2007, in San Rafael at the Guide Dogs for the Blind campus. After about 19 months of training, Elsa was chosen to be part of the Guide Dogs breeding program. Elsa's strong training foundation led Elsa to pass the AKC Canine Good Citizen (CGC) test and become a Delta Society Pet Partner, a VHS therapy dog, and a member of the ARF Pet Hugs Pack. Elsa has earned the AKC Therapy Dog certificate for over 50 hours of service.

Sue Day and Elsa started working as a VHS therapy dog team in June 2009. They have worked at several retirement homes and were at the VA in 2009 and 2010. Elsa has let children read to her at the Paws to Read programs at local libraries. She has had four litters for Guide Dogs. When she is not working with Guide Dogs for the Blind or doing therapy dog work, she enjoys doing freestyle dance, taking hikes, and playing fly ball.

Gandalf II is a Chihuahua/Schipperke mix, born in 2001. He came into Roy Ficken's life during the 2001 holiday season. Roy was attending a Tri-Valley Animal Rescue (TVAR) Christmas Dinner. That evening, a friend told Roy about some puppies she had rescued. She knew that Roy had been looking for that special dog for the past four years. They went to her home, opened the garage door, and saw four small black puppies excitedly jumping up and down. A small black dog, standing behind the three larger puppies, caught Roy's eye. For some unknown reason, Roy said, "This is the dog I've been looking for." He went back to the dinner and showed his new dog off to everyone that evening. He named his new puppy after the family dog, Gandalf, that they had had in the 1960s. The name Gandalf comes from J. R. Tolkien's book, *The Lord of the Rings*.

About three weeks later, Roy started noticing that Gandalf II was acting funny. He took him to the Feline Medical Center in Pleasanton and asked Dr. Marshall to check him over. She told me that Gandalf II has Addison's disease and would have to be on medication the rest of his life. He is doing fine now, and I am so thankful that Dr. Marshall made the right diagnosis and prescribed the right medication.

When he was only eight weeks old, Gandalf II started working with the Pleasanton Police Department as the Public Relations K-9. He also participated in DARE programs and safety presentations to youth groups and students. Although now retired after a ten-year career with the police department, he worked hard while there.

In 2011, he became a therapy dog. He and Roy go to the Paws to Read program at the Pleasanton Public Library, visit residents at the The Parkview, and continue participating in community events and giving safety programs. Stories about his work with the Pleasanton Police Department are also in this book (see Chapter 14), even though he wasn't officially a therapy dog then.

Gunther, a Norwegian Elkhound, was born in July 1999 at Bjorn Lass Kennels in New Jersey, which was operated by Richard Gamsby, a long-time Elkhound breeder, who met his first Elkhound while stationed at California's Fort Ord during the Vietnam era. In November 1999, Paula and David Huettig were looking for a puppy housemate for their dog, Teddy, after his soul mate, Rinda, had passed away. They contacted Richard Gamsby and brought Gunther home when he was four months old.

Gunther was a very happy, outgoing, social puppy who loved both people and other dogs. He spent lots of time playing and entertaining Teddy, and sleeping on Teddy's bed with him when he needed a nap. Gunther loved obedience classes, and quickly became the star pupil, acting as the "demo dog" for the instructor. Gunther moved on to conformation showing, and quickly became an AKC champion.

Gunther became a therapy dog in 2006 and started, in September 2007, going to the VA in Livermore almost weekly. Toward the end of 2008, Gunther began to have difficulty navigating the slippery, shiny floors at the VA. Often, he would slip and fall down, but got right back up again and continued to do his job. In December 2008, his veterinarian told us that Gunther had an 80% tear in the ligament in his knee, and it required a major surgery. He also advised that Gunther not visit the VA until the outcome of the surgery could be determined. Subsequently, he had to retire from that facility as a "Chief Petting Offier." Gunther really enjoyed his time visiting with the veterans and was eager to go every week. He especially related to the men in wheelchairs, who were sometimes amputees. It seemed as though he knew that these veterans would talk to him and give him lots of pets and good firm massages.

While the surgery was successful and he was fully mobile and pain free, he had arthritis in his hips, and no longer had the ability to move safely on slippery, shiny floors at the VA. So he started participating in the Paws to Read program at the Rincon branch library in the spring of 2010. Gunther passed away on January 14, 2011, after a busy career as a therapy dog.

Hunter is a Black Labrador Retriever, born on January 15, 2010, in Prather. Amy Berryhill purchased Hunter from Pat Collom at Windrose Labradors. Hunter loves children and has a naturally sweet, loving, and calm disposition, even as a puppy. He was a natural fit for therapy dog work. Amy started training with him right away and thought the Paws to Read program would be a great match for him and her family. Hunter has been working as a therapy dog since 2011 at Los Perales Elementary School and at the Orinda Library. He is also certified by Tony La Russa's Animal Rescue Foundation (ARF).

Amy can tell he enjoys his work because he is so eager to get to his work destination and then he naturally calms down when it is time for him to listen to the children read. When Hunter isn't working, he enjoys hanging around his family and their friends, and playing with other dogs. He gets lots of exercise because he is part of an active family that likes to be outdoors. He follows all characteristics of a typical Lab. He loves to swim and play fetch, and is extremely friendly with people and dogs.

Jiffy was born in October 1999 in San Rafael. She started working at the Livermore VA in May 2005. She was a Yellow Labrador Retriever, who started her career training to be a Guide Dog, but changed her career to a therapy dog when she couldn't pass all the rigorous tests. Thankfully, she found her way to the Livermore VA where her owner, Vietnam War veteran, Doug Cabral, came for outpatient services.

Doug saw Lawrence at work and asked about bringing Jiffy. Before they knew it, Jiffy was providing her loving services to our veterans as well as many VA staff members. Jiffy visited people in the Main Building in the various waiting areas and provided needed encouragement and pain management for those struggling to improve their skills through physical therapy. She also visited everyone in the Nursing Home Care Unit. Jiffy passed away on November 14, 2009. Prior to her passing, Jiffy attained the rank of "Master Chief Petting Officer" for over 500 hours of service at the VA. Jiffy was remembered at the semi-annual memorial service at the VA on November 21, 2009.

Kane was a Golden Retriever, born on March 30, 2003, in Dublin. Kane came to live with the Rogers' family when he was six months old. Kane was only nine months old when he became a therapy dog. His career started in January 2004 with going to the Pleasanton Public Library for the Paws to Read program and to Merrill Gardens. He also went to Camp Arroyo. He continued working until September 2007, when he became too ill to continue.

Kane really loved being with the children and having them read to him. When not working, Kane enjoyed playing ball, taking long walks, and spending time with "his grandchildren!" Kane passed away of cancer in October 2007, though he made great contributions to people's lives in his short lifetime.

Klaus is a loving German Shepherd/Airedale mix with piercing blue eyes. Born in 2001, Klaus began working as a therapy dog at the Livermore VA in November 2009 until 2011. His owners are Tom and Shari Marcotte. He was rescued from Tri-Valley Animal Shelter in 2004 to be a companion for Tom's mother. The Marcottes were told at the shelter that Klaus was extremely vocal and an escape artist, but friendly with all people and with other dogs as well as cats. Klaus is not the most handsome dog, but has beautiful crystal blue eyes. He also has a unique way of expressing himself by giving soft howls when spoken to or when he wants your attention. Klaus never seems to be in a hurry and moves very slowly. He is very gentle, always just going with the flow.

Unfortunately, Tom's mother passed away in 2006, and, although Tom and Shari already owned two other dogs, Tom offered to take Klaus from his stepfather after his mother's passing. His stepfather said he was undecided if he wanted to keep him or not, but one day asked Tom and Shari to dog sit for a few days and then he never returned for Klaus. This is how Klaus became part of their family. Because Klaus was very therapeutic to Tom's mother during her last few years and brought her such peace and happiness, Tom and Shari felt he was destined to continue his therapeutic gift, and this is how he became a therapy dog. Klaus went to the VA about once a month.

Kody was a Samoyed, born on September 25, 1993, in Benicia. He passed away on July 15, 2006, after a seven-year career as a therapy dog. After his family from Danville moved to Seattle, Washington, he began his career in Seattle visiting the library. When Ellen Waskey moved to Pleasanton, Kody worked weekly at retirement homes, rehabilitation hospitals, and his owner's school, Lydiksen Elementary School in Pleasanton. When he was on the school campus, the rule was that you had to get a book and read it to him. That's how Ellen found out about the Paws to Read program at the Pleasanton Public Library, and they started volunteering there.

Kody loved to work, especially having children read to him. When Ellen got his therapy dog vest and his short leash out, he would bark and dance around in circles. As soon as she opened the car door, he was ready to go. As they turned onto the street where the library is located, he got so excited because he knew where he was going. The moment they walked into the meeting room, Kody was on his best behavior. He absolutely loved the children and having them read to him.

Lady, a Border Collie/Aussie mix, was born on June 1, 2002, in Livermore. She was chosen out of a litter of about 14 puppies that were bred for cattle herding purposes in 2002. Actually, she picked Graham Scott for her owner. As he checked out all the puppies, she continuously pulled at his pants and kept untying his shoes. Graham gave in and brought her home.

With all her energy, he knew that he needed a way to give her a workout. Graham and his wife, Pat, started by throwing a tennis ball and having Lady fetch it. That evolved into throwing and catching discs (aka Frisbees ®). By practicing daily, she has become pretty good. Graham found a disc dog club on the Internet called "Disc Dogs of the Golden Gate." Since 2003, she has competed in several major tournaments and has won a few of them. Even at ten years old, she was still competing in a couple tournaments.

The club owner and good friend, Steve Teer of the Disc Dog Club, told Graham about how he got his dog involved in therapy dog work. About a week later, someone gave a talk at Graham's Rotary Club meeting and mentioned pet therapy. He figured that would be a great job for Lady. He submitted their paperwork and they were approved to work at the VA in Livermore starting in October 2009. She adapted quickly to her new job and has made many friends at the VA. She has also gone to Camp Erin and attended Welcome Home Celebrations. At home, when Lady hears that she's "going to work," she perks up and races to the truck.

The culmination of her disc dog and therapy dog skills were displayed on Memorial Day in 2010 when she showed off her disc catching skills for her friends at the VA. She also did this for the kids at Camp Erin and has had repeated performances at the VA. She enjoys seeing the smiles and hearing the applause for something she loves to do.

Lady is an AKC certified therapy dog and has attained the rank of "Chief Petting Officer" for over 100 hours of service at the VA. When not working or chasing discs, Lady enjoys her daily walks in the park, barking at cows while riding in the truck, and managing her squeaky toys.

Lassie, as one could probably guess from her name, is a Collie. Kay Christensen got Lassie through the Contra Costa Animal Shelter. She was presumably born on July 1, 2004. She started as a therapy dog at the Livermore VA in October 2008 and retired as a therapy dog in 2011.

Her owner, Kay Christensen, found Lassie in a high-kill shelter with only two days left to live. She had been taken from her owner for abuse and was 30 pounds underweight when Kay got her. She was terrified of men for about a year. But she put that experience behind her and became a loving and smart dog, just like the one after which she is named. She tried to come to the VA at least once a month, but had to retire because of her owner's work schedule and the long commute.

Lawrence, the Livermore Lab, a Black Labrador Retriever, was the first Valley Humane Society therapy dog at the VA in Livermore. Born on July 20, 2001, in Palo Alto, his owner Pat Wheeler bought him from a breeder. When visiting the breeder, Pat could not decide which of the eight adorable Black Lab puppies to pick. She asked the breeder to pick one that would be a good therapy dog and he suggested Lawrence. What a great choice!

Lawrence became a therapy dog in November 2002 and immediately began working once a week at Golden Manor (later called Livermore Manor). He continued to go there every week for nine years until it closed. In July 2004, he started at the VA in Livermore. In September 2006, he began going to Easy Living Care Home sites two or three times a month.

He participates in numerous community events (e.g., the First Wednesdays in Pleasanton, the Home Campaign at Lawrence Livermore National Lab, business open houses); marches in parades (e.g., Livermore Rodeo Parade, Veterans Day Parade); performs in concerts (e.g., Golden Gate Park Band in San Francisco, Windjammers Circus Band in Carmichael, San Ramon Symphonic Band); goes to Welcome Home Celebrations for military members returning from Afghanistan, Iraq, and other tours of duty; and visits schools. Lawrence loves being out in public and marching in parades.

He is an AKC Canine Good Citizen and an AKC Therapy Dog. In 2012, he received an Honorable Mention as a Therapy Dog from the AKC Humane Fund Awards for Canine Excellence. As the "lead" therapy dog at the VA, Lawrence is involved with the evaluation of all potential handlers and therapy dogs, and also shows new therapy dogs how to do the job at the VA. His tail has had a workout during his career, and his veterinarian has commented about all the muscle tissue around his tail. When his tail reached one thousand hours of service at the VA in September 2010, Lawrence was promoted to "Rear Admiral." He oversees all the "Petting Officers" at the VA. When not working, Lawrence enjoys lying outdoors in the sun, going for walks with Pat's granddaughters, carrying toys to Pat, and, of course, eating.

Lucky was born on October 18, 2003, in Danville. Pat Jacobson got Lucky when he was a nine-month-old Golden Retriever. The person who originally purchased him had never had a dog before and was hoping that his family would enjoy a dog. But that was not to be, and Lucky was returned to the breeder, who happened to oversee the pet therapy program at the time. Pat had worked with the Paws to Read program with her Golden Retriever, Bizi, from the first day of the program in 2002, but she lost Bizi to cancer. So the breeder offered Lucky to Pat. This was lucky for him as well as for Pat and her family.

Lucky became a certified therapy dog in 2006, and he immediately started in the Paws to Read program at the Pleasanton Public Library as well as at the Pleasanton Nursing and Rehab Center. He also started going to Camp Arroyo that year. In 2010, Lucky began working with special education students at Alisal School. In 2011, he received the "You Make the Difference" award from students at Alisal School for his work in a special day class (SDC). After his family moved to Castro Valley in 2011, Lucky started visiting the Oak Creek Alzheimer's & Dementia Care Center in Castro Valley. When not working, Lucky likes to go for walks and to hang out with the cats and other dogs in the Jacobson family.

Maggie is a Golden Retriever mix who was found wandering the beach in San Felipe, Mexico, very pregnant, in August 2007. The San Felipe Animal Rescue (SFAR) finally caught up with her (after two days chasing her!), and, a week later, she delivered her eight puppies. SFAR knew that the Dennis family was looking for a new dog and emailed a picture to them of Maggie nursing her pups. The Dennises went down a week later, waited until Maggie finished nursing, and brought her home. Her puppies were all adopted out at Pet Smart in Yuma, Arizona.

Maggie is such a calm, loving dog that Dusty decided to have her tested to be a therapy dog. Though Dusty was open to any opportunity, she really wanted to take Maggie to the VA in Livermore since her dad was a veteran, and she feels a special gratitude to the men and women who serve our country. Maggie passed her "test" with flying colors and they have now been going to the VA at least once a month since May 2009. Maggie has reached the rank of "First Class Petting Officer." Since 2009, Maggie has also visited seniors at Merrill Gardens every other week and has participated in the Paws to Read program at the Danville Library where Maggie enjoys having the children read to her. She and Dusty go to Welcome Home Celebrations for military members returning from Afghanistan and Iraq, have gone to Camp Erin, and march in local parades.

Miles is a Golden Retriever, born on September 27, 2005, in Discovery Bay. John Flotten and Miles have been going to the VA in Livermore almost every week since June 2009 to love and comfort our veterans. Miles has reached the rank of "Senior Chief Petting Officer." Miles has been a regular at the Paws to Read programs at the libraries in Livermore and Pleasanton since 2010. He has gone to Marylin Avenue School since 2011. Miles has also attended a Welcome Home Celebration in Pleasanton and marched in the Veterans Day Parade for the Pleasanton Military Families. When not working, Miles likes to go for long walks in the park.

Mitsy is a Havanese/Poodle mix. She was born on June 4, 2003, and lived in Concord before coming to live with her new handler, Judy Butterly, after her first owner passed away. Her owner was 83 years old, and there was no one to keep Mitsy. Now she lives with Judy and her Maltese pal, Sam, who is a year younger. After Judy retired and moved to Livermore, Mitsy became certified as a therapy dog in May 2010. She began going to Special Olympics events with the team in June 2010 and to visit her friends at Eden Villa in July 2010. Mitsy would get so excited when she saw her purple therapy dog vest that Judy knew it was time for Mitsy to do more of what she loved best—visiting friends and hopefully getting some hugs. So Mitsy picked up more therapy dog jobs.

She loved going to visit all her friends at Livermore Manor until it closed in November 2011. Mitsy enjoys it when the children read to her in the Paws to Read program at the Livermore Public Library. She went to the VA in Livermore for a year starting in September 2010 and found that to be lots of fun, but had to cut back on her busy work schedule. Mitsy enjoys making people smile and be happy, and she likes it when they pet her and hold her. She hopes to be a therapy dog for a long time.

Mojo is a Welsh Corgi, born on June 10, 2005, in Livermore. Roberta Davies got him that year from a local breeder who was also an equine veterinarian. He went everywhere with Roberta, finished basic obedience classes, and, at eight months, was certified as a therapy dog so he could take part in the Paws to Read program at the Pleasanton Public Library. Despite his young age, he was and still is amazing with the children. He is a little cuddle bug. Mojo has been in the Paws to Read program in Pleasanton since 2006. When the Livermore Public Library started their own Paws to Read program in 2010, Roberta and Mojo also volunteered there. The Livermore Public Library provides a few Paws to Read sessions each year for special-needs children; Mojo and Roberta go to those sessions as well.

Mojo has been to Camp Arroyo each year since 2007 and has worked events for different groups upon request such as the First Wednesday Event in Pleasanton and parents nights in Livermore. He has made classroom visits to different schools. In 2012, he was recognized as an AKC Therapy Dog. When not working, Mojo likes to lie in the sun with his buddy, Woody, a Chocolate Lab.

Patch, a Golden Retriever, was born on March 25, 1999, in Modesto. He became a therapy dog in 2001 after his owner/handler, Salomé Thorson, read about pet therapy programs in *Parade* magazine. Patch visited Rosewood Gardens in Livermore for several years before starting to visit the Nursing Home Care Unit (NHCU) and Alzheimer's unit at the VA in January 2005. Patch's original visits to the VA were twice a month and then at least once a month starting in 2008, as he began to tire after about one hour. He attained the rank of "Chief Petting Officer" for over 100 hours of service. When not working, he loved to be with Salomé and her family. He was a very sensitive, caring dog. When out on a walk, he seemed to gravitate more toward people than other dogs.

Patch loved it when Salomé would get out his vest to go to the VA. He always got a super brushing or professional grooming, so he would look his best. As soon as Salomé turned into the VA grounds from Arroyo Road, Patch would pace back and forth in the back seat of the truck from window to window. He loved barking through the truck windows at the wild turkeys and deer that live in abundance on the VA grounds as Salomé drove to the NHCU.

Patch passed away on September 11, 2009, from inoperable tumors in his abdomen. Patch was remembered at the semi-annual memorial service at the VA on November 21, 2009. In Patch's memory, Salomé attends Welcome Home Celebrations for our troops since many are serving because of what happened to our country on 9-11 in 2001. Patch had beautiful milk-chocolate brown eyes that penetrated your heart. His fur was several shades of red and was very wavy. His teeth were very white and he smiled all the time because he was happy all the time. He is sadly missed by his family and remembered for his confident gait, wonderful heart, beautiful eyes, and love for everyone he met.

Salomé has his ashes and the cast of his paw print in her home as a remembrance. She will always treasure the time spent with Patch at the VA and the joy that he brought to the residents and staff. He was a true gem and 85 pounds of pure love.

P.I.P. (Pretty Impressive Pooch) was found by Carolyn Vane at the Oakland SPCA in 2004. P.I.P is probably a Border Collie/Cattle Dog mix. He was originally at the Hayward shelter, but when his time was up, the SPCA picked him up. Carolyn knew he would make a great search dog and she was right. P.I.P. was mission-ready just before his first birthday. He then started working for the Alameda County Sheriff Search and Rescue team. He has been on many searches and seems to love his work.

In 2011, P.I.P. started a new job as a therapy dog for the Castro Valley Library's Paws to Read program. P.I.P. sits on a blanket and a child comes and reads stories to him. P.I.P. licks the child and he gets petted. P.I.P. loves this job and loves showing off his tricks for the children. P.I.P. also goes to Camp Erin. When not working, P.I.P. enjoys fetching a ball and licking children.

Poli is a Yellow Lab, born on March 15, 2009, in San Rafael. When Jiffy passed away, Doug Cabral missed having a Yellow Lab at his home and coming to the VA with his dog. So Doug contacted Guide Dogs. A few months later, Poli came to his home, after she did not pass the final screening for Guide Dogs because she did not like working with the harness on. She was ready not only for a new home, but for a career change.

The youngest therapy dog to work at the VA in Livermore, Poli started in September 2010. She comes at least once a month to visit her friends in the Community Living Center. When not working, Poli likes to go for walks and play tug of war with her pull toys. She loves the water and can't wait for Doug to fill the waterfall in their yard so she can play in it.

Rio is the largest dog in the therapy dog program at the VA in Livermore. A 130-pound Bernese Mountain Dog, he is incredibly gentle. His fluffy coat makes him look very large as he comes down the hallway at the VA. Born in October 2005 in Watsonville, he has been a therapy dog at the VA since December 2009.

However, he is also certified by Therapy Dogs Inc. (TDInc) and has been working at senior facilities and with children's programs in Tracy and Lodi since 2008. His owner, Dan Schack, wanted Rio to be a therapy dog because he elicits such positive responses when interacting with people of all ages.

Rivers is a Queensland Heeler mix born in April 2000. She was adopted by Cecile and Rich Porter after she was abandoned when six weeks old at the San Francisco Airport (SFO) in June 2000. She started working at the VA as a therapy dog in July 2010 with her sister, Brooks. She is one very happy, lovable dog. If she isn't "nosing" her way up to you, her tail will let you know you're number one by going 'round and 'round and 'round . . .

Rivers wears the American Legion Riders (ALR) patch. She loves going to Welcome Home Celebrations with the Warriors' Watch Riders (WWR) and Patriot Guard Riders (PGR). She'll do anything for a little attention, a pet, and a hug.

Sailor is a Portuguese Water Dog, born in 2000 in Hilmar. He is independent and gentle, and a dog of purpose. He became a therapy dog in 2007 and started visiting the veterans at the Livermore VA in May that year. He truly enjoys his time with the veterans. He knows as soon as he dons his therapy dog vest what is in store and he takes this very seriously. When entering the VA property, Sailor begins to howl, occasionally bark, and generally gets very excited all the way to the front door, where he settles down and begins providing comfort. He and his owner, Jim Duthie, have attended Welcome Home Celebrations for our troops.

Sailor also has the role of greeter in his owners' storefront, Castle Comforts Interior Design, in downtown Livermore. Each morning, he proudly carries his leash from the car to the door, ready for his day's work. He likes to meet everyone and give people the opportunity to pet him. People respond well to his presence, and, like the veterans, the customers accommodate Sailor's request for petting. The breed is not well known, even though President Obama chose "BO," a Portuguese Water Dog, as the "First Dog." This breed is known for its feet with webbed toes, not shedding, and not causing allergic reactions in humans.

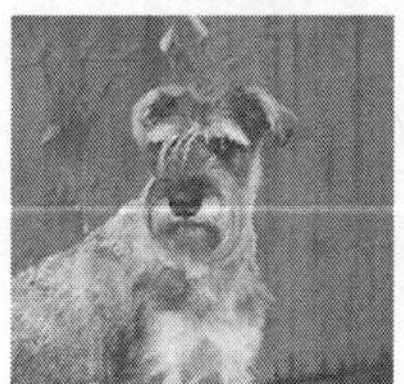

Schnoz, as the name implies, is a Schnauzer, a standard one. Born in October 2000 in Sebastopol, he has been a therapy dog since 2002 and started at the VA in 2006. Schnoz has been trained as a sheep-herding dog and has earned his AKC Canine Good Citizen (CGC) certificate. He is a funny and intuitive dog. Nanci Menise started out taking Schnoz to dog shows, but he enjoyed having people put their hands on him so much that he changed his career from show dog to therapy dog. Of course he is still a show dog, but not at the competitive dog shows. He just loves to show off for people.

Schnoz has worked at the VA in Livermore where he attained the rank of "Chief Petting Officer" for over 100 hours of service. Nanci and he have also worked in the Paws to Read program, at The Friendship Center, at Marylin Avenue Elementary School, and at assisted living facilities and senior centers. He has made many buddies in his work as a therapy dog. When at home, he has a fun time playing with the other two Schnauzers.

Shasta is a Border Collie/Beagle mix and was born in August 2003. She came to Kathy Benn from a kill-shelter in the Central Valley. Fortunately, she was rescued from this kill-shelter by Tri-Valley Animal Rescue (TVAR). It was obvious how much she liked to learn at her basic obedience classes. She continued on with many more classes including Agility for Fun, Agility 1 and 2, Fun with Rally, Come on Let's Go, and Tricks for Fun. Her most important class was the Canine Good Citizen prep class in August 2007 because this class opened the door for her to become a therapy dog! Shasta has worked as a therapy dog at The Parkview since 2007. Shasta also enjoys going to Pleasanton's street fairs and dog parades.

In 2008, Shasta had a starring role on TV Channel 20's "The Dogs Are Back." At the audition, she sat perfectly in the large easy chair and turned toward the TV camera at just the right moment. At home, her favorite thing to do outside is chasing tennis balls. She is extremely fast and loves to run. Unfortunately, this resulted in both of her knees failing. After several surgeries, she had to stay inactive for over one year while she healed. Although she is doing quite well, she cannot chase tennis balls like she used to.

Shasta has a "Skunky" to play with indoors. She shares this and everything else with her little "sister," Bella, a Puggle. She has taught Bella all that she knows. She shares the heartwarming qualities that make her a great therapy dog with other animal companions.

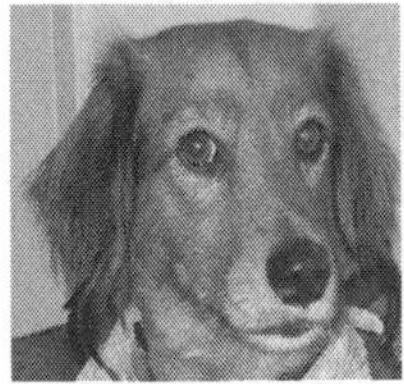

Shazam was born in 1994 in Ripon. She is a Sheltie/ Longhaired Dachshund mix. Kevin Coenen and Shazam started working as a therapy dog team at the VA in July 2007. Even when she was getting old, she still responded to the call of duty and visited the VA in Livermore as regularly as she could to show the veterans how much she loved them—her eyes told the story quickly. She retired from he VA in 2011 as a "Chief Petting Officer."

Since August 2010, she has participated in the Paws to Read program at the Pleasanton Public Library. Starting in 2011, she has also listened to children read books to her at the Livermore Public Library's Paws to Read program at the Rincon branch and visited students at Marylin Avenue School.

Shazam has been the most incredible gift a dog owner could ever have, and was a blessing for all the veterans at the VA. She is very loving, kind, and playful. Her favorite activities are walks around the neighborhood, playing in the park, visiting the veterans at the VA, having children read to her, and, after her long days, sleeping.

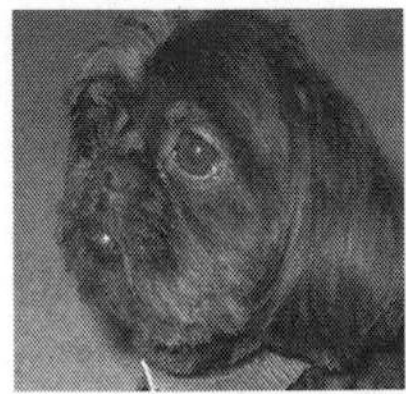

Simon is a Shih Tzu, born on January 28, 1998, in Livermore. Sadly, he passed away on April 25, 2012. Simon volunteered as a therapy dog at the VA in Livermore from May 2010 until December 2011. His owners were Tom and Shari Marcotte. In 1998, Shari shared with one of her co-workers that she was thinking about getting a puppy. Her co-worker mentioned that her friend bred Shih Tzus, and that they just had a litter of puppies and had one puppy left. Spending money on a purebred puppy was not something Shari was considering, and she knew there were plenty of dogs needing a home at the local shelter, but she agreed to go look at the Shih Tzu puppy anyway.

Simon was 12 weeks old and weighed about two pounds when Shari first saw him. He was a tiny little ball of black fur. When asked why all the other puppies from the litter were sold and not him, the breeder replied, "He has a bad under-bite, and has too many colors in his fur. Therefore he could never be a show dog and was undesirable to potential buyers." The woman said she would never be able to get anything for him and offered to sell him for $100. Shari ended up taking him home the same day, and Simon became part of her family.

Shari called Simon her shadow because if she got up, so did he. He was always a few steps behind her and followed her wherever she went. Simon was a quiet, calm-tempered dog. He brought a very calming presence to the hospice patients he visited at the VA, lying in their laps as they stroked his head. If Simon had it his way, he would have spent his whole day curled up in somebody's lap. Simon probably thought he was the one getting the therapy when visiting patients.

Tedi Bear was a Newfoundland dog that came to Hazel Jacoby from Newfoundland Health and Rescue, Inc. at three-and-a-half years of age. She was born on June 3, 2003, in Gavilan Hills. She had some training, but her owner Hazel did not. So they went to classes and Tedi Bear passed her AKC Canine Good Citizen (CGC) test.

Tedi Bear loved water, like many Newfies. Hoses, sprinklers, lakes, beaches, etc. were all fair game. She had some orthopedic issues and was quiet, but she loved people and animals. Whenever she heard a child, she tried to go see them. Hazel began checking into therapy dog opportunities for her. In 2007, Hazel first asked Community Assistance for Retarded and Handicapped (CARH), a group in Castro Valley that works with the developmentally disabled and seniors, whether they had a therapy dog program. They had no such program, but were interested. Their insurance carrier agreed that a Newfoundland would work well in their environment. They went to a couple of CARH's picnics and let all who wished to do so pet and cuddle her. Tedi Bear also went to a Castro Valley rehabilitation center for a few months to let patients chat with her and pet her.

When Castro Valley finished their new public library and began its Paws to Read program to assist children with reading skills, it seemed perfect! Tedi Bear became a certified therapy dog, and Hazel and Tedi Bear began going to the Paws to Read program at the Castro Valley Library when it started in May 2010. Tedi Bear's love of children was obvious, as she treated each child appropriately. She participated in the program until her death in July 2011.

Thunder was found on September 1, 2003, the morning after a huge thunder and lightning storm in the Tri-Valley. Laurie Kerr found him wandering on the Poppy Ridge golf course outside of Livermore, with his tongue hanging out and no identification except a gnawed leash attached to his collar. Laurie was unable to find anyone who recognized him, so she took him to the county animal shelter, hoping his owners would come for him. After six days, no one inquired about him, so he became a new member of the Kerr family. It was estimated that he was born in September 2002 and is thought to be a Boxer/Great Dane mix. Because of the thunder and lightning storms the night before she found him, Laurie named him Thunder, and it turned out to be the perfect name for him.

Thunder made his grand entry into the hallways of the Livermore VA in September 2007. No one can miss him—he arrives with *Thunder and Blazes*! He is very easy to reach from one's bed or wheelchair because of his height, unless he settles on the floor. Thunder is a "Master Chief Petting Officer" at the VA, for having over 500 hours of service there. Thunder also goes to Easy Living Care Home sites two or three times a month, marches in parades, participates in events for veterans, and, at 105 pounds, has been a big hit, literally, at Welcome Home Celebrations for returning military members.

When he is asked, "Are you ready to go to work?" he goes absolutely crazy running around, as happy as can be and anxious to get into the car. Thunder loves people and loves being petted and talked to by people, and, occasionally he even "talks back" while at the VA, letting everyone know that he is there and happy to see them. This job was made for him. When not working, he enjoys going for his long morning and evening walks. He waits for the sun to appear each day in the backyard so that he can do his daily sunbathing. He loves riding in the car and in the motor home. He also runs and catches squeaky toys when Laurie returns home.

Tioga was acquired in 2008 when Frances Roelfsema was looking for a promising new pound puppy to work as her partner in search and rescue. After Frances spent several months looking in a variety of Northern California animal shelters without success, she contacted a good friend of hers that had recently taken a position with the Animal Rescue League of Boston. This friend had spotted a particular puppy that seemed to meet Frances' requirements within an unwanted litter. It appeared to be a Lab/Golden Retriever mix. She made arrangements for Frances to meet the puppy after a quick, unscheduled plane flight to Boston. Fortunately, the puppy was a perfect fit, and, a couple weeks later, was on its way to the West Coast on a plane flight.

Tioga was an unusually quick study at the "find people" game, and he is now certified as both a trailing dog and human remains detection dog with the California Rescue Dog Association and the Alameda County Sheriff's Office Search and Rescue. Tioga is also an AKC Canine Good Citizen (CGC) dog. He has worked as a therapy dog in the Paws to Read programs at the Castro Valley Library since 2010 and at the Pleasanton Public Library since 2011. When not working, Tioga likes to make friends with every type of animal that will let him say hello.

Zito – See **Alfie**

APPENDIX C

HANDLER BIOS

This section provides short bios for the 46 handlers of the therapy dogs featured in this book. In the case of the handlers, two-thirds are females and one-third males, which is the opposite of the gender breakdown for the therapy dogs. About one-third of the handlers have retired from active employment. The most frequent employment category is public safety, though the handlers come from all walks of life. At least ten have served in the U.S. military. They live in communities throughout the Bay Area, from San Jose to Antioch, from Redwood City to Tracy. They report a variety of outside interests, and several of them volunteer for other organizations, both dog-related ones and others.

Dave Becker is a retired electrical engineer. Now he is a therapy dog handler for Bella, his family's Shetland Sheepdog, more commonly known as a Sheltie. They go to The Parkview and the Paws to Read program at the Pleasanton Public Library.

Pat Becker is a retired employee of the State of California. She, too, is a handler for the family dog, Bella, going to The Parkview and the Pleasanton Public Library.

During their free time, Dave and Pat enjoy traveling, visiting grandchildren and other family members, and spending time at their beach cottage in Pacific Grove where they take Bella for runs on the beach and walks in the forest. Dave and Pat live in Pleasanton with Bella.

Kathy Benn has loved animals all her life. As a child, she grew up with a Dalmatian and still has memories of her family taking the dog along to the drive-in movies to see *101 Dalmatians* together! She was sure she wanted to be a veterinarian until her kitty died in her arms as the doctor said, "There was nothing we could do." Kathy wanted to help animals and that was a heartbreaking lesson to learn at so young an age.

Kathy began actively working with dogs at age 13 in a 4-H project. A dog that lived next door had been washed out of the Police Academy because he was too nice. She worked with him daily to the point that the dog seemed to read her mind at times. Kathy studied energy medicine for several years and incorporates that into her work with animals.

She takes her dog, Shasta, to The Parkview. She currently works part time as a registered dental hygienist in a periodontal office. When not working with Shasta as a therapy dog handler, Kathy enjoys hiking, photography, traveling, and knitting. She lives in Pleasanton with her husband, two dogs, and a large Maine Coon cat.

Amy Berryhill runs a professional organizing company called Spiffy Chicks. She also coaches a running and nutrition program for girls, ages 8-12, for a company called LOLA. Her primary job, however, is raising two daughters and taking care of her family, which lives in Orinda. The family goes everywhere they can with their dog, Hunter. Since all family members volunteer in the local community, Amy thought it would be fun for her family to have him volunteer like the rest of them. She decided Hunter would be good for therapy dog work.

Amy wanted to help her friend, Dustie Robeson, get the LP Reads program at Los Perales Elementary School in Moraga off the ground. She never thought about how deeply she would be touched by watching the transformation happen with so many children. Of course, Amy had heard about how effective such programs can be, but she never actually experienced it first hand. She has found out that what these dogs are giving to the world is a wonderful gift, and she is so proud to have one of them in her family.

Now Amy and her dog, Hunter, volunteer with the Paws to Read program at the Orinda Library and the LP Reads program. Amy lives in Orinda with her husband, their two daughters, and Hunter. In her spare time, Amy likes to be active outdoors, running, cycling, hiking, skiing, and swimming.

Judy Butterly finally retired in March 2009, after 35 years in the operating room, the last 30 of which were spent at Kaiser Hospital in Walnut Creek and Pleasanton. For many years, Judy has been very involved with Special Olympics because her oldest grandson has special needs and loves to participate in all the sporting activities.

With both her son and daughter-in-law working, it was easier for Judy to get him to and from his practices. And, to make it easier for Judy, she ended up moving to Livermore from Alameda. Judy chairs the board of a nonprofit, R.E.A.C.H., for special adults in the Tri-Valley. This organization is dedicated to enhancing the quality of life of the individuals it supports by helping them reach their full potential. Judy also co-chairs the annual golf fundraiser for R.E.A.C.H.

Judy has always been an animal lover and has had dogs all of her adult life. On Valentine's Day in 2007, she lost her beloved Black Lab, Jake. He was 13 years old. Since she was still working at the time, she decided it was not the time for another dog. But about three months after Jake's passing, she got a call from a friend who had saved a little dog that was found running on the freeway. Judy came, she saw, and she took Sam, as she called him, home. Sam is a work in progress, but he is ten pounds of love.

Two months later, another call came from the same friend. This time she was fortunate to have Mitsy come to live with her. Mitsy's owner had passed away and the family could not keep her. Mitsy is a Havanese/Poodle mix. Judy knew from the beginning that Mitsy would make a wonderful therapy dog. So, when she retired and moved to Livermore, she had Mitsy certified as a therapy dog. Since June 2010, Judy and Mitsy have been having a wonderful time taking Mitsy to Special Olympics events, visiting the elderly at Livermore Manor and the veterans at the VA in Livermore, and going to the Livermore Public Library where the children read to Mitsy. Judy says this has been a truly rewarding experience for her, and she hopes to keep doing it for quite some time.

Doug Cabral is a retired logistics manager. He served in the U.S. Army and did a full tour in Vietnam in 1967-68. Doug adopted Jiffy from Guide Dogs for the Blind in 2001. In 2005, Doug and Jiffy started working in the therapy dog program at the VA's Livermore facility. Jiffy passed away on November 14, 2009. A year later, Doug started bringing their new Yellow Lab, Poli, to the VA. Poli also came from Guide Dogs for the Blind.

Doug also serves the veteran community through his car club, the P-Town Push Rods. They provide the veterans with luncheons and trips to car shows throughout the year. Doug lives in Tracy with his wife and their dog, Poli.

Kay Christensen is a lover of Collies. She has two, one of which was a therapy dog at the VA in Livermore in 2008-09. Kay could see, that despite a tough background, Lassie loved people and Kay wanted to share Lassie's love with people who badly needed such loving. Kay works with children in playgroups most of the year. Because of her work schedule and the long commute to Livermore, she and Lassie pulled out of the program in 2009. But they had many memorable times at the VA in Livermore. Kay and her two Collies live on the Peninsula near Redwood City.

Lisa Clowdus is a computer programmer in Livermore. She and her husband adopt senior Vizslas who need a good home. Lisa was thrilled to meet Pat Wheeler and become a part of the therapy dog program. Working with Dazzle at the VA and the Paws to Read program was extremely rewarding. Dazzle passed away in 2007. Lisa currently has one Vizsla, but it is too shy to be a therapy dog. Lisa hopes to have another therapy dog in the future that she can partner with to bring joy to others. Lisa and her husband adopted a cat, Max. They live in Livermore.

Kevin Coenen is a National Account Manager for Huhtamaki Consumer Packaging, managing the Nestle USA account since 1990. Kevin remembers seeing an ad for a pet therapy program in the back of a United Airlines flight magazine. He thought Shazam would be great for this program. Kevin said to himself, "I'm going to do this when I get back from my business trip." The day after he got back, he and Shazam were certified as a therapy dog team and the rest is history.

Thinking of his great-uncle, who served in the U.S. Navy, Kevin and Shazam joined the therapy dog program at the VA because Kevin wanted to give something back to the servicemen and women who put everything on the line to protect our great nation. This was his way of showing appreciation for their many years of service and sacrifice so we could be free. Kevin and Shazam have been in the therapy dog program since they started at the VA in July 2007, but he had to officially retire Shazam from the VA in 2011. In August 2010, they started participating in the Paws to Read program at the Pleasanton Public Library, and, in 2011, also going to the Livermore Public Library's Rincon branch and to Marylin Avenue Elementary School.

His family includes his wife, Aleshia; their four children; their three grandchildren; and their nieces and nephews. When not working, Kevin enjoys scuba diving, drawing and painting, and officiating junior college and high school basketball. Kevin lives in Pleasanton with Aleshia and their dog, Shazam.

Roberta Davies has been working full time for Alameda County since 1980 as a human resources technician. Over the years, she has had many dogs of various large breeds including Rottweilers, German Shepherds, Golden Retrievers, and Collies. In 2002, through her sister, Roberta found out about the Paws to Read program at the Pleasanton Public Library. At the time, she didn't have a dog that was suitable for the program, but she was interested in participating in it.

After moving into a house that allowed dogs, Roberta decided it was time to get another dog. Her horse's veterinarian was a breeder of Corgis. She felt it was time to get a smaller breed of dog and liked what she had read about the Corgi breed. After looking into the breed, she thought a Corgi would be a great fit. She waited for the right dog and had the pleasure of getting Mojo in 2005 from a local breeder.

Roberta and Mojo work at two Paws to Read programs—Pleasanton since 2006 and Livermore starting in 2010. They have attended sessions at Camp Arroyo since 2007. They have gone to parents nights at local schools and to public events to make the community aware of the therapy dogs and of the Paws to Read program. Roberta enjoys helping others understand the important role that animals, especially dogs, can play in our lives. Dogs are not judging of new readers. They give unconditional love and help children relax and have fun.

Roberta got married in May 2011 to her wonderful husband, Tony. She has two daughters and one son. She and Tony live in Livermore with their two dogs, Mojo and Woody, a Chocolate Lab, plus two turtles, Fred and Ethel. Roberta also owns a wonderful Morgan horse named Ladd who was born in 1984. Ladd has had the pleasure of teaching young children about horses.

Sue Day has been a longtime volunteer for Guide Dogs for the Blind as a campus volunteer, puppy raiser, and custodian of Elsa, who was selected to have puppies for future guide dogs. They completed the AKC Canine Good Citizen (CGC) test, were certified with Delta Society, and were approved for VHS's pet therapy program. Elsa and Sue participate in the Paws to Read program where the children read to the dogs at local public libraries, as well as going to retirement centers. Sue thought the VA setting would be a good balance and went there from 2009 to 2010, especially since Elsa was trained and certified through the Delta Society in a hospital setting. They are also certified by the Animal Rescue Foundation (ARF). Elsa continues her work as a therapy dog. Sue and Elsa live in Walnut Creek.

Dusty Dennis retired from 20 years in sales/marketing with Xerox Corporation in 1989 and started A.M. Landscaping & Maintenance with her husband, Mike. Dusty is an active volunteer with the Make-A-Wish Foundation (making wishes come true for children with life-threatening illnesses) and volunteers at Loaves & Fishes Family Kitchen, a food pantry. Dusty and Mike have a vacation home in San Felipe, Mexico, where they actively support the animal rescue groups. It was there, in October 2007, that they found Maggie.

Dusty and Maggie became certified as a therapy dog team in 2009, and started going to the VA in Livermore, Merrill Gardens in San Ramon, and the Danville Library for the Paws to Read program. They have also attended Welcome Home Celebrations and gone to Camp Erin. Dusty and Maggie enjoy their visits to the VA in Livermore. Maggie gets so excited when they drive in, and Dusty leaves with wonderful memories of each visit. They get so much from doing this, and thank all the veterans they see for their service and for giving them this wonderful opportunity. They also go to Merrill Gardens two or three times a month and participate in the Paws to Read program at the Danville Library. Dusty, Mike, and Maggie reside in San Ramon.

Sandi DeTata was a special education teacher and is now retired. When Alfie and Zito were puppies, she used to take them to school. They were so mellow, loving, and sweet that the students just adored them. The speech therapist at Sandi's school was involved in pet therapy, and she told Sandi about the program. Sandi thought it sounded just like something that her dogs would be good at.

When Sandi and her dogs became certified as therapy dog teams, she chose the VA as one of the places to visit because she had a friend who spent two-and-a-half months at the VA hospital in Palo Alto in February to April of 2009. She had visited him there with her dogs in the spinal cord injury unit where he was situated. The other patients loved her dogs and so did the staff. Seeing that the veterans in Palo Alto loved the dog visits, Sandi decided to volunteer in Livermore after getting Alfie and Zito certified as therapy dogs.

From April 2009 to June 2011, Sandi and her dogs went to Quail Gardens, an assisted living facility in Livermore, and, in June 2009, they started going to the VA in Livermore. She brings both her dogs to the VA almost every week. Pat Wheeler joins them as a handler for her dogs so both Alfie and Zito can come to the VA at the same time. Sandi is delighted that the veterans seem to really love her two affectionate little dogs, and that they can bring some small measure of joy into their day. They have attended Welcome Home Celebrations and marched in a Veterans Day Parade in Pleasanton. Sandi and her two dogs reside in San Jose.

Bud Donaldson retired after 23 years in the U. S. Air Force and is a Vietnam Veteran. He later retired after 19 years from Lockheed as a systems engineer. He wanted to serve our veterans and became a volunteer at the Livermore Division of the VAPAHCS. He has been a VA volunteer since 1998, setting up a water-based oil art program every Monday starting in 2004 and a music program every Friday since 1999. In May 2012, Bud received the Jefferson Award from KPIX Channel 5 TV, the CBS station in San Francisco, for his volunteer work at the VA. But with the art and music programs, Bud just got to know a small portion of the patients at the VA facility.

Bud responded positively when asked by Pat Wheeler to be a handler for her two dogs, Lawrence and Albert, so she could bring both dogs out at the same time. Bud was amazed at the opportunity to meet all the veterans and how the dogs meant so much to them, as well as reminding them of their relationships to their own animals. It was nice to hear all their stories about their military service, their families, and the challenges they face every day. Bud was able to introduce them to the art and music programs that he does and all the other programs that the VA has to offer the patients. He has also attended Welcome Home Celebrations with one of Pat's dogs. Bud resides in Livermore with his wife, Mary, and two dogs, Cierra and Sporty Guy. They have two daughters and two sons, ten grandchildren, and six great-grandchildren. Mary also volunteers at the VA, as do some of their grandchildren.

Jim Duthie and his wife, Susan, own and operate Castle Comforts Interior Design, located in downtown Livermore. Jim looked at participating in the therapy dog program as a way to give back to those great Americans who have served our nation. He has discovered great personal rewards from participating in the program with Sailor at the VA in Livermore. The response of the veterans to Sailor brings out the best in everyone—the staff, the dog, and the handler. Having served in the U.S. Marine Corps, Jim enjoys the reaction of the veterans to Sailor's name.

Jim and Sailor have also attended Welcome Home Celebrations for our troops. Sailor's name always evokes some military humor. Sailor also spends many days at their store in Livermore, greeting customers and keeping staff happy. Jim and Susan reside in Livermore with their dog, Sailor.

Roy Ficken is a U.S. Air Force veteran and a retired Senior Animal Service Office for the City of Pleasanton's Police Department. During his 30-year career, he encountered many types of animals, often dogs. It was a great job for Roy since he is an animal lover. In fact, he didn't see this as a job per se.

Since retiring, Roy continues to enjoy every day as a volunteer with several citizen and animal groups. This includes being a therapy dog handler with his Chihuahua/Schipperke mix, Gandalf II. They visit residents at The Parkview, participate in the Paws to Read program at the Pleasanton Public Library, conduct safety meetings for Scouts and students, and are involved with various community events.

Roy lives in Pleasanton with Gandalf II and his cat, Gollum. In his spare time, Roy enjoys reading, walking, and being with people.

John Flotten has been an active volunteer with Valley Humane Society since January 2009. He began in the pet therapy program in June 2009 as a volunteer with Miles, his Golden Retriever, at the VA in Livermore. John and Miles also participate in the Paws to Read programs at the libraries in Livermore and Pleasanton, and go to Marylin Avenue School. They have marched in a Veterans Day Parade and been to a Welcome Home Celebration.

In addition, John oversees the AniMeals program for VHS. He coordinates the food pickups from stores and drop-offs to needy families as well as training the AniMeals volunteers. When working, John was a manager. In his spare time, John enjoys spending time with his grandchildren. John and his wife live in Pleasanton with their two cats and Miles.

Caroline Gary is a speech pathologist who has resided with her husband in Livermore since 1985. Together, they have raised their two daughters, three Golden Retrievers, and five chickens. She became interested in volunteering with the pet therapy program because of the gentle and calm demeanor of her dog, Augie. She and Augie went to The Friendship Center for eight years. In her spare time, Caroline enjoys spending time with her family and friends.

Joan Gigliati is a retired secretary/administrator. She worked for almost 30 years for a research and development company in a variety of administrative positions. Always an animal lover, Joan began volunteering at a local humane society (answering phones and doing office work). It was there that she learned of the therapy dog program at the Livermore VA. Joan thought that her English Cocker Spaniel, Belle, had just the right temperament to participate in the program and that this would be an excellent opportunity to share her special animal with those who couldn't be with their own special friends and maybe help to brighten their day a little. Joan has been visiting the Livermore VA since December 2007 when she started bringing Belle each week. Starting in February 2010, she also brought their Maltese mix, Buddy G, with her husband, Lou. She resides in Livermore with Lou and their dogs, Belle and Buddy G.

Lou Gigliati is a retired parks manager. He worked for 30 years managing and supervising several parks within a dual county park system. Lou has been participating in the therapy dog program at the Livermore VA with his dog, Belle, since 2008 and later taking their dog, Buddy G, with his wife, Joan. Lou went into the U.S. Air Force at age 18. He has always felt that the military shaped his life, teaching him discipline, duty to country, and the value of team effort in working towards a common goal. His father served in the U.S. Army during World War II, and Lou is proud to provide some measure of comfort and companionship to any veteran.

Joanne Hamilton and her dog, Buddy H, became involved with the pet therapy program in 2003. They participated in the Paws to Read program in Pleasanton, visited assisted living facilities, and went to The Friendship Center for special occasions. They retired from the program in 2005. Joanne was a stay-at-home mom until their two daughters went to college. In May 2012, Joanne received her Bachelors degree in Family and Consumer Sciences. Now she is working on her teaching credential.

Joanne really enjoyed taking Buddy H to The Friendship Center because it was such a positive place to be. She found that the staff always did a wonderful job of sharing humor with the clients, and the clients so loved to laugh. At the Paws to Read sessions, Buddy H and the other dogs seemed to motivate the children to read. The children were so excited and delighted to interact with the dogs and would read enthusiastically to them.

Joanne immigrated to California from Ottawa, Canada, in 1997. Joanne now lives in Livermore with her husband, Stuart; her dog, Buddy H; and five cats. Her hobbies include cycling, reading, gardening, and cooking.

Frances Hewitt and her dog, Royal King Dog Bosco, became a therapy dog team in 1998. She and Bosco visited the Pleasanton Convalescent Hospital; went to Chardonnay Home Sr. Solutions, Inc., a residential care facility in Livermore; and participated in the Paws to Read program at the Pleasanton Public Library. Bosco continued as a therapy dog until his retirement in 2005.

Since 2004, she has owned her Yellow Lab, Cabo (Bosco's great-nephew). Frances and Cabo visit two schools, Marylin Avenue Elementary School and Emma C. Smith Elementary School, both in Livermore. They also go to The Parkview and participate in the Paws to Read program at the Livermore Public Library's Rincon branch.

Frances has her own marketing business, FHI Marketing Consultants, which helps small- to medium-sized businesses, with marketing, printing, and branding. Frances also started and runs the popular GNON (Girls Night Out Networking) group in the Bay Area with over 1,100 women. Although she is constantly working on marketing projects for her clients, she always makes time on a regular basis for her hobbies. She enjoys running and competing in races, reading, wine tasting, and spending time with her husband, friends, and family. Frances lives in Pleasanton with her husband, Don, and their dog, Cabo.

Paula Huettig moved to California in 2004 from New Jersey, where she spent 27 years working in human resources, specializing in labor relations, at a pharmaceutical company. She and her husband, David, made the cross-country move by car so that Gunther and his housemate, Christy, would not have to fly. They lived in a dog-friendly apartment complex in Fremont for about a year, after which time, they moved to a house with a large yard in Pleasanton. David and Paula, with Gunther and Christy, often took walks in downtown Pleasanton on nice afternoons or evenings, and had lunch or dinner at pet-friendly restaurants on Main Street in Pleasanton. It was on these occasions that they noticed that Gunther was very outgoing, meeting and greeting anyone who looked his way. He seemed to know when they were talking about him, and he loved the attention.

One day, Paula saw an article about the therapy dog program at the VA facility in Livermore and decided to look into the possibility of participation. After evaluation and veterinary certification, Paula and Gunther became a part of the program in 2006 and began visiting the VA every week until Gunther had to retire from the program at the VA in December 2008. In 2011, Paula and Christy started going to the Paws to Read program at the Livermore Public Library's Civic Center and Rincon branch as well as to Marylin Avenue School.

Pat Jacobson taught natural science classes in adult education programs and community colleges from 1977 to 1997. Dogs and dog rescue programs are near and dear to Pat and her family. Pat found her first Golden Retriever at the Pleasanton pound in January 1983, when the female dog was exactly one year old. Pat was her third owner. With lots of love and visits to classrooms, she lived to be over 15 years old.

Pat loved the disposition of the Golden Retriever and knew that any future dog for her would have to be a Golden. Her second Golden, Bizi, was a therapy dog with the Paws to Read program in Pleasanton and also at a rehabilitation center from 2002 to 2004, but unfortunately Bizi died of cancer at the young age of six-and-a-half years.

Then Lucky came into Pat's life. He is also a therapy dog, working since 2006 with children at Paws to Read in the Pleasanton Public Library, the patients at the Pleasanton Nursing and Rehab Center, the youth at Camp Arroyo, and the students at Alisal School. In March 2012, Lucky started working as a therapy dog at the Oak Creek Alzheimer's & Dementia Care Center in Castro Valley.

Pat loves to travel and learn about our natural world. This includes snorkeling and studying tropical fish around the world. Pat lived in Pleasanton for 54 years before moving to Castro Valley in 2011. This move has provided space for her daughter to foster German Shepherd rescue dogs, sometimes as many as ten at a time. Pat has one grown son and one grown daughter plus three grandchildren and seven great-grandchildren.

Hazel Jacoby is retired from her work of over 30 years in the mainframe computer field. She did support work for the data center for IBM computers for most of her career. The last nine years she worked for IBM in their Consulting Group, helping clients manage computers in their company. Although she grew up with dogs, she did not have dogs while working, due to long hours and travel. A year after retirement (and catching up with things), she decided it was time to get back into dogs.

Her childhood dogs were mostly mid-size or larger (including a St. Bernard), so large dogs were the goal. Hazel did some homework and decided on a Newfoundland, and then found out there was a breed-specific rescue. Her inclination was to rescue, so this meant she could have the kind of dog she wanted and still have a rescue. Due to the nature of the Newfoundland breed, being therapy dogs seemed an easy match to do with these dogs. In 2006, Hazel got Chex Mix and Tedi Bear. The dogs became family very quickly! They went most places with Hazel, including some road trips. They visited family in Carmel, and the beach was a favorite place for them.

Hazel and her dogs have gone to activities for Community Assistance for Retarded and Handicapped (CARH) and participated in the Paws to Read program at the Castro Valley Library. Tedi Bear passed away in July 2011. Hazel and Chex Mix attend many of the Welcome Home Celebrations. In her spare time, Hazel enjoys reading, walking dogs, and sewing and other crafts. She is the Treasurer for both the Newfoundland Health and Rescue, Inc. and the Newfoundland Club of Northern California, and helps with events such as water rescue testing and draft testing for the Club. Hazel lives in Castro Valley with her dog, Chex Mix.

Laurie Kerr is retired from a career in public safety with Alameda County. Laurie and Thunder started going to the VA in September 2007, right after they became certified as a therapy dog team. Laurie thought they were going there to accomplish two things. First, she was hoping that they would lift the spirits and put smiles on the faces of the people they met. The second thing Laurie wanted to do was make Thunder very happy because he loves people and loves being petted and talked to by people. Both of these have been accomplished.

The third thing that happened is one that Laurie did not expect and is hard to explain. Some days Laurie feels that she gets more out of the visits than the residents or Thunder. She looks forward to taking Thunder to the VA every week. The two of them create bonds with people that are very special. They have found that they do different things with each person, which makes each visit special and unique. So basically, this has turned out to be a three-way win. The veterans win, the dog wins, and the handler wins.

The one thing that Laurie had not anticipated was the passing away of their "friends." They had become so close to some of the veterans that they felt some emptiness when those residents were no longer there to visit. Laurie says that this has been the hardest part for her. What makes it all worthwhile, though, is knowing that Thunder and she have brought happiness to the veterans, even if it was only for a short period of time, and, for that, she feels very blessed.

Laurie and Thunder also visit the five Easy Living Care Home sites on a rotating basis each month. They have attended events such as the Veterans Day ceremonies in Danville and Pleasanton, marched in Veterans Day parades in Pleasanton and San Leandro, have gone to a veterans event at Las Positas College in Livermore, and been at Welcome Home Celebrations. When not working as a therapy dog handler, Laurie enjoys time with Thunder and her other dog, Sandy, a Jack Russell Terrier mix, and volunteering with the Coast Guard Auxiliary. She also likes taking both dogs on trips in her motor home. They reside in Livermore.

Randy Kirchner was born and raised in Oakland, and served 30 years with the Oakland Fire Department. He volunteered for several charities such as the Elisa Rusch Burn Foundation, Children's Hospital in Oakland, and Special Olympics where he was able to work along with the Oakland A's and the Raiders.

After retirement and having had large dogs in the past, a French Bulldog named Buddy K joined the family. Buddy K is a "people magnet" everywhere Randy takes him. Randy thought he would volunteer his time and spread the joy of Buddy K with the veterans and knew they couldn't resist him. Since Buddy K is called "The Mayor" at the neighborhood dog park, Randy felt that he would also make a good "Petting Officer." Randy started taking Buddy K to the VA in September 2009. They also go to the Paws to Read programs at the two libraries in Livermore and visit students at Marylin Avenue Elementary School. If you get the chance to meet both Buddy K and Randy, you will see the family resemblance. Randy lives in Livermore with his family and Buddy K.

Dan Longnecker is a U.S. Marine Corps veteran, serving over four years (1990-95), including deployments in Saudi Arabia, Kuwait, and Somalia. He has received numerous awards for his service. Dan has always loved dogs, but is unable to have one where he lives. He wanted he serve his fellow veterans. So in February 2010, he became a certified handler for Lawrence, Pat Wheeler's dog. He goes to the VA with Lawrence every week. Dan is a CPA in Pleasanton. In his spare time, he enjoys scuba diving.

Debbie Lunning is a retired mom. She was a Navy wife for many years and studied English and art, working in educational settings from kindergarten to the university level while traveling with her family. She learned about the Paws to Read program while volunteering with the Pleasanton Public Library's literacy program, and, with encouragement from neighborhood children, she realized that a therapy dog program could be a perfect fit for her and Ella, her Cavalier King Charles Spaniel. The concept of dogs comforting people of all ages appealed to Debbie, just as working in education had.

Debbie and Ella began attending Paws to Read sessions at the Pleasanton Public Library in July 2007, visited The Parkview from 2008 to 2009, went to Alisal Elementary School's special day class (SDC) during 2009, and have been with the special needs children at Camp Arroyo in Livermore since 2010. When not taking Ella to work, Debbie enjoys her grandchildren, draws, reads, and sews. She lives in Pleasanton with her husband and Ella.

Shari Marcotte has worked for the VA since 1997. She started as a Nursing Assistant and became a Ward Clerk in 2002. In 2011, she took on the role of Program Support Assistant and now works for Livermore VA's entire Nursing Extended Care Service. She witnessed firsthand the miracles of the therapy dogs at the VA. She dedicated a bulletin board in the unit where she worked to the therapy dogs. Entitled, "We Love Our Therapy Dogs," there were photos of many of the therapy dogs with their names. She planned to have it up for only one month, just prior to a Therapy Dog Awards Ceremony. But the patients, family members, visitors, and staff loved it so much that Shari kept it going for much longer. She could see the bulletin board from her desk and enjoyed watching the onlookers pointing out a dog and sharing their stories with the person they were showing it to. So Shari decided to become involved in the therapy dog program and started taking her dog, Klaus, to the VA in November 2009 for two years.

Tom Marcotte wanted to become part of the therapy dog program along with his wife, Shari, who was already going to the VA with Klaus. They owned three dogs, and, with the two of them as handlers, they quickly added one of their other dogs to the program. Their dog, Simon, became a therapy dog in the spring of 2010. This way, they could go together to the VA, each with a dog. Tom took Klaus to visit the more mobile patients while Shari and Simon would visit the more fragile and bed-bound patients. Sadly, Simon passed away on April 25, 2012.

When not working or being therapy dog handlers, Shari and Tom continue their involvement with the community and are Officers of the Court, volunteering as Court Appointed Specialty Advocates (CASA) for Alameda County's Foster Care System. For fun, they enjoy dirt bike riding, camping, and getting together with friends. They reside in Livermore with their dog, Klaus, and are in the process of trying to adopt a baby.

Nanci Menise retired from the workforce in 2000. She was still relatively young and energetic, and thought about what she would do with all this newfound time. She decided to find a best friend to hang out with. That is when Schnoz came into her life, and they have been best friends ever since, with Schnoz being a total joy in Nanci's life. She found, during obedience classes, that she and Schnoz made a pretty good team. So they became part of the therapy dog program in 2002.

Nanci and Schnoz have visited schools to teach young children about good dog manners. They participate in the Paws to Read program at both libraries in Livermore and visit students at Marylin Avenue School. In the past, they visited several other places including the VA in Livermore, The Friendship Center, and assisted living facilities and senior centers. Nanci feels that she and Schnoz get as much out of being a therapy dog team as the people they visit, maybe more. Nanci lives in Livermore with her husband, Schnoz, and two other Schnauzers.

Lynley Payne was born in New Zealand. She left New Zealand in 1985 and lived in the United Kingdom, Switzerland, Canada, and Australia before settling in the United States in 1995. She has lived in Pleasanton since 2002 with her Canadian husband, Gordon; their three children; and two dogs, Benji, a Collie/Labrador Retriever mix, and Lucy, a Husky/Australian Shepherd mix.

In April 2008, on her husband's birthday, the Paynes lost their beloved dog, Buddy, a Labrador Retriever/Rhodesian Ridgeback mix. Buddy came to them as a three-month-old rescue dog and was only nine years old when he suddenly succumbed to cancer of the spleen. Feeling the void, the Payne family quickly adopted Benji from the same rescue group where they got Buddy. Buddy and Benji looked eerily very similar, an omen in Lynley's eyes that they were meant to have Benji.

In 2009, Lynley read an article about therapy dogs and quickly decided that this was something Benji was born to do. She had Benji certified as a therapy dog. Since 2009, they have been visiting the residents at The Parkview. They participated in Paws to Read at the Pleasanton Public Library in 2009 and 2010.

Lynley is a stay-at-home mom and has kept busy over the years volunteering in both school and sports activities for her children. When her oldest child graduated from high school and went off to college, Lynley became involved as a board member with Open Heart Kitchen, a nonprofit organization that feeds the hungry in the Tri-Valley. Lynley is an avid tennis player and dog lover.

Cecile Porter is a police veteran with over 30 years of experience. Part of her career was working with school children in drug education. In 2012, she is gearing up for retirement, which will come not soon enough. She is a member of the American Legion Riders (ALR) Auxiliary and rides "shotgun" on the back of her husband's Honda Goldwing. Together they welcome home soldiers, representing the Warriors' Watch Riders (WWR) and Patriot Guard Riders (PGR). She enjoys sharing the love of her two "puppies," Brooks (now deceased) and Rivers, and is fulfilled by the light she sees in the eyes of the residents when she brings them for a visit at the VA in Livermore and attends Welcome Home Celebrations. When not working, Cecile enjoys scrapbooking and her newfound hobby of embroidery. She lives in Antioch with her husband, Rich, and their dog, Rivers.

Rich Porter is a U.S. Marine Corps veteran. He served four years in the Marine Corps with one tour in Vietnam. He is a retired police officer with a 21-year career behind him. He now drives charter buses and loves the interaction he gets with the young athletes he transports. He is a member of the American Legion Riders (ALR). He rides his Honda Goldwing with the Patriot Guard Riders (PGR) and Warriors' Watch Riders (WWR), welcoming military personnel and veterans home and escorting fallen soldiers. Their goal is to make sure no soldier feels the resentment that Vietnam soldiers received when they returned home. In addition, his time spent at the VA in Livermore with the residents has added to the fulfillment of giving back to our veterans. In his spare time, Rich likes to ride his Honda Goldwing. There's nothing like the open road, with the sun and wind in his face. He lives in Antioch with his wife, Cecile, and their dog, Rivers.

Frances Roelfsema has worked since 1993 for Kaiser Permanente, and, since 1987, as a mission-ready dog handler for the California Rescue Dog Association where she volunteers with her working canine partner to help find lost people. She has trained and certified a series of dogs—all mixed breed pound puppies—for search and rescue (SAR) work in a variety of disciplines. Her current dog, Tioga, a Lab/Golden Retriever mix, showed an early affinity for young children and that is why she decided to sign up for the Paws to Read program. Frances lives in Castro Valley with her husband and her dog, Tioga, and his search and rescue pound puppy.

Nancy Rogers lived in Maryland until 1977 when her husband was transferred to New Jersey where they lived until being transferred again, this time to California in 1980. They have two children and three grandchildren. One family lives in New York and the other family moved in 2012 to Aberdeen, Scotland, from Southern California. Nancy worked at Johns Hopkins Hospital in Baltimore, Maryland, until their first child was born. She has volunteered at hospitals in all of the areas in which she has lived.

Nancy became involved in the therapy dog program after moving to San Ramon from Walnut Creek in 2001. She has had three Golden Retrievers working with her as therapy dogs—Bear, Kane, and Caper. When she learned about the Paws to Read program in Pleasanton, Nancy and her dog, Bear, began a long journey with these wonderful people. Nancy visited The Parkview with Kane until his death and now she visits with Caper on a regular basis. Kane and Bear also went to Merrill Gardens and participated in the Paws to Read program at the Pleasanton Public Library. Bear was in this program from the start until he passed away. Kane started going to Paws to Read when he was nine months old and continued until he died four years later. Caper started going to Paws to Read in Pleasanton in 2008 and then to programs at the Livermore Civic Center Library and the Rincon branch when those programs began the following year. Both Kane and Caper have gone to Camp Arroyo.

Nancy lives in San Ramon with her husband and their Golden Retriever, Caper. When not taking Caper to work, Nancy enjoys gardening, traveling, and reading.

Dan Schack is a civil engineer and has had his own engineering/architectural firm in Tracy since 1982. He became interested in therapy dog work while watching the interactions between young and older spectators at parades that he attended with his first Bernese Mountain Dog, Braemar. He particularly noted the positive reactions from the elderly. Upon obtaining his current Berner, Rio, the two worked at becoming a therapy dog team right away. Rio has been a big hit with everyone ever since then.

Rio and Dan have visited veterans at the VA in Livermore since December 2009. Before that, they started visiting senior facilities and children's programs in Tracy and Lodi as a Therapy Dogs, Inc. team. Dan lives in Tracy with his wife, Cindy; their dog, Rio; and two cats. They have two grown daughters. The whole family has pets and cares deeply for the humane treatment of all animals.

Graham Scott has been a part owner of a small business since 1978. He and his dog, Lady, a Border Collie/Aussie mix, have been regular disc competitors since 2003. Through some of his fellow players, he learned about therapy dogs. Since Graham served in the U.S. Army for three years, the VA was a natural choice. Graham and Lady have been visiting the VA facility in Livermore weekly since the fall of 2009. They have also attended Welcome Home Celebrations and gone to Camp Erin. Graham resides in Livermore with his wife, Pat, and Lady, plus two other dogs, Charlie and Dixie, both Chihuahuas. In his spare time, Graham likes to play golf, go bowling, and engage in Rotary Club activities.

Harold Swartz was a U.S. Army veteran. He worked for the Contra Costa Sheriff's Department and also at Lawrence Livermore National Lab. Harold started as a certified therapy dog handler with Lawrence at the VA in June 2007. He also went to Camp Arroyo and marched in three Livermore Rodeo parades with Lawrence. Harold passed away in August 2009. Lawrence attended Harold's memorial service. Harold lived in Livermore with his wife, Karen Ballou, and their four Dachshunds.

Salomé Thorson is a Career Coach and Change Management Consultant (under contract with large corporations such as Chevron). She has over 20 years of business experience in the areas of Organization Development and of Employee Learning and Development.

Salomé was raised on a 480-acre ranch in southern Colorado with plenty of cattle, horses, sheep, goats, chickens, and geese to tend to. As a child, she would deliver monologues and speeches to the livestock from atop the corral fence posts. They always proved to be an attentive, if not curious, audience. In addition, the family pets always included numerous cats and working cattle dogs over the years.

After reading about pet therapy programs in *Parade* magazine, Salomé immediately took the steps to have her dog, Patch, a Golden Retriever, certified as a therapy dog. Their first assignment, in late 2001, was to visit the residents at Rosewood Gardens, a retirement community in Livermore, and, starting in January 2005, the VA in Livermore, where she and Patch went until his passing on September 11, 2009. Salomé has attended Welcome Home Celebrations for our troops in memory of Patch. Salomé lives in Livermore with her husband and two dogs, Batman and Porsche, both Chihuahua mixes. She enjoys writing, gardening, bicycle riding, and travel in her free time.

Carolyn Vane worked for eight years as a veterinary technician in Castro Valley, and then as the Executive Director of the Castro Valley Boys and Girls Club for eight years. In 1992, she started working at PETCO where she is the reptile and fish specialist at the store. Since 1980, Carolyn has been a dog trainer. She started training search and rescue (SAR) dogs in 1982. P.I.P. is her third search dog and the last one she will have since she plans to retire when P.I.P. does.

Carolyn has been a 4-H leader since 1986. She has taught many children how to train their dogs, cats, and even a pig. She has enjoyed training P.I.P. and also her horse, Karma. Since 2011, she has taken P.I.P. to the Paws to Read program at the Castro Valley Library, and they have gone to Camp Erin.

She lives in Castro Valley with her husband and many pets including P.I.P., six cats, three lizards, 17 chickens, and a horse. In her spare time, Carolyn enjoys riding and reading.

Paul Wankle and his dog Buddy W have been part of the Paws to Read program since January 2009. His involvement with Paws to Read developed as a result of an article in the local paper that highlighted the uniqueness of the program and its success in Pleasanton and other communities across the country. The article explained how educators and administrators have seen excellent results from children reading to dogs in a positive, non-judgmental environment. He was intrigued with the concept, and the photographs showed a number of Golden Retrievers and Labrador Retrievers as participants.

While his dog, Chamois, was an important part of his immediate family, she was part Chow and exhibited many of the negative, stereotypical Chow characteristics. Chamois was very protective and had a tendency of being somewhat aggressive in unfamiliar or unusual surroundings. She clearly did not have potential as a therapy dog.

When Chamois died, Paul rescued Buddy W, a four-year-old Labrador/ Golden Retriever mix.

Paul and Buddy W have participated in the Paws to Read program at the Pleasanton Public Library since 2009. They went to Camp Erin in 2011. Paul is President of Classic Cars Ltd. in Pleasanton, which sells, purchases, and trades sports, high performance, and unique vehicles. In January 2012, he was elected to Valley Humane Society's Board of Directors. He resides in Pleasanton with his wife Cathy, Buddy W, and Scooter, their older cat, which gets along famously with Buddy W, despite their considerable differences in size and attitude. In his spare time, Paul enjoys traveling abroad, fine dining, and his collection of vintage automobiles. Over the years, he has been an active participant in a wide range of Motorsports activities including vintage racing, historic automobile events, and concourse shows.

Ellen Waskey is a reading specialist at Lydiksen Elementary School in Pleasanton. She and her dog, Kody, participated in the Paws to Read program at the Pleasanton Public Library for five years before Kody's passing in 2006. Ellen also referred many of her students to the Paws to Read program. In her spare time, Ellen enjoys reading and spending time with her three grandchildren. She lives in San Ramon with her two Ragdoll cats.

Pat Wheeler is a retired educational researcher. She worked for almost 25 years for Educational Testing Service (ETS) and then as a consultant to educational, governmental, health, public safety, arts, and recreational agencies across the country. She became interested in therapy dogs while watching "K9 to 5" on *Animal Planet*. Her Black Lab, Lawrence, the Livermore Lab, started as a therapy dog in the fall of 2002 at an Alzheimer's facility in Livermore, where he went each week until it closed in November 2011.

Pat had been volunteering at the VA in Livermore since the mid-1980s. When asked by the VA to help with a therapy dog program at the VA, she jumped right in. Lawrence started in July 2004 and her other dog, Albert, joined the program at the VA in May 2005. As the program grew, Pat was asked to coordinate the program at the VA. Pat also takes Albert each week to Shepherd's Gate and both dogs to Easy Living Care Home sites several times a month. She regularly takes one of her dogs to the Welcome Home Celebrations. When not working with the therapy dogs, she enjoys her grandchildren, plays in several community bands, and travels. She lives in Livermore with her two dogs.

Sandra Wing is a proud U.S. Army veteran. She has volunteered as a therapy dog handler with her dog, Dori, at the Livermore VA and, more recently, at Villa San Ramon, an assisted living facility in San Ramon. She has lived and worked in Pleasanton for over 25 years in executive leadership positions and as an entrepreneur. She is an active community member and a graduate of Leadership Pleasanton. She has a BS and MBA in business management. For ten years, she taught undergraduate and graduate business students at the University of Phoenix. Due to her own battle with two cancers (ovarian and uterine), she founded the Sandra J. Wing Healing Therapies Foundation. She resides in Pleasanton with Dori.

APPENDIX D

ACRONYMS

AAA—Animal-Assisted Activities
AAT—Animal-Assisted Therapy
ADA—Americans with Disabilities Act
AKC—American Kennel Club
ARF—Animal Rescue Foundation, founded by Tony La Russa
ASPCA—American Society for Prevention of Cruelty to Animals
CARH—Community Assistance for Retarded and Handicapped
CGC—Canine Good Citizen Test, offered though AKC
CLC—Community Living Center, residential facility at the VAPAHCS LVD, formerly called Nursing Home Care Unit (NHCU)
DVFB—Diablo Valley Flag Brigade
East Bay SPCA—East Bay Society for the Prevention of Cruelty to Animals
ELCH—Easy Living Care Home
EMS—Environmental Management Service (at the VA)
ENN—Exceptional Needs Network
LARPD—Livermore Area Recreation and Park Department
LPES—Los Perales Elementary School
LVD—Livermore Division of the VA Palo Alto Health Care System
LVF—Livermore Veterans Foundation
NHCU—Nursing Home Care Unit, facility at the VAPAHCS LVD, now called the Community Living Center
PAHCS—Palo Alto Health Care System
PMF—Pleasanton Military Families
PTSD—Post Traumatic Stress Disorder
SDC—special day class
SLAC—Stanford Linear Accelerator
TDI—Therapy Dogs International
TDInc—Therapy Dogs Incorporated

TTFF—The Taylor Family Foundation
VA—U.S. Department of Veterans Affairs
VAPAHCS—VA Palo Alto Health Care System
VAVS—VA Voluntary Service
VHS—Valley Humane Society
WWR—Warriors' Watch Riders

APPENDIX E

SUGGESTED READINGS

Below are some books about therapy dogs and other books about the bond between people and animals. This is not intended as a complete bibliography, but hopefully will supplement what I have presented in this book and direct you to additional sources of information about therapy dogs and related topics. Much more information is available on the Internet, including information on agencies that certify therapy dogs.

On therapy dogs and animal-assisted activities/therapy—

Altschiller, Donald. (2011). Animal-assisted therapy. Santa Barbara, CA: Greenwood.

Crawford, Jacqueline J.; and Pomerinke, Karen A. (2003). Therapy pets: The animal–human healing partnership. Amherst, NY: Prometheus Books.

Davis, Kathy Diamond. (2002). Therapy dogs: Training your dog to reach others. Wenatchee, WA: Dogwise Publishing.

Fine, Aubrey H. (Ed.) (2010). Handbook on animal-assisted therapy: Theoretical foundations and guidelines for practice (third edition). London: Academic Press.

Frei, David. (2011). Angel on a leash: Therapy dogs and the lives they touch. Irvine, CA: BowTie Press.

Grover, Stacy. (2010). 101 creative ideas for animal-assisted therapy: Interventions for AAT teams and working professionals. Henderson, NV: Motivational Press.

Lind, Nancy. (2009). Animal assisted therapy activities to motivate and inspire. Lombard, IL: PYOW Publishing, Ink.

Marcus, Dawn A. (2011). The power of wagging tails: A doctor's guide to dog therapy and healing. New York, NY: Demos Medical Publishing.

Pichot, Teri. (2009). Transformation of the heart: Tales of the profound impact therapy dogs have on their humans. Bloomington, IN: iUniverse, Inc.

Stanart, Lorna. (2002). Working as a therapy dog: Observations and tips from an experienced therapy dog. Palm Springs, CA: Hispen Books.

Vanfleet, Rise. (2008). Play therapy with kids and canines: Benefits for children's developmental and psychosocial health. Sarasota, FL: Professional Resource Press.

Other suggested readings—

Anderson, P. Elizabeth. (2008). The powerful bond between people and pets: Our boundless connections to companion animals. Westport, CT: Praeger Publishers.

Calmenson, Stephanie. (2007). May I pet your dog?: The how-to guide for kids meeting dogs (and dogs meeting kids). New York, NY: Clarion Books.

Dowling, Mike; with Damien Lewis. (2011). Sergeant Rex: The unbreakable bond between a Marine and his military working dog. New York, NY: Atria Books.

Flory, Susy. (2011). Dog tales: Inspirational stories of humor, adventure, and devotion. Eugene, OR: Harvest House Publishers.

Gardner, Nuala. (2008). A friend like Henry: The remarkable true story of an autistic boy and the dog that unlocked his world. Naperville, IL: Sourcebooks, Inc.

Grandin, Temple; and Johnson, Catherine. (2005). Animals in translation: Using the mysteries of autism to decode animal behavior. Orlando, FL: Harcourt, Inc.

Grandin, Temple; and Johnson, Catherine. (2009). Animals make us human: Creating the best life for animals. Boston, MA: Mariner Books.

Hingson, Michael; with Susy Flory. (2011). Thunder dog: The true story of a blind man, his guide dog and the triumph of trust at Ground Zero. Nashville, TN: Thomas Nelson, Inc.

Horowitz, Alexandra. (2009). Inside of a dog: What dogs see, smell, and know. New York, NY: Scribner.

Kopelman, Jay; and Roth, Melinda. (2006). From Baghdad with love: A Marine, the war, and a dog named Lava. Guilford, CT: Lyons Press.

Miller, Jane. (2010). Healing companions: Ordinary dogs and their extraordinary power to transform lives. Pompton Plains, NJ: New Page Books.

Montalván, Luis Carlos; with Bret Witter. (2011). Until Tuesday: A wounded warrior and the golden retriever who saved him. New York, NY: Hyperion.

Olmert, Meg Daley. (2009). Made for each other: The biology of the Human–animal bond. Cambridge, MA: Da Capo Press.

Tonick, Eileen; and McGovern, Mickey. (2008). All dogs are angels at heart. Bloomington, IN: AuthorHouse.

Webster, C. R. (2010). Dogs and soldiers: A WWII love story. Bloomington, IN: AuthorHouse.